P9-APK-270

PATHOLOGICAL LYING, ACCUSATION
AND SWINDLING

PATTERSON SMITH REPRINT SERIES IN
CRIMINOLOGY, LAW ENFORCEMENT, AND SOCIAL PROBLEMS

A listing of publications in the SERIES *will be found at rear of volume*

PUBLICATION NO. 63: PATTERSON SMITH REPRINT SERIES IN
CRIMINOLOGY, LAW ENFORCEMENT, AND SOCIAL PROBLEMS

PATHOLOGICAL LYING, ACCUSATION, AND SWINDLING

A STUDY IN FORENSIC PSYCHOLOGY

BY

WILLIAM HEALY, A.B., M.D.

DIRECTOR, PSYCHOPATHIC INSTITUTE, JUVENILE COURT, CHICAGO
ASSOCIATE PROFESSOR NERVOUS AND MENTAL DISEASES
CHICAGO POLICLINIC; AUTHOR OF "THE
INDIVIDUAL DELINQUENT"

AND

MARY TENNEY HEALY, B.L.

Montclair, New Jersey

PATTERSON SMITH

1969

98248

Originally published as part of the
Criminal Science Monograph Series of the
American Institute of Criminal Law and Criminology

Copyright 1915 by Little, Brown and Company
Reprinted 1969, with permission, by
Patterson Smith Publishing Corporation
Montclair, New Jersey

SBN 87585-063-4

Library of Congress Catalog Card Number: 69-14932

To

MERRITT W. PINCKNEY

JUDGE OF THE JUVENILE COURT
CHICAGO

" Bonus et sapiens et peritus utilitatis
dignitatisque civilis."

EDITORIAL ANNOUNCEMENT

THIS volume is one of a series of Monograph Supplements to the Journal of Criminal Law and Criminology. The publication of the Monographs is authorized by the American Institute of Criminal Law and Criminology. Such a series has become necessary in America by reason of the rapid development of criminological research in this country since the organization of the Institute. Criminology draws upon many independent branches of science, such as Psychology, Anthropology, Neurology, Medicine, Education, Sociology, and Law. These sciences contribute to our understanding of the nature of the delinquent and to our knowledge of those conditions in home, occupation, school, prison, etc., which are best adapted to elicit the behavior that the race has learned to approve and cherish.

This series of Monographs, therefore, will include researches in each of these departments of knowledge insofar as they meet our special interest.

It is confidently anticipated that the series will stimulate the study of the problems of delinquency, the State control of which commands as great expenditure of human toil and treasure as does the control of constructive public education.

ROBERT H. GAULT,
Editor of the Journal of Criminal Law and Criminology, Northwestern University.

FREDERIC B. CROSSLEY,
Northwestern University.

JAMES W. GARNER,
University of Illinois.

COMMITTEE ON PUBLICATION OF THE AMERICAN INSTITUTE OF CRIMINAL LAW AND CRIMINOLOGY.

PREFACE

CAREFUL studies of offenders make group-types stand out with distinctness. Very little advancement in the treatment of delinquents or criminals can be expected if typical characteristics and their bearings are not understood. The group that our present work concerns itself with is comparatively little known, although cases belonging to it, when met, attract much attention. It is to all who should be acquainted with these striking mental and moral vagaries, particularly in their forensic and psychological significances, that our essay is addressed. In some cases vital for the administration of justice, an understanding of the types of personality and of behavior here under discussion is a prime necessity.

The whole study of characterology or the motivation of conduct is extremely new, and there are many indications of immense values in uncovered fields. Some appreciation of this fact may be gained from the following pages which show the possibility of tracing one form of behavior to its source.

We have laid under contribution practically the entire literature on the subject, almost none of which is in English, and also the thorough-going longitudinal case studies made by the Juvenile Psychopathic Institute of Chicago. In the latter material there was found much of value bearing upon the subject of lying, false accusation, and swindling of pathological character.

Our institute, later taken over officially by the Juvenile Court of Cook County, was for five years maintained upon a foundation provided by Mrs. W. F. Dummer.

WILLIAM HEALY

MARY TENNEY HEALY

WINNETKA, ILL.
June, 1915.

CONTENTS

98248

08348

PATHOLOGICAL LYING, ACCUSATION, AND SWINDLING

CHAPTER I

INTRODUCTION

THROUGH comparison of the literature on pathological lying with our own extensive material we are led to perceive the insistent necessity for closer definition of the subject than has been heretofore offered. Reasons for excluding types earlier described as pathological liars will be found throughout our work. Better definition goes hand in hand with better understanding, and it is only natural that formal, detailed contemplation of the subject should lead to seeing new lines of demarcation.

Definition: Pathological lying is falsification entirely disproportionate to any discernible end in view, engaged in by a person who, at the time of observation, cannot definitely be declared insane, feebleminded, or epileptic. Such lying rarely, if ever, centers about a single event; although exhibited in very occasional cases for a short time, it manifests itself most frequently by far over a period of years, or even a life time. It represents a trait rather than an episode. Extensive, very complicated fabrications may be evolved. This has led to the synonyms: — mythomania; pseudologia phantastica.

1

It is true that in the previous literature, under the head of pathological liars, cases of epilepsy, insanity, and mental defect have been cited, but that is misleading. A clear terminology should be adopted. The pathological liar forms a species by himself and as such does not necessarily belong to any of these larger classes. It is, of course, scientifically permissible, as well as practically valuable, to speak of the epileptic or the otherwise abnormal person through his disease engaging in pathological lying, but the main classification of an individual should be decided by the main abnormal condition.

A good definition of pathological accusation follows the above lines. It is false accusation indulged in apart from any obvious purpose. Like the swindling of pathological liars, it appears objectively more pernicious than the lying, but it is an expression of the same tendency. The most striking form of this type of conduct is, of course, self-accusation. Mendacious self-impeachment seems especially convincing of abnormality. Such falsification not infrequently is episodic.

The inclusion of swindling in our discussion is due to the natural evolution of this type of conduct from pathological lying. Swindling itself could hardly be called a pathological phenomenon, since it is readily explicable by the fact that it is entered into for reasons of tangible gain, but when it is the product of the traits shown by a pathological liar it, just as the lying itself, is a part of the pathological picture. It is the most concrete expression of the individual's tendencies. This has been agreed to by several writers, for all have found it easy to trace the development of one form of behavior into the other. As Wulffen says, " Die Gabe zu Schwindeln ist eine ' Lust am Fabulieren.' " Over and over again we have observed the phenomenon as the pathological liar gradually developed the tendency to swindle.

Notwithstanding the grave and sensational social issues which arise out of pathological lying, accusation, and swindling, there is very little acquaintance with the characteristics of cases showing this type of behavior, even by the people most likely to meet the problems presented. Lawyers, or other professional specialists have slight knowledge of the subject. Perhaps this is due to the fact that the pathological lying does not follow the usual lines of abnormal human behavior, unless it be among the insane where other symptoms proclaim the true nature of the case. Another reason for the slight acquaintance with the subject is the fact that almost nothing has been written on it in English.

The important part which behavior of this type sometimes plays in court work is witnessed to by the records of our own cases as well as those cited in the previous literature. The legal issues presented by pathological lying may be exceedingly costly. These facts make it important that the well-equipped lawyer, as well as the student of abnormal psychology, be familiar with the specific, related facts. For such students the cardinal point of recognition of this class of conduct may at once be stated to be its apparent baselessness.

The only method by which good understanding may be obtained of the types of personality and mentality involved in pathological lying, accusation, and swindling, as well as of the genetics of these tendencies, is by the detailed reading of typical case histories. In this fact is found the reason for the presentation of this monograph. Appreciation of the nature of the phenomena can only be obtained through acquaintance with an entire career. Any of us may be confronted by fabrications so consistent as to leave at one or several interviews the impression of truth.

Our selection of literature to summarize needs no explanation. We have simply taken all that we could find which specifically bears on the problem. Lying, in general, especially as a form of delinquency, has received attention at the hands of some authors, notably Ferriani [1] and Duprat.[2] The falsifications and phantasies of children and adolescents have been dealt with by Stanley Hall.[3] None of these goes into the important, narrower field with which we are here concerned. The foreign literature is vitally important in its opening up of the subject, but from the standpoint of modern psychopathology it does not adequately cover the ground.

The fabrications, often quite clever, of the clearly insane, which in earlier literature are confounded with pathological lying, we have discriminated against as not being profitable for us to discuss here, while not denying, however, the possibility in some instances of lies coexisting with actual delusions. We well remember a patient, a brilliant conversationalist and letter writer, but an absolutely frank case of paranoia, whom we had not seen for a period during which she had concocted a new set of notions involving even her own claim to royal blood, confronting us with a merry, significant smile and the remark, " You don't believe my new stories, do you ? "

A short statement on the relation of lying to delinquency may be of interest here. Ferriani's discussion [4]

[1] *Ferriani, Lino*, " L'Enfance criminelle." Milan, 1894. (Trans. Minderjährige Verbrecher. Berlin, 1896.)

[2] *Duprat, G.-L.*, "Le mensonge." Alcan, Paris, 1903.

[3] *Hall, G. Stanley*, "Children's Lies." Amer. Journal of Psychology, Jan. 1890; pp. 59–70.

[4] *loc. cit.*

of the lying of 500 condemned juvenile offenders, with
classification of their lies, ranging from self-defense,
weakness, and fancy, to nobility of purpose, does not
include our field. Nor does he leave much room for
appreciation of the fact we very definitely have observed, namely, that plenty of young offenders are
robust speakers of the truth. Our analysis [1] of the
delinquencies of 1000 young repeated offenders carefully studied by us does not tell the proportion of truth
tellers as distinguished from liars, but it does give the
number in which lying was a notable and excessive
trait. The total number of males studied was 694, of
females 306. Ages ranged from 6 to 22; average about
16 years.

	MALES	FEMALES
Lying — counted only when excessive and a notorious characteristic of the individual,	104	80
	(15%)	(26%)
False accusations — only recorded when of an excessive and dangerous sort,	5	16
	(.7%)	(5%)

The exact number of pathological liars is not deter-
minable in our series because of the shading of this
lying into other types. It would be safe to say that
8 or 10 of the 1000 were genuine cases of pathological
lying according to our definition, that 5 more engaged
in pathological false accusations without a notorious
career in other kinds of lying. Examples of border-
line mental cases showing fantastic lying and accusations are given in our special chapter. Some of the
cases of pathological lying given in this work do not
belong to the series of 1000 cases analyzed for statistical
purposes. The extraordinary number of times several

[1] *Vide* p. 140, in chapter on Statistics, *William Healy*, "The Individual
Delinquent." Little, Brown, and Co. Boston, 1915.

of these individuals appeared in court (resembling in this respect the European case histories) shows that the total amount of trouble caused by this class is not in the least represented by their numerical proportion among offenders.

We have purposely limited our own material for presentation. Here, as elsewhere, we insist on the value of genetics and consequently have busied ourselves at length with those cases where we could gain something like an adequate conception of the antecedents in family and developmental histories and where some measure of the psychogenetic features could be taken. Cases of older individuals with their prolonged and often picturesque careers, equivalent to those recounted in European literature, we have left strictly alone. One ever finds that the older the individual the less one can learn satisfactorily of beginnings of tendencies, just on account of the unreliability of the principal actor in the drama. The cases of older swindlers at first sight seem to offer much for the student of criminalistics, if only for purely descriptive purposes, but in the literature we have failed to find any satisfactory studies of the formative years of such careers. By taking instances of younger pathological liars, such as we have studied, the natural progress into swindling can be readily seen.

In court work we have been brought face to face with many cases of false accusation and, of course, with plenty of the usual kind of lying. Where either of these has been entered into by way of revenge or in belief that it would aid in getting out of trouble, no further attention has been paid to it from the standpoint of pathological lying. Our acquaintance with some professional criminals, particularly of the sneak-thief or pick-pocket class, has taught us that living conditions for the individual may be founded on whole careers of misrepresentation and lies — for very understandable reasons. Self-accusations may sometimes be evolved with the idea of gaining directly practical results, as when a lover or a comrade is shielded, or when there is danger of a larger crime being fastened on the self-incriminator.

In selection and treatment of our material we have confined ourselves as closely as possible to the definition first given in this chapter — a definition that after some years of observation we found could be made and held to. While we would not deny that some of our cases may eventually find their way into an insane hospital, still none of them, except some we have enumerated under the name of border-line types, has so far shown any indication of this. That some of our cases have more or less recovered from a strongly-marked and prolonged inclination to falsify is a fact of great importance for treatment and prognosis.

We see neither reason for including insane cases nor for overlapping the already used classifications which are based on more vital facts than the symptom of lying. Our use of abnormal cases in our chapter, " Illustrations of Border-Line Types," will be perfectly clear to those who read these cases. They represent the material not easily diagnosed, sometimes after long observation by professional people, or else they are clearly abnormal individuals who, by the possession of certain capacities, manage to keep their heads well above the level of social incompetency as judged by the world at large.

We have introduced only the cases where we have had ample proof that the individual had been given to excessive lying of our peculiar type. In the court room and working with delinquents outside the court, it is in rare instances totally impossible to know where the truth finally rests; such have been left out. Then, too, we omit cases in which false accusations have about them the shadow of even a suspicion of vindictiveness. False accusations of young children against parents would hardly seem to have such a basis, and yet in some instances this fact has come out clearly. Grudge-formation on the part of young individuals has all through our work been one of the extraordinary findings; capacity for it varies tremendously in different individuals.

Several forms of excessive lying, particularly those practised by children and adolescents, are not discussed by us because they are largely age phenomena and only verge upon the pathological as they are carried over into wider fields of conduct. The fantasies of children, and the almost obsessional lying in some young adolescents, too, we avoid. There is much shading of typical pathological lying into, on the one hand, the really insane types, and, on the other hand, into the lying which is to be explained by quite normal reactions or where the tendency to mendacity is only partially developed.

It has been a matter of no small interest to us that in planning this monograph we conceived it necessary to consider part of our material under the head of episodic pathological lying and that later we had to omit this chapter. Surely there had been cases — so it seemed to us at first — where purposeless lying had been indulged in for a comparatively short time, particularly during the adolescent period, without expression of a prevaricating tendency before or after this time. When we came to review our material with this chapter

in mind we found no sufficient verification of the fact
that there was any such thing as episodic pathological
lying, apart from peculiar manifestations in cases of
epilepsy, hysteria, and other mental abnormalities.
A short career of extensive lying, not unfrequently met
with in work for juvenile courts and other social
agencies, seems, judging from our material, to be always
so mixed up with other delinquencies or unfortunate
sex experiences that the lying, after all, cannot be
regarded as purposeless. It is indulged in most often
in an attempt to disguise undesirable truths. That
false accusations and even self-accusations are engaged
in for the same purpose goes without saying. The
girl who donned man's clothes, left home and lived for
months a life of lies was seeking an adventure which
would offset intolerable home conditions. The young
woman who after seeing something of the pleasures of
the world was placed in a strict religious home where she
told exaggerated stories about her own bad behavior,
was endeavoring to get more freedom elsewhere. A
young fellow whom we found to be a most persistent
and consistent liar was discovered to have been already
well schooled in the art of professional criminalistic
self-protection. So it has gone. Investigation of
each of these episodic cases has shown the fabrications
to emanate either from a distinctly abnormal personality or to partake of a character which rules them out of
the realm of pathological lying. In our cases of temporary adolescent psychoses lying was rarely found a
puzzling feature; the basic nature of the case was too
easily discoverable.

A fair question to ask at this point is whether pathological lying is ever found to be the only delinquency of
the given individual. We should hesitate to deny

the possibility of its being the sole offense, but in our study of a long list of cases, and after review of those reported by other authors, it seems practically impossible to find a case of this. The tendencies soon carry the person over to the production of other delinquencies, and if these do not come in the category of punishable offenses, at least, through the trouble and suffering caused others, they are to be regarded essentially as misconduct.

The reverse of the above question deserves a word or two of attention; are there marked cases of delinquency which do not show lying? Surveying the figures of Ferriani [1] who enumerated thousands of lies, belonging to his nine classes of prevarications, which a group of 500 young offenders indulged in, one would think that all delinquents are liars many times over. But as a matter of fact we have been profoundly astonished to discover that a considerable percentage of the cases we have studied, even of repeated offenders, have proved notably truthful. Occasionally the very person who will engage in a major form of delinquency will hesitate to lie. Our experience shows this to be less true, however, of sex delinquency than perhaps of any other. This statement is based on general observations; the accurate correlations have not been worked up. Occasionally the professional criminal of many misdeeds is proud of his uprightness in other spheres of behavior, including veracity. But even here one would have to classify carefully, for it is obvious that the typical swindler would find lying his best cloak of disguise. On the other hand, a bold safe-blower may look down with scorn upon a form of criminality which demands constant mendacity.

[1] *loc. cit.*

Realizing that pathological lying is a type of delinquency, and following the rule that for explanation of conduct tendencies one must go to youthful beginnings, we have attempted to gain the fullest possible information about the fundamentals of developmental and family history, early environment, and early mental experiences. Fortunately we have often been able to obtain specific and probably accurate data on heredity. The many cases which have been only partially studied are not included. Successive cross-section studies have been made in a number of cases, and it has been possible to get a varying amount of after-history. Observational, historical, and analytical data thus accumulated have given us a particularly favorable opportunity for discerning the bases of this special delinquent tendency. The results of the various kinds of social treatment which have been undertaken are not the least interesting of our facts.

To enumerate the results obtained on the many mental tests given in most cases seems quite unnecessary for the purpose of this monograph. We have referred to a few points of special interest and rarely have designated the results on tests in our series. In general, the reader probably will be better off with merely the statement of the principal findings and of the mental diagnosis.

Of much interest for the present subject is the development of psychological studies of testimony or report. Because of the natural expectation that the pathological liar might prove to be an unreliable witness our studies on this point will be offered in detail. For years we have been giving a picture memory test on the order of one used extensively abroad. This " Aussage " Test is the one described as Test VI in our monograph on Practical Mental Classification.[1] More recently our studies on the psychology of testimony have led us into wider fields of observation, and here the group of cases now under discussion may have to stand by themselves. The picture, the record of testimony on which is given in some detail in our case histories, is that of a butcher's shop with objects and actions that are universally comprehended. After careful and fair explanation of what is about to be undertaken, the picture is exposed for ten seconds, and then the examinee is asked to give a free recital of all he saw. When he states that no more is remembered he is questioned on omitted details. (All told, there are about 50 details of varying importance in the picture.) During the progress of this part of the examination he is asked if he saw 7 objects which might well be in a butcher shop, but which are not in the picture. This is the test for susceptibility to suggestion. All points are carefully scored. Norms on this test, as on many others, it seems hardly fair to give by averages — there is much variation according to mentality and even personality groups. Practically all of our cases of pathological lying range above the age of young childhood, so it is not necessary here to discuss the characteristics of young children's testimony. Perhaps it is sufficient to say that the ordinary individual recalls voluntarily or upon questioning upwards of 20 items, and does not give incorrect items to any extent. On questioning he may perhaps accept one or two of the seven suggestions, but when details in general are asked for he does not add fictional items more than are

[1] "Tests for Practical Mental Classification," by *William Healy* and *Grace M. Fernald*, Monograph No. 54.   Psychological Review Pub. Co., 1911, Princeton University, Princeton, N. J.

accounted for by some little slip of memory. One can find definite types of intellectual honesty, even among children of 10 or 12 years of age, when there is no tampering with the truth; if an item has not been observed, there is no effort to make it seem otherwise. For discussion of the results on this test among our pathological liars we refer to our chapter on conclusions.

The short summary of causative factors given at the end of the case study deals only with the factors of delinquency. To avoid misinterpretation of the coördinated facts, what they are focused upon should ever be remembered. The statement of these ascertained factors brings out many incidental points which should be of interest to lawyers and other students of criminalistics.

It should be needless to state to our professional readers that the personalities represented in our case histories are entirely fictitious, but that alterations have been made only in such facts as will not impair scientific values. We confess to no particular pleasure in writing up this rather sordid material; the task is undertaken because such studies offer the only way to gain that better understanding which is necessary for adequate treatment of special types of human beings.

CHAPTER II

PREVIOUS STUDIES

THE subject of pathological lying was first definitely brought to the attention of the medical and legal professions by the studies of Delbrück.[1] The aim of this work was to follow the development of a symptom but little commented upon up to this time, a symptom, as he says, found in every healthy person in slight degree, but in some cases rising to pathological significance and perhaps dominating the entire picture of abnormal traits — thus becoming pathognomonic. This symptom he at the outset calls lying.

Through an elaborate and exhaustive investigation of the lies told by five patients over a period of years, he came to the conclusion that the form of falsifying in these cases deserves a new and separate name. It was not ordinary lying, or delusion, or false memory, these words express only part of the conception; hence he coined the new term, pseudologia phantastica, to cover the species of lying with which he was concerned. Later German writers have also adopted his terminology.

To emphasize the method by which he arrived at this

[1] " Die pathologische Lüge und die psychisch abnormen Schwindler. Eine Untersuchung über den allmählichen Uebergang eines normalen psychologischen Vorgangs in ein pathologisches Symptom, für Aerzte und Juristen." Pp. 131, Stuttgart, 1891.

14

conclusion and to gain at the same time some knowledge of the problems he dealt with, we may review in bare outline his case-studies.

The first patient presented by Delbrück was an Austrian maid-servant who in her wanderings through Austria and Switzerland had played at various times the rôles of Roumanian princess, Spaniard of royal lineage, a poor medical student, and the rich friend of a bishop. Her lying revealed a mixture of imagination, boastfulness, deception, delusion, and dissimulation. She romanced wonderfully about her royal birth and wrote letters purporting to be from a cardinal to herself. She fled disguised as a man from an educational institution to Switzerland where her sex was discovered. It appeared that she was subject to contrary sex feelings and thought of herself as a man. She was under the observation of Krafft-Ebing at one time. He considered it at least as a case of paranoia. Others had determined the girl to be a psychopath who indulged in simulations and lies. Delbrück denominated it a case of direct lying with a tendency to phantasies, delusions, and dissimulations. Delbrück from this case argues that a mixture of lies and delusions is possible, comparing such a state with dreaming and with the hypnotic condition in which one follows the suggestion of the hypnotizer and is still aware of the fact. It was evident at times that this girl half believed her own stories, then again that she had forgotten her former lies. In her, Delbrück considers perverted sex feeling and hysteria revealed a brain organization abnormal from birth. There was the instinctive tendency to lie.

The second patient, an epileptic girl, had been many times imprisoned and also sent to the Charité for examination into her sanity before Delbrück saw her. Her peculiar method was to approach strangers, claiming to be a relative coming from another city to visit. If cordially received she would stay as long as her welcome lasted, then depart taking with her any of their possessions her fancy chose. Many prominent physicians examined her and were unable to decide as to her responsibility; judges and others said she was a willful deceiver, a refined swindler. Delbrück, looking deeper, found that she was suffering from hysteria, having hystero-epileptic seizures with following delirium, or rather twilight states. Though her delinquencies seemed to show cunning and skill, a careful investigation revealed the fact that this was merely aberrant. Generally her thieving was undertaken in feebleminded fashion; many times she stole things worthless to herself. Evidences of her pathological mentality were that she would give orders for groceries, would buy children's clothes, or send for a physician under an assumed name. She might not go back for the groceries, but after ordering them would say she would return with the carriage. The characteristic fact throughout her career was that she wished to appear to be some one wealthier, more influential than she was. Delbrück classifies her as high-grade feebleminded, suffering from convulsive attacks and peculiar states of consciousness, with a morbid tendency to lying. She possessed no power to realize the culpable nature of her acts when she was performing them.

His third patient as a boy appeared normal both mentally and physically. In his youth he went through the gymnasium and then studied theology. He spent money very freely on clothing and books, but at this period neither stole nor lied. After finishing his theological studies, he preached in his home town and was regarded as a young man of great promise. Then came a change; he began to write strange letters, telling of some positions offered him, he borrowed money freely from relatives and friends who were willing to give because they believed in his coming career. When studied, it was concluded by Delbrück that this was a case of constitutional psychosis, hysteria, moral insanity, and psychopathy — all of these forms being interrelated. Outside of masturbation, begun in early childhood and indulged in excessively at times, no causal factors were discovered. He considered that this case offered a good illustration of the peculiar coexistence of real lies and delusions in the same individual.

His fourth case was that of an artful, deceitful, arrogant, selfish boy, always clever in excuses, who had stolen from the age of twelve, often stolen things that he threw away. Though of Protestant family, he delighted to draw Catholic insignia and embroider religious characters. He finally entered the university, always lying and stealing. At the end of three months he was taken home in debt 2000 marks. He later became a Catholic. Outside of normal expense he had cost his father 28,000 marks. By the time he was studied he had already taken opium for four years, having started because of neuralgia. There had been a severe operation on account of some trouble with the teeth. It was discovered that there was contrary sexual feeling in this case also. The patient had a great inclination for doing woman's handwork. Delbrück again considered the early appearance of character anomalies and perverted sex feeling to prove a deep-seated abnormality of nervous constitution.

He diagnosed it as a case of constitutional psychosis; the extent of the abnormalities showing the individual to be irresponsible.

His last patient was an alcoholic adventurer, early life unknown, who had an idiotic sister. He had lived long in America and returned to Germany full of stories of his wonderful achievements over seas. This case does not concern us except to emphasize the influence of alcohol in the development of such cases.

This outline is sufficient to show the justification of his conclusion, namely, that just as in healthy people a mixing of lies and mistakes may occur, so the same combination may reach a pathological height, and one can diagnose a mixture of lies with delusions or false memories.

These studies focus our attention on the following points which are valuable to emphasize for the purpose of this monograph: the complexity of details to be examined in the life of any one patient in whose delinquencies pathological lying is a factor, the variety of cases in which this factor may occur, hence the difficulties in the way of determining the extent to which the patient is responsible for his deeds and whether he belongs in a reformatory or an insane hospital. From the standpoint of society Delbrück's work has great use, since it reveals so plainly the menace that these liars are to their families and to the community as a whole, their unscrupulousness in financial dealings, their tendencies to bring false accusations involving families and friends alike in useless expense and litigation.

German studies on pseudologia phantastica since Delbrück's time have followed the line of amplification of his views and clarification of the subject by the addition of new types.

Köppen [1] attempted to differentiate sharply and to analyze more accurately the conception of the pathological lie. He found it impossible to make an absolute separation between pathological lies and normal lies. The lies of the mentally diseased are seldom pathological. They lie, but their lies do not differ from those of the mentally sound. We cannot call the results delusional lies. Among imbeciles we find a peculiar disposition to lying, especially among those of criminal inclination. Their lies do not separate themselves either in content or in relation to the rest of their ideas from the lies of the mentally diseased. Here follows his positive contribution to the conception; the pathological lie is active in character, a whole sequence of experiences is fabricated and the products of fancy brought forward with a certainty that is astonishing. The possibility that the untruth may be at any minute demolished does not abash the liar in the least. Remonstrances against the lies make no impression. On closer inspection we find that the liar is no longer free, he has ceased to be master of his own lies, the lie has won power over him, it has the worth of a real experience. In the final stage of the evolution of the pathological lie, it cannot be differentiated from delusion. Pathological lies have long been credited to hystericals, they are now known to arise in alcoholics, imbeciles, degenerates. All pathological liars have a purpose, *i.e.*, to decorate their own person, to tell something interesting, and an ego motive is always present. They all lie about something they wish to possess or be.

Köppen offers three case studies: I. A man who had suffered from many epileptic seizures came from a

[1] " Ueber die pathologische Lügner," Charité-Annalen, 8, 1898. Pp. 674–719.

family in which there was insanity. He gave himself many false titles, and from his childhood pathological lying had been a prominent symptom. As an example, when he married against his father's will, he at the wedding read a false dispatch, pretending it to be congratulations from his family. Köppen suggests that this individual was incapable of meeting life as it really was and he therefore wove a mass of phantasies. II. A young man charged with grave falsifications. He had come from an epileptic family and himself had slight attacks in childhood. He bore various pathological stigmata. Köppen considered that the patient believed his own stories about his rather superior education and that in general his lies became delusions which influenced his actions. He diagnosed the case as psychotic; insane in a legal sense. III. A young man undoubtedly insane brought forward his pathological lies with such force that Köppen was persuaded that the patient believed in them.

Bernard Risch [1] has seen many cases of delinquents with more or less marked psychopathic signs in which pathological lying was the focal point. He reports five cases at great length, in all of whom the inclination to fabricate stories, " der Hang zum fabulieren," is irresistible and apparently not to be repressed by efforts of the will. Risch's main points, built up from study of his cases, are worthy of close consideration: 1. Mental processes similar to those forming the basis of the impulse to literary creation in normal people lie at the foundation of the morbid romances and fancies of those afflicted with pseudologia phantastica. The

[1] " Ueber die phantastische Form des degenerativen Irrseins, Pseudologia phantastica." Allgemeine Zeitschrift für Psychiatrie, 65, 1908, H. 4; pp. 576–639.

coercive impulse for self-expression, with an accompanying feeling of desire and dissatisfaction, plays a similar part in both. That the making up of tales is an end in itself for the abnormal swindler, just as it is for the normal author, seems clear to Risch. 2. The morbid impulse which forces " zum fabulieren " is bound up with the desire to play the rôle of the person depicted. Fiction and real life are not separated as in the mind of the normal author. 3. The bent of thought is egocentric, the morbid liar and swindler can think of nothing but himself. 4. There is a reduction of the powers of attention in these cases; only upon supposition that this faculty is disturbed can we account for the discrepancies in the statements of patients. One has the impression that their memory for their delinquencies is not clear. Careful investigation proves that they do not like to remember them and this dislike has to be overcome. 5. There is a special weakness in judgment, which for general purposes is sound. The train of thought is logical, but in ethical discernment the lack appears. The pathological liar does not face openly the question of whether his lies can be seen through.

Then follows a closer analysis of the qualities possessed by pathological liars: (a) Their range of ideas is wide. (b) Their range of interests is wider than would be expected from their grade of education. (c) Their perceptions are better than the average. (d) They are nimble witted. Their oral and written style is above normal in fluency. (e) They exhibit faultiness in the development of conceptions and judgments. Their judgment is sharp and clear only as far as their own person does not come into consideration. It is the lack of any self criticism combined with an abnormal egocentric trend of thought that biases

their judgments concerning themselves. (*f*) Psychic
traumata arise perhaps through a striking reaction in
the emotional realm towards external occurrences.
(*g*) Nearly all of Risch's cases were burdened with bad
inheritance. He maintains that, above all, these cases
show instability and psychic excitability. The entire
symptom complex arises upon a basis of degeneracy.

Essential similarities run through all of Risch's
cases; it is perhaps valuable here to cite a couple of
them. His Case I is that of a soldier, who after being
released from prison at 23 years had begun his military
duty and in a short time attempted suicide. He was
then studied for insanity. It was found that he gave
long accounts of his experiences as a chauffeur, rendering
his story with fluent details about hairbreadth escapes
and other adventures. He also told at length of his
love affair with a young girl. These stories were discovered to be false from "A to Z"; he did not clearly
remember them later. The evolving of such fabrications was all along one of his chief characteristics.
Examination showed no gross intellectual defect, but
there were certain psychopathic signs which had been
displayed from early childhood: he had little endurance
and was unable to stand criticism. Emotions befitting
his stories were correctly expressed by him; there were
no facial evidences of conflict or discomfort. It was
impossible to tell from his physiognomy that he was
engaged in untruths. Mentally he was well oriented
and his thoughts flowed in orderly sequence. Despite
rather limited education he demonstrated very good
style in his conversation and his letters. The train of
thought was expressed coherently and logically, so
well that one could speak of him as having literary
ability. Physically he was quite normal. Investiga-

tion of antecedents showed that he was born of an exceedingly nervous mother (more exact diagnosis not given) and that he had a feebleminded brother. During his school career he was considered to have quite fair ability. He learned no trade, and after stopping school would leave a position upon the slightest provocation. Before he was 23 he had been legally punished many times for stealing and had spent, all told, over three years in prison. Once before he had attempted suicide. After the thorough study of him at 23 he was placed in an asylum. There he was occupied at basket weaving and was chiefly notable for keeping up the characteristics that were peculiar to him before. He continually lied and, indeed, seemed to get his main pleasure out of telling fabulous stories to the other patients.

Case IV was a man of 31 years, a decorative painter by trade, who presented himself at the states attorney's office and stated that in a fit of jealousy he had shot and killed a man. Taking up the case it was soon found that this was quite untrue and that the man was a chronic liar. He seemed much astonished when he was told that the man he claimed to have killed was still alive. Further study of this self-accuser showed that he had been punished by the law every year since he was 16. His offenses consisted of embezzling, theft, forgery, and swindling. In all he had served about $6\frac{1}{2}$ years. His lying was so much a part of his mental life that he seemed to be unable to discriminate between his real and his fancied crimes. He not only invented stories, but was much inclined to play some rôle created by his fancy. There seemed to be a method in his cheating and swindling which added to his undoubted pleasure in lying. His peculiar career was much furthered by the possession of a fluent style and a good memory through which his creations were built up in most plausible fashion. He proved to be willingly introspective and stated that his inclination to lie was a puzzle to him, and that while he was engaged in prevarications he believed in them. He always was the hero of his own stories. He further declared that inner unrest and love of wandering drove him forth even when he was living under orderly conditions. He considered that his feeling of restlessness was a weighty motive in the deeds for which he had been punished. At one time this man had simulated attacks of epilepsy and attempted in connection with these to swindle physicians and others. His schooling had been continued to the gymnasium, " untertertia," then he had taken up his trade. His intelligence and memory were considered excellent. He had an insane brother.

Vogt [1] has made a thorough analysis of six cases of pathological liars, ranging from the very stupid to the intelligent. I. A girl, who had done poorly in school was unable to hold a place and became a thief. Her mother was epileptic. Examination showed intelligence not equal to that of eight years with moral inferiority on account of this weakness. II. A feeble-minded girl of vacillating, weak judgment. Father insane. Her lies were marked by their fantastic nature. III. Lively, fanciful, unstable, hysterical girl. Poor record at school. IV. Hysterical liar with peculiarities united with splendid mental ability. V. Unusually intelligent, 15 years old, illegitimate child; normal mother who later had five sound children; father drunkard. Her lies were neither of suggested

[1] " Jugendliche Lügnerinnen." Zeitschrift für Erforschung d. jugend. Schwachsinns., Bd. 3. H. 5. 1910; p. 465.

nor dreamy type, they were skillfully dramatized means to an end in her fight for social position. In the psychiatric examination she was found mentally normal. VI. Girl thoroughly intelligent, good at figures and puzzles, with no signs of degeneracy.

Vogt characterized the pathological lie as active, more elaborately constructed, more inclusive, and leaving the ground of reality more readily than ordinary lies. Such lies he does not always find egocentric. To the pathological liar his own creation is reality, so he walks securely, is open and amiable. All these cases are gifted with lively imaginations and inclined to autosuggestion. Vogt calls the pathological lie a wish psychosis. This statement opens the way to an interesting and valuable interpretation of the psychological significance of this phenomenon of the mental life. He finds many more girls than boys among his cases; boys lie from need of defense and protection, girls more from autosuggestion. This type of lie is of greater interest to social than to clinical psychology. He emphasizes the point that very refined and complicated lies appear in healthy young people in the stress of difficult situations. Obstinate and stubborn lying of itself is no disease among children; examination must reveal that the lie has a morbid cause.

The resemblance of pathological lying to poetic creation was first suggested by Delbrück [1] in a reference to Keller's "Der grüne Heinrich," a German novel in which the lies of a boy of seven years, lies of a creative type of the nature of retroactive hallucinations, are described. Hinrichsen [2] discusses at length the

---

[1] loc. cit.

[2] " Zur Kasuistik und Psychologie der Pseudologia phantastica." Arch. für Kriminal Anthrop. und Kriminalistik, 1906.

resemblance of pseudologia phantastica to poetic creation in Goethe, Grillparzer, Hoffman, and others.

In an inaugural dissertation Anna Stemmermann[1]
presents exhaustively a series of cases. These cases
were studied over a long period catamnestically. Commenting upon one case she says : It is worthy of note
in this history that the patient in a hypnoidal condition,
with headache and flushed face, crochets in a senseless
way and thinks she is weaving a wreath for her
mother's grave, her mother being still alive. We often
meet with actions like this. Characteristic is the report
of spontaneous, fearful headache, without the patient's
putting this in relation to her peculiar behavior. We
lay more stress upon this condition than has been
done previously in the literature. We believe that
this symptom is wanting in no classic case of pseudologia phantastica. Often in this condition of narrowed
consciousness, the daydreams are spun and have such a
power of convincing that they later make the basis for
pathological lies and swindling. In this hypnoidal
state a strongly heightened suggestibility exists and
trivial external causes give daydreams their direction.
The general trend of fancy reveals naturally the inclina-
tions and ideals of the affected individual. Stemmermann also maintained that the pathological lie is a
wish psychosis. Even outside of the hypnoidal state,
these cases are more suggestible than the general run
of people.

Of Stemmermann's own cases, ten in number, only
four at most were normally endowed, the remainder
were either stupid or slightly imbecile. This agrees
with the experience of previous writers. Study of her

[1] " Beiträge und Kasuistik der Pseudologia phantastica." *Geo. Reimer,*
Berlin, 1906, pp. 102.

cases showed that there was report of previous mendacity, four had been liars from childhood. She found in them the combination of the general habit of lying underneath the more accentuated form of pseudologia phantastica. One case had perverted sex feeling, one was a prostitute at sixteen years.

In her dissertation some points for the differentiation of the pathological lie have been added to those offered by Delbrück, Risch, Köppen, and Vogt. The pathological liar lies, not according to a plan, but the impulse seizes him suddenly. This propensity grows stronger. Under strict supervision it comes to only an abortive attack, similar to what happens in cases of dipsomania, or of tendency to rove in which the repressed outbreak expresses itself in tormenting psychical and physical unrest. While the normal liar and swindler is forced to be on his guard lest he divulge something of the actual state of affairs, and is therefore either taciturn or presents an evil and watchful appearance, or, if a novice at his trade, is hesitating in his replies, the pathological liar has a cheerful, open, free, enthusiastic, charming appearance, because he believes in his stories and wishes their reality. The inconsequential way in which such persons go to work is to be explained by the fact that consciousness of the real situation is partly clouded in their minds. In any special act it is impossible to say whether the consciousness of the lie, fancy, or delusion preponderates. Inability to remember delinquencies Stemmermann regards also as added proof of pathological lying.

She speaks of another class of prattlers, chattering people that might be confounded with pathological liars from the stories they tell in full detail. But they have no system which they develop, often change their subject and do not paint in a lifelike way because they do not believe their own stories or live in them in a self-centered manner.

Of the 17 cases Stemmermann studied from the literature (Delbrück, Hinrichsen, Jörger, Redlich, Koelle, Henneberg, Wellenbergh) 10 were periodic. Of her own 10 cases, 6 were periodic. Sex abnormalities were present in 5 out of the 17 in the literature. Among possible causes of pathological lying she places any factor which narrows consciousness and increases suggestion and weakness, such as pregnancy, over-exertion, chronic alcoholism, monotonous living, long, close work, head injuries.

Concerning prognosis she finds little detailed in the literature. The general opinion is that such cases arising from a background of degeneracy are incurable. One of her cases was free from attacks for two periods of three years each, and had been blameless in an honorable position as editor for seven years at the time of the publication of her monograph. She suggests that the profession he has chosen may be particularly suited to the talents of the pathological liar. She also ventures to state that where pathological lying is merely an accompaniment of puberty it may disappear.

The fact that so many of the cases cited by Stemmermann were clearly abnormal and found places in insane asylums makes much citation of them by us, in turn, hardly worth while. However, a short summary of a couple of her more normal cases will show the problems and conditions as she found them. I. Annie J., 19 years old, father a tailor, had been employed in several places as a servant. Aside from the fact that it was stated she always had an inclination to lie, nothing more was known about her early life. She complained

98248

of headaches and fainting attacks, and mourned over the death of her fiancé.   She said he had gone to Berlin to learn tailoring and had died there of inflammation of the lungs.   He left her 650 marks which her mother got hold of.   On investigation it was found that this man was still alive and never had been engaged to her. She then accused her mother of taking 50 marks from her and said that a man, purporting to be her real father, came from another town and told her she had been brought up by foster parents.   Through the quarreling which arose from these various stories Annie was taken before the police physician and pronounced mentally unsound.   Then she told of another engagement with the brother of her departed fiancé, who had discovered her real mother.   The latter was going to leave her 30,000 marks.   He had formed a plot with the foster mother to put Annie out of the way and to divide the money.   He followed her on the street and threw a drugged cloth over her head.   She fainted and was carried home.   She said she brought action for attempt to murder.   (Whether this fiancé and the rich mother were real persons is not known.)   Later in the same year, Annie being again at large, a new father, der Graf von Woldau, appeared and bought her beautiful clothes costing 100 marks.   He wanted to take her away, but quickly disappeared and was not seen again. When Annie told this story she was employed by a woman who attempted to get traces of the count, but failed.   Later this employer missed a sum of money equivalent to that spent for the clothes.   Annie's responsibility by this time was still more questioned and she was sent to an insane asylum.   There she was found normally oriented, orderly, industrious, but suffered from periodical headaches.   When questioned

in the asylum concerning her tales she hesitated and
would say, "Now I believe them and now I don't."
It is remarkable in this case that her different employers
believed all her fabrications and took the girl's part
against the supposed offenders. For a year she engaged in a sort of orgy of pathological lying and then
this phase of her career stopped. After a few months
in the asylum she returned home and later married.
The last report from her mother was that she was
nervous and easily excited, but showed no further signs
of insanity.

II. This was a boy, Johann P., who was studied
mentally first when he was 16 years old. A thoroughly
good history was forthcoming. He was brought for
examination on account of his extreme changeableness,
his failure in several occupations, his tendencies to
swindling and his extreme lying. As a young child his
mother had to correct him much for prevarications.
Soon after he was 9, when both his parents were already
dead, he forged a school certificate and was felt to be a
bad influence in the home of his guardian. About that
time he also stole money from pockets on a number of
occasions. In school he was regarded as an undesirable
pupil on account of his underhanded behavior, and one
teacher who had observed him for long wrote that he
showed marked inclination towards lying. At the
time he was 15, he was somewhat retarded in school
life, but was told he had to decide upon an occupation.
After a stormy period he announced he would become a
gardener. After doing well for a month or so at his
first place he began to tell compromising stories about
the wife of his employer. He gave himself out to be
the son of a general who was going to inherit a large
sum of money. On the strength of this he managed

to get hold of expensive articles he desired. A short time afterward he wrote to his guardian he was fitted for higher pursuits than that of gardening. Soon afterward he ran away to a large town. He now wrote that the word freedom sounded like the sweetest music in his ears. He acknowledged that he had started on a career of criminality, but decided to do better. At this time he attempted to make his way by offering his compositions at a newspaper office where they were declined either because his productions were immature or his authorship was doubted. One editor loaned him some money, but he got much more by representing himself to be a collaborator of this editor. He soon failed to make his way and attempted other things, including entrance into the merchant marine. He finally turned up again at his guardian's house, and when his box was opened it was found to contain a very curious lot of material such as money accounts, business cards, letter heads, catalogues. It was at this time that he was placed for observation in an asylum and it was soon found that his alleged compositions were plagiarized. He claimed to suffer from headaches. Outside of that he was in fine physical condition. He frequently wrote sketches in proof of his ability. A general statement was finally made that he showed slight traces of hysteria, was a sufferer from headaches, and showed periodic tendencies to wandering and lying. No special defect in the ethical discriminations was present. He had good insight into his own tendencies. He was finally released to his guardian, and Stemmermann offered the prognosis that Johann might well develop into a typical pathological swindler. He came of a family of five brothers and sisters, one of whom was incarcerated for a year on account of stealing.

One sister was noted for her tendency to prevarication. Several of them were remarkably unstable, at least early in life. All of them are said to have learned very unwillingly in school. One brother of the father was exceedingly nervous.

Jörger [1] presents a case of a boy of poor parents who was from childhood possessed of the idea of becoming a teacher. He was always a solitary child, endowed with great religious fervor. In spite of poverty he obtained an education, studied the classics, and did excellent work. He developed early religious eccentricities, became unsound on money matters, boasted of his father's millions, spent freely as a benefactor, bought expensive books. Then developed an outspoken tendency to swindling. Finally he was adjudged insane and committed to an asylum. Commenting on this case, Jörger points out the marks of abnormality from childhood, such as solitariness and religious intensity. He was above normal in intellectual ability, but lacking in moral development. He did not love parents, brothers, sisters, or teachers; he was very egotistical. Jörger defines this as a case of constitutional psychosis. When older, pseudologia phantastica controlled him; it was like hypnotic influence, his dreams of wealth were like paranoia. His hypnotic condition grew to such an extent that there was an interruption of consciousness with following amnesia.

Henneberg [2] cites another case of a highly educated young man who told wonderful stories in childhood and

---

[1] " Beiträge zur Kenntnisse der Pseudologia phantastica." Vierteljahrschrift für gerichtliche Medicin und öffentliches Sanitätswesen, 1904, Bd. XXVII; pp. 189–242.

[2] "Zur kasuistischen und klin. Beurteilung der Pseudologia phantastica." Charité-Annalen, XXV, XXVI.

later obtained money under false pretenses with elaborate deception. From an eccentric grandmother, and a mother who was very excitable and suffered from hysteria, he inherited a nervous system which was not calculated to bear the strain which his own overzealous efforts in pursuing his studies and his spiritual exaltation put upon it, hence the mental and moral breakdown. This is a very interesting case because it does not fit into the usual group of pathological liars.

Wendt [1] enlarges the field in which we may look for such cases. He finds pseudologia phantastica a symptom, not only of hysteria, alcoholism, paranoia, but also of sex repression, and neurasthenia. He takes a more philosophical view of the subject than previous authors. He understands by pseudologia phantastica not merely the bare habit of telling fantastic lies, and what they bring forth, but rather the yielding up of consciousness of reality in the presence of the morbidly fantastic wish in its widest consequences. Since the wish in order to exist is not permitted to lose entirely the conscious presentation of what it hopes for, so memory and recognition of reality emerge disconnected in consciousness, and a condition described as double consciousness arises. In this state of mind two forms of life run side by side, the actual and the desired, finally the latter becomes preponderant and decisive. Such a psychic make-up must lead unconditionally and necessarily to swindling and law breaking. A degenerative alteration furnishes the basis from which a wish or wish-complex arises, increasing in force until it becomes autosuggestion, hence it is pathological. Then follow the practical consequences, and we have developed,

[1] "Ein Beitrag zur Kasuistik der Pseudologia phantastica." Allgemeine Zeitschrift für Psychiatrie, LXVIII, Heft 4; pp. 482–500.

on the one side, pathological lying, and, on the other, swindling, *i.e.*, criminality. Purely symptomatically pseudologia phantastica is characterized by the groundlessness of the fabrications, the heightened suggestibility of the patient, and in its wake arises double consciousness and inadequate powers of reproduction of reality.

Wendt gives at length the history of a precocious boy, the son of an official of medical rank, who had lived always with older people. He lied from early childhood. He was a chronic sufferer from severe headaches. Between the ages of 15 and 17 this boy showed evidences of literary talent, but was poor in mathematics. From a tender age he had an overmastering desire to become great; he said he wished to become a jurist because only jurists get the high offices. He entered a South German university, rented a fine apartment, stated he was accustomed to a Schloss, his father was a high state official. He later called himself Graf Friedrich Gersdorf auf Blankenhain. The young man's deceits grew rapidly, he obtained much money falsely, traveled first class with a body servant. He passed to other universities, was always quiet and industrious. After many adventures he fell into the hands of the law and was adjudged insane. Most interesting was the fact that he discussed intelligently his career. " My capacity for considering my thoughts as something really carried out in life is unfortunately too great to permit my having full conception of the boundary between appearance and reality."

The family history of the above case included swindling, hysteria, and epilepsy. His fabricating tendency first reached its height at 14 years, thus showing the influence of puberty. Wendt regarded the etiological factors as family degeneracy, a wish-complex which in activity amounted to autosuggestion, double consciousness, and a periodical preponderance of the wished for personality.

Bresler [1] in proposing two reforms in the German "Strafgesetzbuch" undertook a discussion of pathological accusations, as material using cases reported by several authors. He attempted a classification as follows: 1. Deliberately false accusations based upon the pathological disposition or impulse to lie; the content of the accusation being fabricated. 2. False accusation upon a basis of pathologically disturbed perceptions or reasoning. Content of the accusation is here illusion, hallucination, or delusion. 3. Accusations correct in content, but pathologically motivated.

The first group nearly always is the action of hystericals, and many are centered on sex affairs. Bresler's cited cases of this class seem merely to impress the idea of revenge, or of protection from deserved punishment. A very complicated case was that of a girl who had been rejected in marriage after the discovery by her lover that she had attacks of major hysteria. She entered into a conspiracy with her mother to destroy him. She first maliciously cut grape vines and accused him and his brother of doing it. Then she slandered his whole family. A year later, suddenly appearing wounded, she accused his uncle of trying to kill her and obtained a verdict against him. Then she attempted the same with another uncle who, however, maintained an alibi. After this her rôle changed, for her mother summoned people to see her daughter lying with a wreath around her head, brought by an angel, with a scroll on which was inscribed "Corona Martyri."

[1] "Die pathologische Anschuldigung." Juristisch-psychiatrische Grenzfragen, Band V, Heft 8, pp. 42.

The church now took her part and she toured the country as a sort of saint.   Later she returned to her former tactics, she set fire to a house, cut off a cow's udder, and accused her former lover of these deeds.   Now for the first time it went badly with her.   She was finally imprisoned for life on account of attempts to poison people.

In Bresler's second group he places the false accusations of alcoholics, paranoiacs, querulants (whom he calls a sub-class of paranoiacs) and sufferers from head injuries.   Besides these, he here classes the false accusations of children.

The third class is so rare that it receives almost no discussion.

Longard [1] reports an interesting case of a chronic liar and swindler, a man who on account of the peculiarities of his swindling was placed under custody for study. Upon detention he went into convulsions and later seemed entirely distracted.   He was then 24 years old. Investigation of his case showed that his abnormalities dated from early life and were probably due to the fact that in childhood he had a bad fall from a height. When he was 23 he had served six months on account of swindling.   At that time he had been going about in the Rhine country dressed as a monk, begging things of little worth, such as crucifixes, candles, medals, etc. His pious behavior and orderliness gave him a good reception.   He sometimes took money or begged it in order to read masses for poor souls.   In one village he said he had come to reconnoiter for a site to build a hospital.   Some cloister brothers in one place took him for a swindler and decided he was overwrought reli-

[1] "Ein forensisch interessanter Fall. Pseudologia phantastica."   Allg. Zeitschrift f. Psych. LV, p. 88.

giously, and that he really thought he was what he wished to become. He was studied at length in prison where he had one attack of maniacal behavior and tried to hang himself. The physician there thought him a simulator. He was excused from his military service because of stomach trouble. At that time mental abnormalities were not noticed. After this he again acted the part of a monk, wandering through France and Germany, living in monasteries, and being helped along by different organizations, Protestant as well as Catholic. He was arrested in Cologne when discovered to be a fraud. He lay four days in jail apparently unconscious and then appeared stupefied and staggered about. When questioned he responded, "I am born again." He spoke mostly in Biblical terms and was fluent with pious speeches. He was found quite sound physically. He ate a great deal and was known to take bread away from other prisoners at night. He was sentenced for 15 months for swindling. He himself related that in youth he had seen many monks and had become possessed of the idea of being one. He was a sex pervert.

The author considered this not a pure case of simulation; the patient was an abnormal being, none of his keepers thought him normal. His entire appearance, his excited way of speaking, his gestures and play of features were all striking to a high degree. His method of going about begging was unreasonable; he gained so little by it. His tendency to untruthfulness stood out everywhere. He imitated the pious as he chattered without aim. The man had lived himself into the rôle of a cloister brother so completely that he was not clearly conscious of the deceit. The author thinks the case presents some paranoiac features with a pathological tendency towards lying. Thus this pathological liar presents the phenomenon of a mixture of lies and delusions.

From the Zürich clinic of Forel several cases of pathological swindling have been reported at length.[1] It must be confessed that the success of much of the misrepresentation cited in these case histories seems to be as largely due to the naïveté of the country folk as to the efforts of the swindlers themselves. Two of the cases were clearly insane and were detained for long periods in asylums after their study in the clinic. But even so, it is to be noted that one of these when absenting himself from institutional care succeeded in going on with his swindling operations. The third case was regarded as that of an aberrational individual with special tendency towards lying and swindling, but the opinion rendered did not end in the man being held as insane. He was simply regarded as a delinquent, and after serving his sentence he went his old way. These cases are interesting to one who would learn the extent to which swindling among a simple minded population can be carried on.

From French sources we have not been able to collect such a wealth of material as we found in German literature. One study by Belletrud and Mercier[2] compares favorably in elaborate working out of details with the work of German authors. A Corsican boy, from childhood moody, fond of adventure, inclined to deception, had attempted suicide several times before he was

---

[1] " Gerichtlich-psychiatrische Gutachten aus d. Klinik von Prof. Forel in Zürich; f. Aerzte u. Juristen, herausgegeb. von Dr. Th. Koelle." Stuttgart, Encke, 1902.

[2] " Un cas de mythomanie; escroquerie et simulation chez un epileptique." L'Encephale, June 1910, p. 677.

twenty years old. He was married at that time and
went to France, where he was employed in several
towns. His life following this included an immense
amount of lying and swindling. He had a mania for
buying costly antique furniture and jewelry which he
obtained on credit. He frequently disappeared from
localities where he was wanted on criminal charges,
and changed his name. He wandered through Italy,
Tunis, and South America. Returning to France he
was taken into custody and mental troubles were noted.
He showed delirium of persecution and was removed to a
hospital for the insane. Experts studied him for a year
before they could decide whether he was insane or
merely simulating insanity. Finally they thought he
was not simulating. A few months later he escaped,
went to Belgium, Italy, Corsica. Turning up at a town
in France under an assumed name, he was arrested
again and elaborately examined. At this time he had
frequent attacks of unconsciousness and frothing at the
mouth. At times he was melancholy. Summarizing
the case, the authors say that the psychic peculiarities
of the patient were congenital, and included habitual
instability of character with defective development of
the ethical sentiments, and tendency to deceit and
swindling. Epilepsy here is, of course, the central
cause of mental and moral deterioration.

From a pedagogical point of view Rouma [1] tells of the
marvelous stories of a five-year-old boy in the Froebel
school at Charleroi. His stories were generally suggested by something told by the teacher or other pupils.
He referred their anecdotes to himself or other members
of his family and greatly enlarged upon them. He also
made elaborate childish drawings and gave long ac-

[1] " Un cas de mythomanie."   Arch. de Psych. 1908, pp. 259-282.

counts of what they meant. Going into the question of heredity Rouma found this boy's mother very nervous; the father was a good man. She had worked steadily at the machine before his birth. Two of their children died with convulsions; of the two living, one was well behaved, but weakly. Rouma's case had stigmata of degeneracy in ears, palate, and jaw. Tested by the Binet system, he did three out of five of the tests for five years satisfactorily. He was easily fatigued, refused at times to respond, said he had been forbidden to reply, said he would be whipped if he did. In school he was always poor at manual work, wanted to be moving about, to go out of classes on errands, was always calling notice to himself in a good or bad way. He paid very little attention to his lessons, played alone or with younger children, leading them often into mischief. It was found that he got much of his material for stories from his older brother who told him of robbers and accidents. From his good father he got the form of his tales, because the father was wont to tell him stories with a moral.

In summary, Rouma stated that this child possessed senses acute beyond the average, and was of very unstable temperament, refusing regular work, not submitting to rules, rebelling at abstractions. There were evidences of degeneracy on the mother's side.

Remedies in education for such children are: Suppress food for imagination, such as came from the stories of father and brother. Direct perceptions to accurate work. Systematize education of attention, exercise the senses, use manual work, such as modeling and gardening. Give lessons in observation in the class room and on promenades.

Meunier [1] tells of three girls in a well known Parisian school who indulged in wonderful tales. The first, in the intermediate grade, told stories of the illness of her father to account for her not having her lessons. The second, 11 years old, said that her mother was dying; she came bringing this news to the teachers at two different periods of her school life. She was a calm, thoughtful, analytical child with no reason for lying. Family history negative. The third, 13 years old, told of an imaginary uncle who was going to collect funds for needy children; she kept up the deceit for two months. She was an anemic, nervous, hysterical child with a nervous mother. Meunier calls these cases of systematized deliriums. The development of such delirium annihilates, so to speak, the entire personality of the subject, and his entire mental life is invaded by abnormal extra and introspection — the delirium commands and systematizes all acquired impressions. There is a veritable splitting of the personality in which the new " ego " is developed at the expense of the normal " ego " that now only appears at intervals.

[1] " Remarks on Three Cases of Morbid Lying." Journal of Mental Pathology, 1904, pp. 140–142.

CHAPTER III

CASES OF PATHOLOGICAL LYING AND SWINDLING

In the group of twelve cases making up this chapter we have limited ourselves to a simple type in order to demonstrate most clearly the classical characteristics of pathological liars. How pathological lying verges into swindling may be readily seen in several of the following cases, *e.g.*, Cases 3, 8, 10, 12, although only two, Cases 3 and 12, have had time as yet to show marked development of the swindling tendency. For the purpose of aiding in the demonstration of the evolution of lying into swindling, and also to bring out the fact that facility in language may be the determining influence towards pathological lying and swindling, we have included Case 12, which otherwise possibly might be considered under our head of border-line mental types.

In any attempt to distinguish between pathological accusers and liars, cases overlapping into both groups are found — so some of the material in this chapter may be fairly considered as belonging partially to the next chapter.

In discussing the possibility of betterment, a fact which we as well as others have observed, consideration of Cases 1, 4, and 7 is suggested.

CASE 1

Summary: A girl of 16 applied for help, telling an elaborate tale of family tragedy which proved to be totally untrue. It was so well done that it deceived the most experienced. Shrewd detective work cleared the mystery. It was found that the girl was a chronic falsifier and had immediately preceding this episode become delinquent in other ways. Given firm treatment in an institution and later by her family, who knew well her peculiarities, this girl in the course of four years apparently has lost her previous extreme tendency to falsification.

Hazel M. at 16 years of age created a mild sensation by a story of woe which brought immediate offers of aid for the alleged distress. One morning she appeared at a social center and stated she had come from a hospital where her brother, a young army man, had just died. She gave a remarkably correct, detailed, medical account of his suffering and death. In response to inquiry she told of a year's training as a nurse; that was how she knew about such subjects. In company with a social worker she went directly back to the hospital to make arrangements for what she requested, namely, a proper burial. At the hospital office it was said that no such person had died there, and after she had for a time insisted on it she finally said she must have been dreaming. Although she had wept on the shoulder of a listener as she first told her story, she now gave it up without any show of emotion. We were asked to study the case.

Hazel sketched to us a well-balanced story of her family life; one which it was impossible to break down. It involved experiences at army posts — she stated her only relatives were brothers in the army — and her recent work as a " practical nurse." She finally led on to the death of her brother, as in the tale previously told. When asked how she accounted for the fact that no such person was found in the hospital, she answered, " Well, I either must have been crazy or something is the matter, and I don't think my mind is that bad." The girl evidently was suffering from loss of sleep; her case was not further investigated until after a long rest.

The next day Hazel started in by saying, " It's enough to convince anybody that I was not in the hospital when Mrs. B. and I went there and found out that they said I had not been there. Truthfully I don't know where I was. If I was not there I must have been some place or I must have been in a trance." The long stories told in the next few days need not be gone into. They contained descriptions of life with her family in several towns when she was a child, of her graduation from the high school in Des Moines, and of her experience as a nurse in Cincinnati and Chicago. Our cross-examination disclosed that she knew a good many facts about obstetrics, in which she said she had had training, and about the cities where she said she had lived. For instance, she gave a description of the Cliff House at San Francisco, the seals on the rocks there, the high school in Des Moines, and so on. She also knew about life at army posts. The point that made us skeptical was when in mentioning the names of railroads she placed the wrong towns upon them. For instance, she told us her brother worked on the L. S. & M. S. at Kenosha.

Hazel's stories were successfully maintained for several days until a shrewd detective, who got her to tell some street numbers in Chicago, ferreted out her family. She had persistently denied the existence of any of them in Chicago, and, indeed, stated that her father and mother had died years previously. One of the most convincing things about her was her poise; she displayed an attitude of sincerity combined with a show of deep surprise when her word was questioned. For example, the moment before her mother was brought in to see her, she was asked what she would say if anyone asserted that her mother was in the next room. Her instantaneous, emphatic response was, " She would have to rise out of her grave to be there."

We soon learned that not a single detail the girl had given about her family was true. She was born and brought up in Chicago and had never been outside of the city. She had never studied nursing nor had she ever nursed anybody. In public school she had reached eighth grade.

Hazel came of an intelligent family and we were able to get a good account of the family and developmental history. Heredity seems completely negative as far as any nervous or mental abnormalities are concerned. She is one of seven children, four of whom are living, three having died in infancy. The father had just recently died of tuberculosis. There has been no trouble with the other children of any significance for us. Pregnancy with Hazel was healthy, but the mother suffered a considerable shock when she stood on a passenger boat by the side of a man who jumped overboard and committed suicide. The birth was difficult. The child weighed 12 lbs. Instruments were used; it was a breech presentation. At 2 years of age Hazel was very ill with gastritis and what was said to be spinal meningitis. She had some convulsions then. Had both walked and talked when she was about 16 months of age. During childhood she had a severe strabismus and at 8 years of age was operated upon for it. Vision has always been practically nil in one eye. Several diseases of childhood she had in mild form. After she was 2 years of age she had no more convulsions, or spasms, or attacks of any kind. From the standpoint of general nervousness Hazel was said to be one of the calmest in the family, although she was accustomed to drink five or six cups of coffee a day. Menstruation at 13 years, no irregularity.

On examination we found a very well nourished and well

developed young woman of slouchy attitude and normal expression. Vision very defective in one eye and $\frac{10}{20}$, even with glasses, in the other. Slight strabismus. General strength good. Examination otherwise negative except for the fact that she had been infected with the diplococcus of Neisser.

Mental tests proved her to have quite normal ability. Neither special ability nor disabilities of significance were discovered. For present discussion it is of interest to note that in the "Aussage" Test she gave a functional account, enumerating 16 items, 2 of which were incorrect, and accepted none of the suggestions which were offered.

The mother and sister brought out the facts that Hazel had been giving an assumed name recently and lying about her age. She had alleged that she was married. In the last year she had run away from home on several occasions. At one time had written to her mother about her happy married life. One letter reads, "Dearest Mother : — I can picture your dear face when you receive my letter. I know you have your doubts about the matter, the same as I had the first few days. But mama, you know I love him and I have the satisfaction of being a married woman before Annie is." In the letter she describes the appearance of her imaginary husband, tells about her new dress and gloves and "the prettiest little wedding ring that was ever made." In another letter she says, "It is just one o'clock A.M. and Jack has just gone to sleep and so I stole a little time to write," etc. (It was later shown by the stationery used, and by the girl's final confession, that these letters were written in the rest room of a department store.)

Hazel's lying began, it seems, when she was a little girl. She would come home from school and out of whole cloth relate incidents which occurred on the way home. One of her earliest efforts was about being chased by a white horse. The mother states that for years she has had to check Hazel because she recognized her remarkable tendencies in this direction.   The father's death was somewhat of a shock and it seems that after this the girl's other delinquencies began. Prior to the time she first went away from home she had some sort of hysterical spells when she said she could see her father lying in his coffin before her in the room.   Her behavior became quite outrageous with some young man in her own household at just about this time.   Not that she was immoral, although she once suddenly blurted out in the parlor a grave self-accusation: "Now, John, mother thinks you must be careful.   You know I am a prostitute." When we first saw her she had been away from home four times, on this last occasion for three weeks.   Before she went she had said she wanted to kill herself.   Mother had notified the police but no trace of her was found.

From Hazel's own story told at this time and even after she became more stable it seems very likely that her bad tendencies began with her acquaintance with a certain rather notorious woman.   Her mother came to believe that this was undoubtedly the fact.   Our inquiry into beginnings brought to light the fact that Hazel while a school girl for long associated with this woman who taught her about sex immoralities.   "I don't believe my mother knows what this Mrs. R. did to me or she would have her arrested. She started me on all this.   When I was about 11 years old I first knew of those things.   The first I ever heard was from that woman's daughter.   I never said anything to my mother.   I was always ashamed of myself to say anything about it.   After I got to working with factory girls I heard a lot about it."   The mother told us later that she thought it probable from what she now knew that this Mrs. R. may have been largely responsible for Hazel's tendency to delinquency.   Hazel kept this association of several years' standing quite to herself.   The mother remembers now how

Hazel once stayed for hours after school and told a story in explanation that they felt sure was untrue. The teachers used to tell the mother that Hazel seemed as if she couldn't pay attention to her school work. One teacher reported to us that she remembers Hazel as a girl who seemed peculiar and hysterical. The other girls called her queer and used to steer clear of her.

The mother reports Hazel as being for several years impulsive, erratic, talkative, untidy, and rather dishonest in other small ways besides lying — all this in spite of vigorous home discipline. The girl at one time under the influence of revival meetings left the religious faith of her parents. However, they thought if any form of religion would make her better it would be all right.

At our last interview with Hazel before she was sent away, an interview which she prefaced by saying, "I want to apologize for everything I did," the girl showed herself unable to avoid prevarications. Coming back, for instance, to the subject of her schooling she tells us how she won a graduating medal. This her mother said was untrue.

About her own lying tendencies she confessed that sometimes she hardly knew whether things were really so or not. Asked about her knowledge of other cities; "I read a whole lot and learn things in that way. I used to have to write compositions and imagine we were going places. I was pretty good at that." One felt very uncertain about Hazel's mental condition when in almost the same breath she denied having said anything about the seals on the rocks at San Francisco, or about obstetrical cases, but, of course, the denial may have been itself another falsification. Her knowledge of army affairs was gained through her acquaintance with young soldiers. An unusual amount of what she heard or read was photographed with the greatest clearness in her mind and was recalled most vividly.

A peculiarity of Hazel's case which was quite obvious was her lack of apperception concerning her own interests. Her lies all along, after her identity was discovered, were so easy to trace, and they so quickly rebounded upon her, that there seemed every reason for her to desist. Nothing so clearly proved the absence of self-realization as her feeling under detention that other girls with whom she was in forced association were much beneath her in quality, although many of them were not nearly so untidy and had not been nearly so immoral. During all this period of several months, beginning with her running away and her writing the house-wifely letters about her imaginary married life, and ending with her appeal for aid at the social center, Hazel was indulging in veritable orgies of lying. When away from home she several times picked up men on the street and stayed at hotels with them.

At the time of our first studies of this case we hardly dared to offer either a mental or moral prognosis.

In the institution for delinquent young women to which she was sent Hazel's traits were long maintained. She proved very troublesome on account of lies to her family, to the officers, and to the other girls. The latter soon discovered, however, the peculiar lack of foundation for her stories. In the institution was also noted the tendency to untidiness of which her mother spoke. The authorities steadily persevered with Hazel. They secured another operation on her eye, which successfully straightened it, and she became fully "cured" of her pelvic disease. She received instruction in a form of handicraft in which she quickly showed special dexterity and skill. Her tendencies to falsify gradually became less. About two years later the mother again assumed control with great success.

This is the remarkable interest of Hazel's case, to wit, that with proper discipline and the development of new

interests her fabricating tendencies have been reduced to a
minimum. She has made a wonderful improvement and
has long been a self-supporting and self-respecting young
woman with her own relation to the world realized in a
way that before seemed entirely lacking.

Mental conflict: About early secret   Case 1.
                    experiences.   Girl, age 16 yrs.
Mental conditions: Either mild psychosis
                       or extreme adolescent
                       instability.
        Bad companions: Early.
Delinquencies: Mentality:
  Extreme lying.   Normal ability.
  Running away.   Psychosis (?).
  Sex.

Case 2

Summary: A girl of 19, under partial observation for three
years, was during all this time a great mystery. Brought at first
to us by her family as being insane because she was such a great
liar and unreliable in other ways, we never could find the slightest evidence of aberration. No satisfactory explanation was
forthcoming until the remarkable dénouement when we learned
that the mother, whom we had come to know herself as an extreme falsifier, was not the mother at all. It seems clear that
the girl's behavior was largely the result of mental conflict
about certain suspected facts, and psychic contagion arising
from the world of lies in which she had lived.

Beula D. has been known in several cities and in more
than one court as the "mystery girl." She has appeared
on the scene in various places, giving a fictitious name and
telling elaborate stories of herself which always proved to
be without foundation. She ran away from home on several

occasions, but except in one instance which we know about, has never been seriously delinquent. We saw her on many occasions and tried to get at the truth of her stories of ill treatment and the like. Investigators found there was unquestionably some truth in her statements, but never from first to last in the many interviews which we had with her was there ever any possibility of separating truth from falsehood. The girl simply did not seem to know the difference between the two. What was more, we found that the mother presented the same characteristics. She also, by her most curious and complicated fabrications, led even her most rational sympathizers into a bewildering maze. A woman of magnificent presence, tremendous will, and good intelligence, she nevertheless was soon found to be absolutely unreliable in her statements. This woman's numerous inventions, so far as we have been able to ascertain, have been quite beside the mark of any possible advantage to be gained by her or her family. Naturally we here thought heredity played an important rôle, until our final discovery that the two were not related. The details which we know about this case would cover scores of pages. In summary it stands as follows:

On the physical side Beula at 17 was a striking looking young woman, but of very poor development. She was only 4 ft. 7 in. in height and weighed 102 lbs. Expression was quiet, pleasant, and responsive. Unusually clear and pleasant voice. Typical Hutchinsonian teeth. All other examination negative. Menstruation first at $13\frac{1}{2}$, normal and regular.

Notwithstanding the mother's report of her being subnormal mentally, we found that she had fair ability. Her range of information was good. She was always desirous of writing compositions, she wanted to be a story writer, she said, but her diction was very immature and her spelling

was poor, making altogether a very mild production.   Never
did we see any essential incoherency in her mental processes,
or any other signs of aberration.   A series of association
tests given in an endeavor to discover some of the facts
which her mother maintained she herself was desirous of
knowing (but really could not have been), failed to elicit
anything but the most normal reactions, even to ideas about
which we considered there must be some feeling-tone.

On the "Aussage" Test only ten items were given from
the picture upon free recital.   On questioning twelve more
details were reported correctly, but no less than seven of
these alleged facts were incorrect.   Only one out of the five
suggestions offered was accepted.

No purpose would be served in recounting the details of
falsehood which were told by this girl about family affairs,
about the places she had worked, about the facts of home
treatment, etc.   Her lying was not done cleverly, but it
served to create much confusion and gave considerable trouble
to a number of social agencies that came in contact with
the family.   Even when she was applying directly for help her
lies stood greatly in the way of achieving anything for her.
The confusion was vastly added to by the many vagaries of
her alleged parent, but, even so, one of the chief accusations
of the prevaricating mother was that the girl herself was a
terrible liar.   The whole situation was rendered completely
absurd and needless by the behavior of both the woman
and the girl.

After we had known this case for about three years and
the truth about Beula's antecedents had come to light as
the result of a new person stepping in on the scene, the girl's
tendency to falsification seemed quite inexplicable.   No one
who came to know the circumstances, even as we previously
had been acquainted with them, felt they could blame
Beula much for her attitude of dissatisfaction and her ten-

dencies to run away. We felt, too, that the mystery which
had always hovered about this girl was sufficient to have
led her to be fanciful and imaginative and that the fabrications of the self-styled "mother" did not form an atmosphere
in which the girl could well achieve respect for truth.   But
Beula's almost confusional state concerning the facts of
her family life seemed quite explicable in the light of what
we at last ascertained.   Soon after we first saw the girl the
woman had told us a most remarkable tale of how it was she
happened to be the mother of the child, and the attempt
was then made by several to straighten out the apparent
doubt in the girl's mind.   But it seems that the clever and
tragic tale of the mother, although well calculated to do so,
did not entirely cover the points remembered by this girl
of her earliest childhood.   Evidently for a time Beula tried
to correlate the two, but doubt grew apace.   It seemed almost
as if her doubt as to who she was led her to say first one thing
and then another.   It was particularly at a period of stress
of this kind that she was figuring in other cities as the "mystery girl."

The earlier facts of the case probably never will be known.
Of the many details known by us it is sufficient to say that
the woman adopted Beula as a young child and proceeded
by devious methods to weave a network of lies about the
situation of their relationship.   Who Beula's parents really
were neither she nor any one else of whom we have heard,
ever knew.

Beula showed such delinquent tendencies after a time
that she had to be sent to a corrective institution.   After
coming out she made off in the world for herself before we
could give her the information soon afterwards obtained
by us.   At her last visit we felt that her report in a terribly
tragic mood on the family conditions was totally unreliable.
She went forth to weave, no doubt, new fabrications.

Early experiences: Peculiar treatment and excessive misrepresentations in home circle.	Case 2. Girl, age 19 years.

Mental influences: Contagion from long continued untruthfulness at home. Mystery of antecedents.

Mental conflict about the above.

Heredity and developmental conditions (?) Hutchinsonian teeth only clew.

Delinquencies: Lying. Running away. Sex.	Mentality: Fair ability with poor educational advantages.

CASE 3

Summary: In its wonderfully clear presentation of characteristics this case classically represents the type. A woman of 27 years (usually claiming to be 17), during a career of 7 or 8 years has engaged in an excessive amount of misrepresentation, often to the extent of swindling. Alleging herself to be merely a girl and without a family, she has repeatedly gained protection, sometimes for a year or more, in homes where her prevaricating tendencies, appearing with ever new details, have sooner or later thwarted her own interests. By extraordinary methods she has often simulated illnesses which have demanded hospital treatment. For long she was lost to her family, traveling about under different names, making her way by her remarkable abilities and unusual presence.

This case illustrates, again, two points we have often made, namely, that the difficulty of getting safe data concerning genetics increases rapidly with age, and that the chance of altering tendencies after years of character formation vastly diminishes. These features appear strongly here, yet our long knowledge of the person and of the many details of her career gives the history great interest.

A young woman, whom we will call Inez B., a name she

once assumed for a time, arrived at a girls' boarding home in Chicago with merely a small traveling bag and money sufficient only for a few days. In appearance and conversation she gave distinct evidences of refinement. She showed indecision and confessed she knew no one in the city.

Just at this time a wealthy eastern girl, Agnes W., was missing from her home, and the police everywhere were on the lookout for her. A detective who was ordered to visit the boarding club showed a picture of Agnes W. to the matron, who instantly discerned a likeness to Inez and informed him of her recent arrival. Inez was questioned, but could or would give no satisfactory response concerning her own home. She maintained she was just 17 and had come to Chicago to make her own way in the world. After some account of herself, the details of which were somewhat contradictory, it was inferred that she might be Agnes W. She vehemently denied it, but being the same age and some likeness being discerned, the questioning was continued. Various matters of Agnes W.'s antecedents were gone into and after a time Inez burst out with, "Well, if you must have it so, I am Agnes W." The girl was thereupon taken in charge by the police authorities, and she herself registered several times as Agnes W. After the family of the latter had been communicated with, however, it was ascertained that Inez was not the lost heiress.

She now said that anyhow she really was a runaway girl. She had left her adopted parents because they were cruel and immoral. It was her unhappy brooding over her own affairs that led her to lie about being the other girl. She insisted she was sorry for the many lies she had told various officers, but felt, after all, they were to blame because their obvious desire to have her tell that she was Agnes W. led her on. They deceived her first because they misrepresented themselves and did not say they were police officials.

Nevertheless, she makes much of how she hates her false
position, being registered under a false name and figuring
as a deceiver.

The significant points in the long story of Inez, as told
to us in the days of our first acquaintance with her, are
worth giving. (At this period she was with us thoroughly
consistent; at all times she has appeared self-possessed
and coherent.) Inez states she is 17 and has just come from
a town in Tennessee where she has been living for a couple
of years with some people by the name of B. who adopted
her. At first they were very good to her and she loved
them dearly. She was quite unsophisticated when she went
to them and did not realize then that they were not good
people. She met them at an employment agency in St.
Louis where she had gone after leaving the Smiths, the
people who had brought her up. At that time the B.'s
appeared fairly well-to-do, but Mr. B. had been running
up debts that later carried him into bankruptcy. Inez
was sick and exhausted now from having worked so hard
for them. She finally ran away from that town because the
B.'s wanted to go elsewhere, leaving her in a compromising
position with a young man who rented their house. She
first tried boarding in two places, however, before she ven-
tured to go.

The Smiths were the people she lived with until she was
14. She remembers first living with them, but faintly
recalls bearing the name of Mary Johnson before that.
Who the Johnsons were she does not know, but she feels
sure of the fact that she was born in New Orleans. However, Inez does not worry about her parentage even though
it is unknown. Mrs. Smith was an elderly woman of wealth
who was very good to her, and by the time she was 14 she
had studied German and French, algebra and trigonometry.
She had a French tutor and took lessons on the piano.

Always did well in school and loved her work there. The Smith children, who were much older, were very angry with their mother for all the money she spent on Inez — they would have preferred its being expended on their children. The son grew quite abusive and Mrs. S. was made to suffer so much that the girl came to feel that she was largely the cause of the old lady's unhappiness. After one particularly deplorable scene she slipped away from their home in New Orleans, traveled to St. Louis and went to an employment agency where she found the B.'s. At the present time, above all things, she does not want the Smiths to know about her when she is temporarily a failure. She will never go back to them until she can help the old lady who was so good to her.

Inez tells us she is now suffering from a wound still open as the result of an operation for appendicitis performed two years previously. She also suffered from tuberculosis a few years ago. (She was found to be running a slight temperature, and some slight hemorrhages in the sputum were observed.)

It may strengthen the portraiture so far sketched to give our impressions as stated after our first study covering a week or two; nor will it lessen the reader's interest to remark that it was not for lack of acquaintance with the pathological liar type that we failed to correctly size up this individual. Indeed, we had already studied nearly all the other cases cited in this monograph. Our statement ran as follows: "This girl is very frank and talkative with us. With her strong, but refined features and cultivated voice she is a good deal of a personality. She is sanguine and independent. Very likely she does not exaggerate the hard times she has had in going from one home to another. One cannot but respect this unusual young woman for wanting to keep her early history secret. It would be fortunate if some one

would care for the girl and get her ailments cured. With
her very good ability she might easily then be self-supporting."

A woman of strength and judgment undertook to look
after Inez. The girl's personality commanded interest.
In a few days she complained more vigorously of her abdominal trouble; an operation seemed imperative and was
performed. (An account of this will be given later.) Later
the girl was taken to a convalescent home and then to a
beautiful lake resort. While here she suddenly was stricken
desperately ill. Her friend was telegraphed for, a special
boat was commissioned, and the girl was taken to a neigh-
boring sanitarium. The doctors readily agreed that the
case was one of simulation or hysteria. She was brought
back to Chicago and warned that this sort of performance
would not pay. After being given further opportunity
to rest, although under less favorable circumstances, in a
few weeks she was offered work in several homes, but in
each instance the connection was soon severed. Then without letting her guardian-friend know, Inez suddenly left
the city.

Inquiries had brought by this time responses telling something of the career of Inez in the past two years, but nothing
earlier. She was the "mystery girl" in the Tennessee town,
as she was in Chicago. The B.'s kept a boarding-house and
took Inez as a waitress, knowing her first by still another
alias. She worked for them about a year and then went
to Memphis, where she was sick in a hospital. She had
now taken the B.'s name. They were regarded as her
guardians (on the girl's authority) and they finally sent for
her again out of pity, although they felt she had a question-
able past, and they knew she had lied tremendously while
with them. Then the B.'s moved away and turned Inez
over to a respectable family. While with the B.'s Inez had

been regarded as a partial invalid; their physician diagnosed the case as diabetes and found it incurable. In fact, the B.'s went into debt for her prolonged treatment. Another physician, who was called in after the B.'s left, said the trouble was Bright's disease. At any rate, all regarded her as suffering from some chronic disorder. Except for her extraordinary lying, of which she made exhibitions to many, and some little tendencies to dishonesty mixed with her lying, Inez was regarded as being quite normal. The two other families with whom she lived for a time found it impossible to tolerate the girl on account of her lying. Finally, obtaining money by false representation, telling the story of a rich uncle in Chicago to whom she was going, Inez departed, taking with her a trunk containing valuables belonging to the B.'s.

Dropping our chronological account of this case we may from this time deal with it as a whole, putting together the facts as they developed by further study of Inez herself and by the receipt of information from many sources.

Since we have known her, Inez has been under the observation of several skilled medical specialists. She all along has been in good general physical condition. Having been treated previously for diabetes, special examinations were repeatedly made, but never a trace of this trouble was discernible. Her own story of having had tuberculosis, and the traces of blood in the sputum, which she presented on handkerchiefs, etc., led to repeated tests for tuberculosis. These also proved absolutely negative. Before all this, there was found on the left side of the abdomen a mass which, from the history the girl gave, was surmised to be a tubercular abscess. At this time she was running a little temperature. An operation was performed and an encysted hairpin was removed from the peritoneal cavity. This had undoubtedly found entrance through the old appendi-

citis wound; the hairpin had evidently been straightened
for the purpose. Both wounds now speedily closed. Gynecological examination showed no disease and established
the fact of virginity. Thorough neurological examination
showed that the girl was not of nervous type and that
there was no evidence whatever of organic disease. There
was complaint of frequent headaches, but no signs of acute
suffering from these were ever witnessed and by this time
no reports of subjective symptoms could be credited. No
sensory defects of any importance. It was always easy to
get a little variation upon visual tests and the like, however.
Weight 130; height 5 ft. 1 in. Color good. Head notably
well shaped with broad high forehead. Strength good.
Very normal development in all ways.

Most important to note as bearing on her social career
was the fact that Inez was possessed of markedly strong,
regular, pleasant features, including a good set of teeth well
cared for, and an unusually firm chin. In attitude and
expression she seemed to give complete proof of great strength
of will and character. Her face suggested both frankness
and firmness. When with quiet force and dignity asserting
her desire for education and a place in the world, Inez presented a most convincing picture. Perhaps even more
significant is the fact that Inez possesses a speaking voice of
power and charm, well modulated and of general qualities
which could belong apparently to no other than a highly
cultivated person.

During a year there has been no variation in the general
well-being of Inez, although she has been taken to hospitals
in at least two more towns and has figured again as a sufferer
from tuberculosis and appendicitis, and has written several
times to friends that she was about to be operated on.

The diagnoses of several competent medical men are
that the girl is a simulator or is an hysterical, and their

findings show that she has lied tremendously about her past. (There were never any positive signs of hysteria, and our own opinion is that the case is much better called one of extreme simulation and misrepresentation, as in the diabetes and sputum affairs, etc., and of self-mutilation, as with the hairpin.)

We have had ample opportunity to become acquainted with Inez's mental qualities. She has repeatedly been given tests for mental ability. As judged by the average of those seen in our court work we are forced to regard her as having ability clearly above the normal. Her perceptions are keen and quick. She works planfully and rapidly with our concrete problems and shows good powers of mental representation. It is notable that she is very keen to do her best on tests and takes much delight in a good record. Her psychomotor control is astonishingly good. In a certain tapping test, which we consider well done if the individual has succeeded in tapping in 90 squares in 30 seconds, she did 117 and 129 at two successive trials with only one error in each. This is next to the best record we have ever seen. Our puzzle box, which is seldom opened in less than 2 minutes, she planfully attacked and conquered in 52 seconds. She also rapidly put it together again, which is an unusual performance. Reaction times on the antonym test, giving the opposites to words, were very low; average 1.4 seconds. Her immediate memory for words was normal, but nothing extraordinary. She gave correctly, although not quite in logical order, 18 out of 20 items on a passage which she read herself. On a passage read four times to her she gave 11 out of 12 items in correct sequence. The Kent-Rosanoff association test showed, to our surprise, nothing peculiar. Notwithstanding her known social characteristics, there were very few egocentric or subjective reactions.

Nor did the "Aussage" test show great peculiarity. On free recital she gave 17 items, two of which were incorrect. They were misinterpretations rather than inventions, however. On questioning she added 15 items. She was incorrect on 5 more details, but all of these were denials of objects actually to be seen in the picture. Not one was a fictitious addition. She rejected all the 6 suggestions proffered.

Our psychological observations were important beyond the giving of formal tests. We found her to be a fluent and remarkably logical and coherent conversationalist. Her choice of words was unusually good. Questioned about this she said she had always made it a point to cultivate a vocabulary and was particularly fond of the use of correct English. (This was all the more interesting because we later knew that she had been living recently with somewhat illiterate people and that her original home offered her very little in the way of educational advantages.) Inez told us that she had earlier carried her desire for self-expression in language to the point of writing stories and plays, but we were never able to get her to do anything of the kind for us. One of her constant pleas was that she might get the chance to become a well-trained teacher of English. Her letters never showed the same skill with English that her conversation denoted, but her meagre education probably accounted for this.

Characteristic of Inez, also, is her intense egoism and her abundant self-assertion under all circumstances. It often seemed to us as if for her the world revolved, with passing show, around a pivot from which she regarded it as existing only for what it meant for her career. These qualities have led to her statements, and perhaps to the actual feelings, that she was the aggrieved one, and had been badly treated on many occasions. This seemed to reach almost paranoidal heights at times, and yet, before passing judgment on this, one should be in position to know, what probably will never be known, namely, the actual facts of her earliest treatment. Occasionally Inez showed most unreasonable bad temper and obstinacy. This only came out when she was asked to do things which she considered occupationally beneath her. In general she felt herself much above the ordinary run of people. When she could be patronizing, as with children, she acted quite the grand lady. Indeed, in asserting herself on numerous occasions she has assumed just this attitude, which is all the more strange because our further information shows that it was not justified by any social station which her family ever held.

Going further with psychological considerations it is to be asserted that Inez showed marked lack of normal apperceptive ability in not appreciating the necessarily unfavorable results of her own lying. For that matter, she also fails to learn by experience, for very frequently she has suffered from her own prevarications. It might, however, be argued that to Inez the thought of a possible humdrum future in which there was no adventure, no roving, and no playing the part of a successful personality, was a worse choice than that of lying, which might and, indeed, often did serve the purpose of making friends with people, who otherwise would not have entertained her. So one could hardly judge her deficient even in this particular. (Of the character of her lying and the special observations on that point more later.)

We found Inez, then, neither mentally defective nor insane. To even say that she was without moral sense would be beyond the mark, for in many ways she showed great appreciation of the best types of behavior. Her peculiarities verging on the abnormal are, however, undoubted; they render her a socially pernicious person. They are to be summed up in terms of what we have discussed above, namely, her excessive egoism, her faulty judgment or apperceptions, her astounding tendency to falsification.

Inez was next heard from in Iowa where she wrote that two doctors had pronounced upon her case and said an operation was again imperative. She asked her recently made friend for permission to have this done, and also for $150 to cover expenses. Neither, of course, was forthcoming, on the grounds of there being no guardianship. (Her age was then unknown.) Inez wrote, "I just thought I was compelled by law to let you know of my whereabouts, for I understood I could do nothing without your consent." In the same letter, replete with other lies, Inez asks, "Please forgive me now for all my willfulness and wrongdoing. I will do my best never to do it again, and Oh ! I do so want to be good so that you may feel proud of me some day in the near future."

A month or so later this friend was called up by the director of a religious home for girls in Chicago, who stated that Inez had just come to them and had been taken seriously ill. Advice was given to discount her symptoms, but she was sent once more to a hospital. Here she produced more blood as if from a pulmonary hemorrhage and more symptoms were recounted, but the doctors decided after careful examination that she was falsifying. Her illness ceased the minute she was told to leave the hospital. Matters were serious, for Inez was now without home, money, or relatives. She was once more taken under protection and greater effort was made to trace her family. They were discovered through letters containing remittances sent by Inez herself from Iowa, after years of silence. Much of her career was soon brought to light. By this time, we may note, several observers had insisted that from a commonsense standpoint the girl certainly was insane.

While affairs were being looked up, Inez conferred with us from time to time. She started by telling a thoroughly good story, the general import of which was the same as she told months previously, but there were differences in many details. In the first place she still insisted she was 17 years old and gave us an exact date as her birthday — this was in response to the mild suggestion that she might be considerably older. Since her letters, although showing very good choice of words, were incorrectly punctuated, we inquired further about her education. She said she had received 18 credits in a noted girls' seminary in the south, but later reversed this and stated she had very little education. She told us her experiences of the last few months when she had been introducing literary works in the towns of Iowa. She had done well for a beginner at this, we found from other sources, but had made misrepresentations and had talked too freely, against her employers' wishes and advice. Finally she had sent in forged orders. This was quite unnecessary, for her salary was assured and sufficient, and her employers had regarded her as an extremely promising representative. In Iowa she was receiving mail under two different names; she still found it convenient to represent herself sometimes as Agnes W. In her peregrinations she had again made close friends with some substantial people, who found out, however, in short order that she was untruthful, and her chances with them were at once spoiled.

In the next weeks, when under observation, Inez varied her story from time to time even with the same persons. She was now 17 and now 19 years old. She had an operation first in one town and then it was in another. Her antecedents in many particulars varied from time to time. Inez seemed to have lost her desire or ability to be consistent, and in particular appeared to have no conception of the effect upon the adjustment of her own case which her continual lying was likely to have. (At this time again some non-professional observers insisted strenuously that Inez was insane. They based their opinion upon the fact that she showed so little apperceptive ability, so little judgment in relating the results of her continual lying to its necessary effect upon her career.) It requires too much space to go over the complicated details of her many stories, but some of her expressions and behavior are worth noting.

We always found Inez most friendly, sometimes voluble, and she ever dealt with us in a lady-like manner. Again we noted that many a society woman would give much for her well modulated voice and powers of verbal expression. Without any suggestion of melodrama she would rise to strong passages in giving vent to her feelings of indignation and ambition. At this time we were still wondering where she could have obtained her education; it was not until later that we comprehended that her abilities represented sheer native traits.

She first came to us much hurt because a certain official had warned her, after one of her simulating episodes in a hospital, never to deceive again. "My trying to get sympathy! I don't want any sympathy. I told her I was independent and always wanted to make my own way in the world. If they thought I wasn't sick in the hospital why didn't they say so. The doctor told me to stay in bed.

"Doctor, yes, I did lie to you about my age before; why shouldn't I? I have been deceived on all sides and have found that people are against me. If they want to leave me alone, they can get the truth, but when one is deceived one has to tell lies sometimes. I've had many troubles. Oh, doctor, if you knew what I've been through and what's in my heart you'd think I do pretty well. I would rather starve than have it cast up to me that I had asked for anybody's help or sympathy. I want to make my own way. I must have an education. In September I plan to go to the M. Academy and work my way through. I am just past 18 now.

"The B.'s are ashamed of me I suppose. I ran away from them. They are refined people. But I can't be treated in that way. They adopted me. They said that I got some money dishonestly, but, doctor, it is not in me to be bad. I feel that through and through.

"Well, I know that I'm a Yankee by birth, on both sides. My people came from Mayflower stock. I will make my way in the world, I will succeed, and you'll see, doctor. I will have an education. As to going back to the Johnsons, I would commit suicide rather than do that. It was not true that I had a good education as I told you. They did not treat me well. They can write as they please and talk about forgiveness for what I have done, but it is they who were cruel and abusive. Suppose they do say I'm their child. I know I am not because I was not treated the same as the others. I was 12 or 13 when I ran away from them. How could I belong to the family? They are all so much older than I am."

Inez now gave us, most curiously, some addresses which opened up knowledge of her career over several years. But what she told us about these new people was directly denied by return mail. At one interview her first words were, "Do you know now, doctor, that I was in a State hospital?" Having made this challenging statement she went no further, merely involved herself in contradictions as to the place, and would say nothing more than that she had once suffered from an attack of nervous prostration. She absolutely denied items of information 'about herself which we had gradually accumulated, and this type of reaction obtained all the way through our last period of acquaintance with

Inez, even after we had the detailed facts about her early life from her parents.

Inez never lost an opportunity to impress upon people whom she did not regard as her equals that she considered herself much of a lady and quite above housework. On one occasion, when held as a runaway girl, she had a terrible outbreak of temper simply because she was asked to clear the dinner table. This was no momentary affair. Her recalcitrancy was kept up the larger part of one day, and she made the place almost unbearable that night by screaming and moaning. Telling me about the incident, she said it was because she would not allow herself to cater to such people. "If a person asks me, I may do things, but nobody can tell me to. I would not give in. I would not do it."

To some of us it has seemed highly significant that at moments which would ordinarily be expected to bring out great emotion Inez showed almost none. For instance, when going to an important interview about the disposition of her case, she first plaintively said she did not know what to say, and then immediately began to dwell with evident pleasure upon the costume of the person addressing her. Many normal emotions were seen expressed, however, and many moral sentiments were undoubtedly held, but there seemed to be curious displacements upon these levels of her mental life; there was faulty mental stratification. Probably the force which caused this is egocentrism.

In relating what we now know of the past history of this case we shall put together that which we have heard from many different sources. There is no question about all the important facts — correspondents largely corroborate each other.

Inez came from a family of French extraction, apparently stable and normal tradespeople. The old mother at 74 years wrote us an unusually well-thought-out, detailed account of her daughter's early life. The paternal grandfather was insane and an aunt had epilepsy. Defective heredity in other respects is denied. We get no history of convulsions in the immediate family, nor of any other neurotic manifestation, except that one sister is "very excitable."

Inez came when the mother was unusually advanced in life, and the brothers and sisters, of whom there were five, had long since been born. There was a difference of 10 years between Inez and the next older. In telling the facts, the mother dwells much on this and the bearing which her chagrin during pregnancy may have had upon the girl's physical and mental development. She was born, then, after a troubled pregnancy, a weak and sickly child, "almost like a skeleton."

Inez was rather slow at walking, but at one year spoke her first words. We do not know with accuracy about the earliest factors in the mental environment. (Inez has told various stories about early family friction, and even about contracting an infection at home, much of which seems highly conjectural.) Between the ages of 7 and 10 several sicknesses, diphtheria, measles with some cardiac complication, etc., kept her much out of school. Part of the time she lived in New Orleans, and part of the time in a country district. She only went to school until she was 14, and was somewhat retarded on account of changing about and illnesses. However, it is said she always liked her school and showed fair aptitude for study. At 14 she returned to New Orleans and, desiring to be a dressmaker, started in that trade. She worked in several places, but finally went back to her home.

At the age of 18 Inez met with what, according to her family, was a decisive event in her life. She was in a trolley car accident; after being knocked down she was unconscious for some time. No definite injury was recorded. Her family marked an entire change of character from that time. They say she then began lying in the minutest detail about people and seemed to believe in her own falsifications. Besides this she started the roving tendency which she has shown ever since.

The extensive information which we have received concerning the later history of this remarkable case we can only take space to give in summary. We know definitely that Inez has received attention, during periods varying from a few days to six months, in no less than 18 different hospitals. Besides this she has been under the care of physicians at least a score of times. Her swindling in this matter was so flagrant in one eastern city to which she had journeyed that she was handled through the police court and was sentenced to a state hospital for the insane for a term of 6 months. The charge was that she was an idle person and a beggar, and she was regarded as perhaps being unbalanced. The report from this town is that she would be taken with "spells of apparent violent illness on the street, in the trolley cars, at railroad stations, and so be carried to various hospitals and doctors' homes." She has visited numerous cities, getting her sustenance largely through hospitals and physicians.

After being admitted into one famous hospital and showing some of her curious manifestations she was transferred to a state institution in the vicinity to be studied for insanity. Correspondence with one physician tells the story of how five years ago he was called from a medical meeting to attend this "girl" who had been taken from a trolley car into his home. She was apparently suffering great pain in the region of the old appendicitis scar and she was conveyed in an ambulance to a hospital. After investigation for a few days, it was decided she was hysterical or a simulator.

On numerous occasions her feigned illness has been so apparently overcoming that she has had to be transferred in an ambulance to a hospital. One of her usual performances has been to get into some home or institution and then keep others awake all night with her signs of distress. It is interesting that she has used the same methods over and over again, but has been adroit enough to vary the illnesses which she has simulated. At one time investigation in a hospital seemed to show that she was neurasthenic. She has been given chances in homes for convalescents, but has never maintained herself in such a place for long. We note she was sent back from one of these to the main hospital on account of having vomited the medicine she had been given. In fact, she has repeatedly been found resisting the treatment which had been prescribed.

The record of admission and treatment given in one hospital is of peculiar interest. She was received there four years ago and evidently had been unable just previously to take care of herself properly on account of roaming. Her clothing was dirty and her head unclean. She was found to have the old appendicitis scar, which contained a small sinus. She remained in bed after admission, complaining of much pain in her abdomen, not well localized however, and would lie moaning, crying, and rolling across the bed. She was then running a slight temperature. After a time an operation was decided upon and a hairpin was found in the abdominal wall, undoubtedly inserted through the scar by the patient herself. (The findings of the surgeon in Chicago, then, revealed a repeated performance.)

At another place the patient maintained she was unable to urinate, but at the same time strongly resisted catheterization. From the variability of her complaint it was found it could not be caused by a local condition, and examination showed no reason for the difficulty. Analysis of her symptoms undertaken at this time led to several stories, one about urethritis, which Inez claimed to have contracted from her brother at 3 years; an episode when she had received a great fright during micturition; an incident when she had seen a man exposed when she went to the toilet. (Of course, our experience with this type of case leads us to appreciate the difficulties of psychological analysis with extreme liars.)

On one occasion she entered a hospital, claiming to have been recently injured; she had been taken in a supposed fainting condition from a car. Then it was she maintained that she had been struck by an iron bar and that a spike had entered her back. She also claimed at this time to have had her toes frozen. Study of the case here, too, showed no signs of injury or frost bite. On another occasion she told of having been dropped by a nurse while being lifted from a bed. Altogether her stories and her simulations have been convincing enough to get for her on many occasions good attention during at least a few days.

We can get no account of true hysterical signs being discovered by any one. There has been no showing of anything but that she is a liar and a simulator. In the hospital records the portions devoted to previous history are thoroughly vitiated by her untruthfulness, and they contain statements which offer great contradictions, one to the other.

Inez has been observed, then, for two long periods by psychiatrists. While at the end of neither period were the observers willing to state that the young woman was *compos mentis*, still their verdict in this matter had to be made up from considerations of her social behavior rather than from what they were able to discern by direct observation of her mental processes. From one case-record we read that "The patient was quiet, pleasant, and agreeable, replied promptly and intelligently to questions, and talked spontaneously of her affairs. She was quite clear as to the environment, had apparently a satisfactory memory, with the exception of a recent period preceding admission. Her statements, too, were probably not altogether truthful, but frequently a reason for the untruthfulness was made out. She thought that her mind was all right, but complained of having occasional difficulty in thinking."

Another prolonged study of her mental status was made four years ago. From the record we learn that there were no apparent reactions to hallucinations. Consciousness was clear and the patient was completely oriented for time, place, and persons. The train of thought was coherent and relevant. Questions were readily answered and attention easily held. Memory was fair for most events. School knowledge was reasonably well retained. Judgment, to this observer, seemed impaired, although no definite delusions could be elicited. Emotionally she was found more or less irritable, fault finding, and at times a trifle despondent. (Certainly the latter would be a natural reaction under the circumstances.) Often, however, she was found cheerful and contented. No special volitional disturbances were noted. Was found to act in an hysterical manner when she felt ill. She was neat, tidy, and cleanly in her habits. Appetite was good and she slept well. Such was the report from the institution where she was held for six months. There was no material change in her condition during this time; she showed herself very proficient with the needle; she was discharged when her sentence expired.

We note a statement from one hospital that this " girl " gave no evidence of having had any direct sexual experience, or that she had ruminated much over these matters. Her story about frequent fainting attacks given at this time was not corroborated by observation. The diagnosis from one hospital was neurasthenia, but investigation of her case in most places seems to have led merely to the conclusion that she was a tremendous liar.

Notwithstanding our long record of this case and the accounts which have been handed in to us of experiences with her in other localities, we do not presume to know a tithe of the places Inez has been to or lived in during the last eight years. It is more than likely that she herself would find it difficult to give any accurate account of her rovings. At the time we first saw Inez her parents had not heard from her for about three years. Shortly after this we found that she had renewed correspondence with them and had sent them money as if she were now prosperous. Her family have all along, in spite of her stories, been poor. At one period she visited several cities in the southeastern states and was at a hospital in one of them. In Charleston there is a family by the name of B. (spelled the same as the name of the people she was with in Tennessee). These were the people Inez asked us to write to in an appeal, because they had long known her and were wealthy, for a chance to get an education. She stated they were immediate relatives of the B.'s in Tennessee, and that she had visited them once at their fine home in Charleston for three or four months. These people replied to us that they had been receiving letters for years from associations and organizations in regard to this girl whom they had never seen. They were convinced she had assumed their name because she had understood they were well-to-do and liberal. "We know nothing about her education, but judge she has enough to dupe people with; posing as poor at one time, sick at another, and anxious for an education at another, as you inform us."

From another correspondent with whom Inez had lived in Alabama for a few weeks we had a marvelous tale which they heard from her. She had told them she formerly lived in the most beautiful part of New Orleans and when 5 years old was placed in a convent, and then taken to a boarding-school, from which she was kidnapped and taken to a small town in Georgia. She was later placed in another boarding-school and there met the wealthy B.'s of Charleston who took her home with them. While there she had to go to a hospital on account of some infection. One day she was thrust into a taxicab, taken on a boat, landed at another city, etc. The B.'s of Charleston have thus figured long in her story, and we learned from several correspondents that this kidnapping has figured over and over as a big event in her life.

Once, years ago, Inez was taken into a private home accompanied by a trunk, we hear, which was found to contain a considerable amount of jewelry. This was pawned in the name of the people with whom she then lived and was redeemed later by some one else. Inez laid claim to the jewelry after a time, but apparently was unable to produce anybody who could vouch that it was really hers. Its ownership has remained unknown.

When she went to St. Louis at one time she had stated she was to meet a relative there, but the person, we have come to know, was a certain very decent young man who had become acquainted with her through a correspondence bureau. He had thought well of her and warned her not to come to that city, but when she did so he met her and took her at once to his own home where the womenfolk looked after her until she was found a place elsewhere. The deliberate attempt to throw herself upon his protection was thus frustrated by his relatives. Many other reports of the misrepresentations of Inez have been given us. She has discovered that borrowing money on the strength of invented statements is sometimes possible, particularly for her with her good presence and convincing manner. The B.'s complained that when she left Tennessee there were in her trunk many dollars' worth of articles that belonged to them.

Throughout our long experience with Inez we have never been able to make up our mind whether or not she remembered all of her past. Her lying always stood in the way of getting at anything like the real facts. On no occasion has she truthfully dealt with her career as we know it. She has professed absolute lack of knowledge of her accident, and of the time and place of its occurrence. It is interesting that none of her acquaintances mention this. Although Inez has told long stories of her past to many people, and with some inclusion of truth, she never seems to have mentioned this important event of which we learned from her family. We cannot, then, decide about possible amnesia for this occurrence.

On occasion Inez has expressed the same desire for religious experience as for education, and has written to friends that she had become imbued with the Spirit. Her story of her religious upbringing is altogether unreliable and contradictory, but while in one hospital she professed belief, took communion, and was baptized in a certain faith. Her behavior was not, however, in the least modified by this.

One serious minded woman took Inez at her word when she said she wanted to study algebra and offered her a good opportunity which was never accepted. This demonstrated clearly that the desire was a matter of words only. Inez' constant assertion of independence has been one of her main sources of temporary success. Kindly people have speedily taken up with her. Sympathy is undoubtedly, in spite of her statements to the contrary, one of the strongest needs of her nature. In one of her letters we note her expression of satisfaction in a certain situation where she found herself much "mothered" by kind nurses. All her chances, however, have been spoiled by her indulgence in lies.

Inez has remained adamant to every plea and suggestion made by many well-wishing friends that she reform and begin again. After her parents and other relatives were found and communicated with, her career partly known, and her mother's need of sympathy shown to her, she still refused to change her story in many particulars — even when she knew that we had discovered about her writing home within recent months. She steadily refused to acknowledge her true age. When the evidence was complete, showing that she could not be held as a runaway girl, but must be treated under the law as a woman, she went forth to begin, as we heard from many other sources, her old misrepresentations of herself, which speedily got her into further trouble.

We were not astonished, even after we had accumulated almost the entire knowledge of the career which we have outlined above, and Inez knew that we had done so, to be visited by two fine philanthropic women who wanted to consult with us about an unfortunate girl who had won their sympathy, and who had been placed by them in a leading hospital after having shown some signs of acute bronchitis. In fact, she was in such a bad condition that she had to be transferred in an ambulance. But her illness had rapidly cleared up and now after ten days of observation an eminent diagnostician had thoroughly scolded her for simulation, and the girl was once more on their hands. Indirectly they learned that we knew of the case of this "girl of 16." They realized that they had been taken in, but it had been done so cleverly, and, as they expressed it, Inez showed herself such a splendid actress, that they wondered if she had not extraordinary histrionic abilities which could be utilized. (It remains to be seen whether anything constructive can be done by following this lead. We feel that previous psychiatrists who gave earlier an unfavorable prognosis in this case were perhaps quite right. But perhaps we should not let our opinions in this be swayed by the fact that my associate, Dr. Bronner, who went to this last hospital was met by an absolute denial on the part of Inez of the essentials of the above career, by her insistence that she was not the same person as the daughter of the Smiths, and that she was only 17 — all this in spite of her knowledge of our correspondence with her family and others, and her own previous acknowledgments of lying.)

Summary: In summarizing the characteristics of this woman we may first insist that she has ambition, push, and energy in high degree. Her personality as expressed in general bearing, features, and facial action is remarkably strong and convincing. Her ambition was shown in her work on our tests as well as in her social behavior. (We have wondered if it was not her desire to shine which prevented the typical performance of the pathological liar on the "Aussage" test.) Her self-confidence as expressed on numerous occasions is no less striking. "I tell you, doctor, that I have told lies, but you will see that I will come out on top."

Inez has been free from the overt problems of sex life. We have repeatedly been informed that she has been a girl of good character in this respect. "I ran away from home for a good cause. I'm not one of those girls who is crazy about the boys." Usually Inez shows a very even temper. It is only when her own personality is trod upon that she grows angry, and obstinacy is then her leading reaction. Some pathological liars may be weak in character, but not Inez. She is the firmest of persons. On occasions her attitude is entirely that of the grand lady.

Her type of lying is clearly pathological. It would often be very hard to discern a purpose in it, and over and over again she has defeated her own ends by further indulgence in prevarications. To her the utterance of lies comes just as quickly and naturally as speaking the truth comes to other people. Even in interviews with us when she was voluntarily acknowledging her shortcomings in this direction she went on in the same breath to further falsifications.

The medical aspects of the case come under the same category as the lying. The dysuria, the spitting of blood, the sugar in the urine, the hairpins found twice in the abdomen, the simulated pains, neurasthenia, and bronchial attacks, together with her stories of accidents and fainting spells illustrate her general tendency. This behavior, like her lying, serves to feed her egocentrism, her craving for sympathy and for being the center of action. As with the lying, repetition of this type of conduct probably is largely a matter of habit.

The bearing of this case on the problems of testimony is interesting. As shown in our account of tests done, when objective concrete material was considered by this woman she reported it well. It is only when her egocentrism is brought into play that she becomes so definitely unreliable. This is a line of demarcation that students of this subject would do well to recognize.

Causative Factors: Our study of causation in this case, as we intimated at first, is necessarily incomplete. But some things, probably explanatory, stand out very clearly. Heredity is moderately defective. Inez was the outcome of an unfortunate pregnancy and was a poorly developed infant. She suffered early from a number of illnesses, which, however, left no perceptible physical defects. Her unusual relationship to the other children, based on the difference in age, was perhaps a starting point for the development of her inventional theories of her own origin. She has given us many hints of this in speaking of her earliest remembrances of hearing the Smiths whispering something about adoption, and of her feeling that the other children were too old for her to belong to their family.

Then we insist on the positive bearing which this woman's native traits have had in the production of her career. Her facility with language marks her as possessing one of the chief characteristics of the pathological liar. Added to this she showed the other personal traits which we have described in detail, leading to her success in misrepresenting herself. Her strongly developed physiognomy has caused many people to believe her older than she stated, but still one has seen such lineaments belonging to girls of 17.

The bearing which the accident at 18 had upon the case it is impossible for us to estimate. Her family are very clear on this point; they maintain that all her bad conduct has developed since then. Through unwillingness, or barely possibly real amnesia for the injury, Inez has not helped us to know the facts. Dr. Augusta Bronner, who has studied this case with me, cleverly suggests that just as anyone becomes confused in distinguishing really remembered experiences from what has been told by others was one's experience, so Inez gets confused between what has really happened and what she herself has told as having happened. This finally involves a pathological liar in a network which is difficult to untangle. Part of the causation of the present lying, then, is the extensive lying which has been done previously.

Psychological analysis in such a case is most difficult because of the unreliability of the individual's own statements about her life, inner and outer. Psychoanalysts will be delighted, in the light of what we long afterward found out, at the pregnant opening sentence of an interview, recorded above, when Inez blurted out that she was once in a State hospital. However, from what we ascertained, we may see clearly that here is an individual with a past that she desires to cover up. Much more delinquency may be involved of which we know nothing. As the result of circumstances and traits she finds herself, despite her very good ability, inadequately meeting the world. Her forceful personality carries her into situations which she is incompetent to live up to. The immediate way out is by creating a new complication, and this may be through lies or the simulation of illness, at which she has become an adept. Altogether, Inez must be thought of as one who is trying to satisfy certain wishes and ambitions which are too much for her resources. Towards the goal to which her nature urges her she follows the path of least resistance. Being the personality that she is, the social world offers her stimulation which does not come to others.

To discuss the problem of her responsibility would be to introduce metaphysics — it is sure that in the ordinary sense she is not insane. The cause of her career is not a psychosis, although we readily grant that out of the materials of her mental experience she may ultimately build up definite delusions.

CASE 4

Summary: A girl of 15 had been engaged in an extraordinary amount of clever shoplifting under the influence of her " mother." In the courts where the cases against her were heard there was much sympathy with the girl, but it was difficult to carry out any measures for her benefit because of the excessive prevarications which had characterized her for a long period. Under oath she falsely accused her " father " of sex immorality with her. She was removed from her home, and with knowledge of the mental conflicts which beset her, splendid efforts to " cure " this girl met with success. It is another case where supposed inherited traits turn out to be the result of environmental influences.

Through frequent communication with the highly intelligent woman with whom Edna F. was placed in a small western city after she was taken from her previous miserable environment, we have been able to keep close check on the progress of the case for several years. It was also very fortunate for our understanding that a nurse who knew the girl's real mother in New York, where Edna was born, appeared on the scene and gave us data upon which we could base some opinions of the outcome. The case in its entirety had proved very baffling to detectives because of the mass of contradictory lies told by both the girl and her "mother."

Our attention was first called to this girl when a number of court people were trying to solve the mystery. She had been arrested for shoplifting and her curious attitude and statements had made some believe she was not quite right mentally. Once before she had been detected stealing things in a shop. One of her remarkable statements this last time was that her parents were implicated in the thieving and she named certain stolen articles which might be found at their home. She went with the detectives and accused her "mother" of wearing a dress which she, Edna, had stolen. The woman was forced to give up the dress and other articles, but it was found later that these goods had been actually bought and paid for by the parents. Later it was found that the woman was a party to the girl's stealing and this made the girl's story seem all the more strange, for if she were going to involve the people at all why did she not pick out the actually stolen articles? However, long study of the case brought out the fact that this type of statement was a characteristic of Edna's. Her word on even important points was absolutely unreliable and her own interests were frequently thwarted by her prevarications.

The case in its different aspects came up in court again and

again until finally most of the truth was ascertained, enough
to justify radical measures being undertaken. During this
period the mother was discovered to be an atrocious liar;
even with her last bitter confession that all she had said
about her motherhood had been untrue, she manufactured
more quite unnecessary falsehoods. In the meantime the
family physician and the family lawyer had both informed
me of the peculiar mysteries of the case and of the perfect
mass of lies into which the statements of both mother and
daughter led. This sort of thing had been going on for
years. It is of no small interest to note that the woman was
greatly over-dressed and made up. On numerous occasions
she appealed to us to study the girl and find out why she
lied so much and why she had such an inclination to steal,
in the meantime attempting to fill us up with many inventions about the girl's antecedents.

Physical examination showed a perfectly normally developed girl. No sensory defects. Pleasant features. Well
shaped head. Weight 101 lbs; height 5 ft. 1 in. We found
no hysterical stigmata. Menstruation had first occurred
at 14. No trouble or irregularity was reported. We learn
the girl has never had any serious illness. She herself
told of fainting spells after being whipped and so on, but
these were undoubtedly falsifications. The family physician
informed us he had operated on the girl for appendicitis
about three months previous to the time we first saw her.
He had found some evidences of an old appendiceal inflammation, but it is quite likely from the various accounts which
we heard that her symptoms recounted to him were largely
fabrication and that the signs which he found, at least in
their excessive phases, were partly deceptions. The most
important point for the court proceedings was his findings
that the girl had never been sexually tampered with and had
no local disease. At the time when we knew Edna she was

being treated for a local infection which must have been recent and superficial, for it rapidly subsided.

We had ample opportunity to test Edna's ability and found it quite normal. She had been out of school much and had been careless in general about her education, but she had finally finished the grammar school. A long list of tests was done almost uniformly well. Where a prolonged task which required concentration was asked, Edna was inclined to work carelessly, but in general her capacities proved to be decidedly good. She was accustomed to read nothing but the lightest literature and fairy stories and her interests were of the superficial sort. Neither in powers of imagery or imagination, nor by anything else ascertained about her mental abilities did we come to know of any point of special bearing upon her behavior.

On the "Aussage" picture test, she gave only 12 details, all correct, on free recital. Upon questioning she gave 28 more items and almost the only variation from accuracy was in respect to the colors. Evidently she let her fancy run when she could not remember correctly; through this she got 6 items incorrect. She readily accepted 3 out of 4 suggestions.

Our earliest impressions of Edna state that she seemed much confused in her stories and in her manner of telling them, leaving sentences unfinished and trying to explain inconsistencies by other inconsistencies. At this time she was referring constantly to her doubts about her age, her family, and her origin. She then seemed highly suspicious of every one and talked of suicide. However, when she was showing these signs she could be diverted, for she worked with much pleasure at the tests, particularly certain memory tests on which she did well.

On account of the difficulties of the solution of this case under the law considerable time and effort were spent in looking up her record. It was found that some years ago Edna had run away from home and there was a newspaper article published about her. Even at that time an officer who went to the home was unable to ascertain the truth in the case. The family had frequently moved and the mother asserted it was because of the bad reputation which the girl's actions had given them. The neighbors complained of the cruelty of the parents to Edna, but this meant only the whippings which the mother had given her. By all accounts the father was a good man who insisted that affairs between his wife and Edna were not his own. (Edna always maintained that this man had been unusually good to her, although she so strangely made in court the false accusations of prolonged sex immorality on his part and reiterated these statements even to us. It was not until many months afterward that she acknowledged the falsity of her accusations, although we knew from her physician that they were not true.)

The first time Edna was in court was when she was about 14 years old. At that time she had been observed by a department store detective stealing hosiery and a bracelet. She perceived she was being shadowed and walked up to the counter and ordered some children's garments, having them charged and sent to a fictitious name and address. The detective thought this a masterpiece of slyness, this endeavor to throw them off the track. Since the family, who really kept an account at this store, appealed to the manager to have Edna let off as it was an ordinary trick of a growing girl, the charge was withdrawn. Detectives who had been employed from a private agency made a very poor showing on getting at the real facts. The husband was doing well in his business and there never seemed to be any reason to suspect his wife of being directly or indirectly connected with the shoplifting. Earlier there was some intimation that Edna was not the child of these people, but the persons who suggested this did not know the true facts and were found to have a grudge against the mother. In the meantime the latter had strongly maintained her relationship.

It was months after this and just before we saw the case when a detective, who had kept the case in mind, went to the house to get the goods which Edna maintained had been stolen. There he found the "mother" and another woman smoking and thought he detected signs of their being drug habitués. Later, I myself felt sure of this point, but we were never able to state to what drug they were addicted. Edna frequently stated she had been accustomed to buying morphine for these women, but her statements about its appearance and its cost were so at variance with the facts that though it is likely she had bought something of the kind, yet no amount of inquiry brought out the definite facts. The woman's appearance and her remarkable lack of veracity were both highly suggestive of a drug habit.

In our several interviews with this woman we were amazed by her strange self-contradictions. It was not only that she stated something different from what she had said a week before, but even at different times on the same day her statements would be changed. Concerning her relationship to Edna she gave us the facts of the girl's birth and laughed off the idea that she was not the girl's mother. "Why, I can remember every moment of my pregnancy with her." It was anomalous that this woman had hired a righteous man as a lawyer to represent her and the girl. This attorney, consulting with me, soon came to the conclusion that the only interest he would serve in the case was that of the girl, and then only in the effort to save her from the miserable influences of her mother.

Edna's school record was most peculiar. She had been frequently changed on account of her dishonesty. In one sectarian school she was said to steal all sorts of useless things — bits of string, pieces of pencils, and articles no one else would want. She also stole a two dollar bill from a grocery store; the cashier followed her and recovered the money from her person right there in the school. Edna always denied that she took things. While in another school she had flowers sent to all the teachers and the florist's bill was presented to her there. In still another school she took a pair of shoes from a boy at recess, wore these and left her old ones in the locker room. Her word was everywhere recognized as being most unreliable.

After the case had long been in court and Edna still stoutly maintained that she was not the child of these parents, but had complicated her story by adding incidents which were known to be untrue, such as her "father's" immorality with her, that there had been another adopted child in the family, that even the dishes the family used were stolen by her, and so on, the woman came and suddenly blurted out that she herself had been lying all along and that this was not her child. She then alleged the parentage was so and so, but this matter was in turn looked up and found to be false. It was adjudged that these people had absolutely no parental rights, and then work was begun on constructive measures of redeeming the girl if possible. It was not long after this that the nurse came to us who had known the girl's real mother in New York and who had taken charge of Edna as an infant before her foster mother had taken her. It seems that the mother was an American, that this child was illegitimate. A few months after her birth the mother abandoned her, became dissolute and is said to have since died.

Edna had run away from home on several occasions and slept in hallways for a night or two at a time. She had not been sexually immoral until just previous to our seeing

her. Then while away from home she had gone with a
man to a hotel, and probably had also been with boys.
These were her first and last experiences of the sort, but how
much these affairs had been on her mind we obtained some
intimation of from herself.

"My mother took me to S's when I was 8 years old and
told me to take anything I could and I got into the habit of
it. I can't stop myself. I take anything I want. Mother
said she would kill me if I told the truth. I had to say lots
of things that were not so. I had to lie and say mother did
not beat me, but she had a horsewhip that was plaited,
father burned it. Then they bought a little one, but she
beat me with a rubber hose and everything. The first
thing I think I stole was jewelry in a store down-town.
The woman I call 'auntie' said if I would give her the goods
she would pay me for them."

"My mother fixed it up that if she got the goods and got
caught she would get a clerk to make out receipts and get
them stamped paid. She has not done this yet, but I think
she will in this case." (This was a statement at the very
first interview with Edna and no doubt had reference to
the fact that the mother could produce receipted bills for
the dress and other articles which Edna had maintained to
the detective she herself had stolen. Of course the girl's
story of this was untrue; the receipts were genuine.)

"One of my sisters is adopted, but my father does not
know it. She ain't real. It was this way. When my pa
was out west for a year ma asked me to look in the papers
for a baby and I looked and found an advertisement about
one. Ma said she must not be redheaded because that ain't
like the family. We went and got her and ma went to bed
for nine days and pretended it was her baby. She took a
shawl and gave the nurse $25 and made out adoption papers.
She took me with her. It was a month old. She made me

go and tell my aunt I had a little sister. My aunt said it looked kind of big for 3 days old, but ma said she had been keeping it in an incubator. She had padded herself out before, and pretended it was her own child. Pa came home when it was six months old and he loved the baby just like his own. I ain't jealous, but it makes me sick to hear such lies."

This alleged fact, reiterated to us and testified to in the court, was in itself a source of the whole case being farther followed up. The nurse was found who took care of Edna's "mother" during her confinement and it was found that Edna's whole story was quite untrue. It was evidently an elaborate fabrication representing the facts as they might have been about Edna herself. The only part of it that was true was that one of the younger children had been for a time in an incubator.

"Since I was 10 years old I have known about that. I have known I was not her child. She said something that sounded queer to me once when I ran away. It made me think she was not my mother.

"Why do I tell lies? I got started at it when I was small. She used to make me tell lies to my father. I began to steal when I was about 8 years old. My little sister has started to take things already. She is only 4. I was trying to break her and mother said, 'Let her alone.'

"She's had about nine different servants. She never can keep any. She used to make me forge letters. She made me sign a girl's name to a receipt for wages which the girl never received. The girl had no case against her because she had the receipts. The poor girl lost it.

"I am going to tell the truth. There's going to be lots of things come out. I am going to tell the judge I lied when I told him I did not steal the things. Why did I lie? Well, she gave me just one look and I knew what she would do to me when I got home. Everything I told you about my father is the truth. Where else would I get that disease? I was never allowed to go out with boys."

At another time when we inquired what bothered or worried her more than anything else we obtained an account of her sex repressions. Of course there would always be difficulty in knowing just how true the details were but probably she gave us the main factors in her mental life.

"I used to be out in the streets all the time. There were hardly any houses around there then. I used to hear mother talk about things. She would send me out of the room and say it was not for me to hear. Then boys lived near me and they asked me to do bad things. I first heard about those things from a boy on the porch. I was 7 or 8. I was always thinking about it — what my mother said at that time, I mean. She did not explain it enough. I am always fidgety, always nervous. My hands and feet are always going. Whenever I would see a boy it would always come up in front of my eyes. It was mostly when I saw boys. If she had explained it more it would not have come up that way. I know a girl who does that thing. She's bad. She does it with boys too. The people said so. When I was little I imagined there were some bad girls. You can't tell, but you can guess a little. That boy had lots of things. I don't know if he took anything. It was when I was about 4 until I was 8 that I played with him. These things never came up in my mind when I was taking things. It was only when I was not busy. I was always thinking about it when I haven't anything else to do. These few little words were not enough to explain. I remember I asked my aunt once. I tried to put things together what I heard, and what words about it meant."

The above excerpts from many interviews with this girl represent points upon which there is the least contradiction.

It is obviously useless to give any more of her story because of the variation from time to time. Even on the last occasion when we talked earnestly to her before she was taken to her new home, she lied to us about a number of points. Any attempt at an accurate analysis of her impulse to steal seemed quite beyond the mark in the light of her ever-ready fabrications.

The after-history of this case is of the utmost importance. A woman of strong character took Edna and surrounded her with new interests. Conference was had with us on the nature of the case. For the next few months reports came that the girl was a liar through and through and grave doubts were entertained of ultimate success. It was after she had been tried in her new environment for 3 months that, seeing us again, she confessed that her stories about her foster father were absolutely untrue. From about this time on there has been steady improvement. No more elaborate fabrications have been indulged in. On several occasions when Edna has been late from school she has lied about it, but even that tendency for the last year has been nearly obliterated. A good deal of interest in boys has been maintained, but not with any show of immorality. There has been nothing but normal flirting; accounting for the occasions when Edna has been late from school.

At two or three periods during her new life Edna has engaged in stealing. She has taken articles for which she had no particular use and has told lies about the matter. The thieving has not been a single event, but each time has seemed to represent a state of mind she has been in, and for a week or so numerous articles have been taken. We warned her good friend to make a study of her social and mental influences at such periods. It was found then that Edna was undergoing special stress on at least one such occasion. A young man had been making up to her, and later she confided that this given period was one of great turmoil because of the renewed arousal of many ideas about sex affairs. After this there was still more attempts to win Edna's confidence about her daily experiences, including such as the above. There has been the gradual development of character, and Edna is now, two years after she was taken from her bad environment, only very occasionally guilty of falsifying, and she is otherwise trustworthy.

Our study of the causative factors of this girl's delinquency and particularly of her extraordinary lying led us to see that perhaps all of the following have a part: (a) Heredity. Father unknown. Mother a free-living woman. (b) Home conditions. Mental and moral bad influences in the home life on account of the foster mother conniving at stealing and being herself an extreme liar. (c) Psychic contagion from the atmosphere of lies in which the girl has been brought up. (d) Mental conflict arising from the suspicion of her parentage, early acquaintance with sex knowledge, and the irregular morale of her home life. (e) Bad companions, including her foster mother's friends, and boys and girls.

Mental Conflict.   Case 4.

                                      Girl, age 15 yrs.

    Home influences: Extremely bad, including excessive lying.

      Bad companions.

      Heredity (?).

Delinquencies: Mentality:

  Much stealing. (Shop lifting, etc.)   Fair ability.

  Excessive lying. False accusations.

  Sex immorality.

CASE 5

Summary: A young woman of 20, bright mentally, strong physically, " confessed " to a professor of a university where she was studying that she had shot and killed a man. The facts were known to only three or four people and she was terribly worried about it all. Upon her information the affair was taken up by a group of professional men, one of them a lawyer of large practical experience. She aided in an investigation which attempted to uncover the " white slave " feature of the case. The data of verification proved most elusive. Later, the young woman implicated herself in a burglary, and altogether an elaborate story of her life was evolved. It was found that from early years she had been a great fabricator.

While a first year student at a university Marie M. begged for an interview with one of her instructors at his home and there, with him and others, she told a detailed story of how some months previously she had escaped a difficult situation by killing a man.

The exceedingly long account which was given at intervals to several professional men and enlarged upon in response to inquiry, or as the occasion otherwise demanded, we are not justified in taking space to retell. This case figures, as a whole, in somewhat anecdotal fashion among our others, we freely confess; it is cited to show the extent to which apparently purposeless fabrication can go. It has been found impossible to gain a satisfactory idea of the genesis of this young woman's tendency, quite in contrast to the other cases we have cited. It forms the only instance where we have drawn from our experience with merely partially studied cases.

Marie's story involved many items of her life since she was about 12 years of age. A distant relative who had come to know her whereabouts (she was an orphan living with friends) figured extensively in her narrative. This relative had hounded her in an effort to get her to engage in an evil life. His attentions varied greatly ; sometimes for months she was not bothered with him.   Once when she was on her way to Milwaukee a gray haired man approached her on the train, said he knew her relatives, they were rather a bad lot of people, and he wanted to protect her from them.   Then came a long account of being driven in a carriage, changing her clothes in a hotel, having her picture taken in an immodest costume, signing a paper at police headquarters, and, at last, safely returning home, all guided by the mysterious gray haired man.   Another trip led to an encounter with a man who took her in an automobile under the promise of meeting a friend.   Entering a building where men carried revolvers and girls were given hypodermic injections, just as she was about to receive the needle in her arm, she reached the man's revolver and shot him in the back.   Events follow swiftly in her tale, but all is thoroughly coherent, and a number of facts are included which could be substantiated. The professional men could not help being impressed and spent much valuable time before they felt convinced that it was a fabrication.   The exact locations could not be discovered, but then Marie was a stranger in the city.

When we saw her the whole story was reiterated with but few changes, which, however, from the standpoint of testimony were most important.   We soon found we could get direct testimony on physical features which were provably untrue.   For instance, the description of a certain hallway in a building where she had gone with one of the men interested in the events was totally unlike anything that existed there.   Then, too, certain embellishments, which by this time included the payment of a large check to her as hush money, a check which she as easily gave away again, seemed altogether improbable.   Marie by this time was implicating herself in a burglary with this relative, and some other curious incidents were given.   In all of these, as we later found, there was a central event about which her statements *might* have been true.   There was such a burglary; she had said in previous years that she was hounded by a man, and so on.   We, too, were struck by the uselessness and lack of purpose in the lying — for we soon felt assured that it was such.

Physically we found Marie to be a decidedly good speci- men.   She weighed about 140 lbs.   Strong and firm in carriage.   Vivacious in expression.   The physical examina- tion at the university had shown her to be without notable defect of any kind.   We can summarize Marie's characteris- tics by stating that from the earliest age of which we can get satisfactory record, when she was about 10 years old, she has been persistently addicted to falsehoods.   Even then she made up, without any basis, stories which puzzled many people.   It is much to the point that she has been a great loser on account of this tendency; it has injured her repu- tation on numerous occasions and destroyed many of her good chances.   When she was about 15 it was noticed that she was a great day-dreamer.   She thought she could write stories and once began a novel.   Much more peculiar than this was the fact that she repeatedly wrote letters to her friends which were simply a mass of fabrications, de- scribing such things as imaginary excursions.

Tests for mental ability were not given in this case, there was no need for it.   Her marks in the preparatory course were just fair.   It had been noted by her teachers, as well as by her foster parents, that she was prone to have periods when attention to her work seemed difficult.   Aside from her peculiarities, which showed themselves entirely in her fabricating tendency and her assumed illnesses, nothing much out of the way in her mental life had ever been noted. On several occasions she had taken to her bed, but when a physician was called, a diagnosis was given of simulation, or hysteria. Nothing like major hysterical attacks at any time occurred.

From most excellent sources of information we have obtained an account of the family history. No instance of insanity is known, but it is said there is much evidence of ignorance and superstition. Marie's mother bore a good character, but was decidedly ignorant. At about the age of 50 she made a homicidal attack upon a second husband and then killed herself. The father was an industrious and sober laborer, but unable to support his large family. At his death in Marie's early childhood the family was broken up and the ten children were distributed about. None of the children is said to be abnormal mentally, but there has been a tendency to free living, even on the part of the older sisters. It seems very sure that no other member of the family was given to telling false stories. The brothers have been inclined to be shiftless and to roam, but then the environmental conditions often have been against them. However, some of them have done well. In general, as far as Marie is concerned, it may be said early home environment was not bad except on account of poverty. Marie bears no traces of having suffered from defective conditions before or after birth. Her early developmental history appears to be negative. She has lived about in several different homes, the longest stay being about seven years. In one place she was suspected of masturbation, but we were unable to get a perfectly definite statement that she was addicted to the habit.

Two years prior to the time we knew Marie she had worked up a story of adventure in which she was the heroine. She used the telephone to call for help, stating that she stood with a revolver covering a burglar. From this incident she gained a good deal of notoriety. The police found there was nothing to the case and later Marie herself made a confession.   By the time we saw her this story varied somewhat from her original statement, but was still persisted in, although she must have known that we could readily trace the actual occurrence.

After Marie had continued her stories for a few weeks while attending the university they had grown so that they included night visitations in her boarding-house from the man who was said to be hounding her, she was found once more impossible to deal with and, as her work became poorer, she had to leave.   At this period it was most significant to us that in spite of her expressed desire for freedom from persecution she did not want us to look further into her case because of certain mysterious letters which would incriminate her.   We felt entirely convinced that the several reports which we received of her career in preceding years gave a satisfactory clew to her character, although we were never able to analyze the case far enough to ascertain the genetic features.   Thus it is impossible to make any summary of causative factors.

Case 6

Summary: A thoroughly characteristic example of the type of pathological lying which led to the invention of the term pseudologia phantastica.   A young woman, well endowed physically and mentally, for years has often been indulging in extensive fabrications which have no discernible basis in advantages accruing to herself.   The peculiarities of the falsifications have given rise to much trouble for her, her family, and for many others who have been incidentally connected with the situation. The genesis of the tendency was finally found in early experiences about which there have been much mental repression and conflict.   In the background there was also defective home control and chronic neuropathic tendencies in both parents and in their kin.

Janet B., 19 years old, we saw first in an eastern city at the request of her parents.   There she had become involved

in troubles which seemed particularly hard to unravel.
However, we were told that this was an old story with her.
A diagnosis of her mental condition was asked, and recommendations for the future. Janet had told some very peculiar stories at her place of employment where she was
doing very well as a newcomer, without any seeming reason
for fabrication. Several who had become interested in her
were wondering if she were quite sane.

After having made her way alone to New York, Janet
readily obtained employment. After a couple of weeks she
approached a department manager of the concern for which
she worked and related a long story, which at once aroused
his sympathy. She told him that her father and mother
had died in the last year and that she was entirely dependent
upon herself. When she was about four years of age she
had been in a terrible accident and a certain man had saved
her life. Naturally, her father had always thought very
highly of this person and had pensioned him. Formerly he
lived up in the country with his family, but at present was
old, penniless, and alone in the city. Now that her parents
were dead she was in a quandary about keeping up her
father's obligation to the old man. Out of her $8 a week it
was hard to make both ends meet. She had to pay her own
board and for this man also. She found that he needed to
be taken care of in every way; she had to wash his face and
dress him, he was so helpless. She made no demand for
any increase of salary and the story was told evidently
without any specific intent. The services of a social worker
were enlisted by the firm and the girl reiterated the same
story to her, even though it was clearly intended that the
case should be investigated. Janet's boarding-house was
visited and there she was found to be living with distant
relatives whom she had searched out upon her arrival in
the city. They knew she had run away from home and,

indeed, by this time the mother herself was already in New York, having been sent for by them.

The situation then became more complicated through the girl's giving more explanatory details to the social worker, somewhat accusing her own family. It was at this time I first saw her. She then acknowledged that this story of a man who had saved her life was purely an invention. Now she stated that in the western town where she lived she had been engaged to a young man who was discovered to be a defaulter and who had recently died. When this fellow was in trouble, his mother, while calling on Janet's family, used to make signals to her and leave notes under the table cover, asking for funds with which to help him out. This was a great strain upon Janet and even more so was his death. She could stand it no longer and fled the city. Her lover's stealing was a secret which she had kept from her own family.

Before we had become acquainted with the true facts about the family this girl gave us most extensive accounts of various phases of her home life which included the most unlikely and contradictory details. For instance, they had a large house with beautiful grounds, yet before she left home she bought a sewing machine for her mother, which she is paying for on weekly installments. Her $8 a week is very little for her to live on because she is paying this indebtedness. Janet wishes now to take out a twenty year endowment policy in favor of her mother. Her brothers and sister are all very bright, she tells us, but she has never been particularly close to any member of her family except her mother. The others always remind her that they are better educated than she is. She expects to take up French and Spanish in the evenings because they would be very helpful to her commercially. She does not care to grow up, prefers simple enjoyments, and has no desire for social affairs.

She is only desirous of improving her education. She relates her success as a Sunday School teacher. She thinks at times she is very nervous, and especially when she was in the high school she showed signs of it. Then she used to stutter much, but of late she has been able to control this.

At another time, very glibly and without the slightest show of emotion, she continues with her story. Tells of frequent fainting spells when she goes from one attack into another. She has not had them just recently, but she used to have them at home. Tells us now that her mother has been very sick and she has been worrying much about her. She wanted to send money to her and help support her. 'It's awfully hard on one to know your mother is terribly sick and to think you can't reach her if anything should happen." (It is to be remembered that all this was told when the girl must have known, if she had thought at all, that we would certainly get the full facts in a day or so.)

On the physical side we found a very well developed and well nourished young woman. Weight 148 lbs. No sensory defect noted. Moderately coarse features, broad deep chest, quiet and strong attitude. No signs whatever of nervousness. Her only complaint at present is of headaches and "quivering" attacks. (We could get no corroboration at all of either of these from any one else.) She frequently spoke of herself as entirely healthy except for these slight ailments. Some months later, *vide infra*, it was discovered that Janet had a chronic pelvic trouble. The most notable finding was Janet's facial expression when confronted by some of her incongruities of behavior. Then she assumed a most peculiar, open-eyed, wondering, dumb expression. When flatly told a certain part of her story was falsehood, she looked one straight in the eyes and said in a wonderfully demure and semi-sorrowful manner, "I am sorry you think so." Her expression was sincere enough to make even experienced observers half think they must themselves be wrong.

On the mental side she demonstrated good ability in many ways. She had been through two years of high school and showed evidences of her training. We tested her for a number of different capacities and, with one exception, we found all through that she did fairly satisfactory work, showing herself to have normal mental capabilities and control.

This exception was in the "Aussag " or testimony test. Here in reporting on our standard picture she gave in free recital 17 items, which is a fair result, but she added several incorrect details. On questioning she gave 12 more items, but invented still more details. Of the seven standard suggestions offered she very curiously accepted only one, and that not important. As an example of how she would supply details from her fancy is the following: The picture represents a little girl standing by the side of an older person. Janet said it was a little boy, that he had his hands in his pockets, a muffler on his neck, a stocking cap on his head, and black shoes and stockings. All of these were voluntarily offered and all were incorrect.

Beyond this curious performance, and her peculiar lack of foresight and shrewdness, or whatever it is that causes her so readily to falsify and fabricate, we found not the slightest evidence of aberration. Her conversation was coherent and to the point.

In the information obtained from the intelligent parents the following points stand out clearly. The heredity is of interest. There has been no known case of feeblemindedness, insanity, or epilepsy on either side, but there is a great admixture of very good with quite unstable qualities. This is true of both sides. Some members of the family have taken high positions in the community, and been exceptionally endowed mentally. Others have been notoriously lack-

ing in stability.   We are informed that on one side some have
shown a marked inclination for tampering with the truth,
and it is suggested that Janet's tendency is the result of
early influence.   The care of an incompetent grandmother,
whose word was notoriously untrustworthy, devolved upon
the family and it was impossible to prevent Janet from being
much with her.   All of the children were aware of the old
lady's untruthfulness.   One of Janet's parents had been addicted to narcotics, but had managed to shake off the habit.
The other parent has had a severe attack of "nervous prostration," largely induced, it is maintained, by worry over
family affairs.   It is most interesting to note that the other
children, two boys and one girl, have turned out remarkably well; two being university graduates, and all being
very stable in character.   Both parents are people of good
moral ideals, and in spite of their own nervous defects have
given their children very good care.

The pregnancy with Janet was not entirely healthy, but
no worse than with the other children.   Her birth and infancy were normal.   Walked and talked early.   Started to
school at 6.   Menstruated first at 13; not irregular.   She
never had any severe illnesses of any kind.   As a child she
once fell down some steps and was unconscious for a few
minutes, but the accident was not known to have left any
bad effects.   Janet's own stories of fainting are much exaggerated.   In fact, the mother has never really seen her
faint, nor is there any evidence of any minor lapses of consciousness.   At times the girl would feel faint and ask that
water be poured on her forehead — that was all there was
to it.   She was removed in the middle of her high school
course on account of general nervousness.   The doctor felt
she was working too hard.   Her parents are sure she was
never a great sufferer from headaches.   Nothing else of importance could be found in her physical history.

The story of this girl's falsifications and fabrications as obtained from her people is exceedingly long. As a young child she was not over-indulged in fairy stories, and the parents noticed nothing peculiar about her then. She was not regarded as a child who had any unusual powers of imagination. Somewhere about 12 years of age, her parents cannot be certain just when, they noticed she began the exaggeration and lying which has continued more or less ever since. In the past two or three years this has grown upon her and she has been making not only untrue statements, but has been concocting peculiarly long and intricate fabrications. The curious thing to the family is that Janet seems to have little shrewdness in lying; of normal ability in other things, she seems to have the mind of a child in this. Very many deceptions are discovered in short order, but even then the girl will sometimes argue at length that what she has said was really the truth. The parents insist she must know that she is lying, but her anomalous behavior has been so excessive that they have long felt she should be studied by a psychiatrist. Her mother asserts there is some periodicity in Janet's tendencies. She maintains she has noticed that most of her lies are told in the two or three days preceding menstruation. (This was certainly not true during the period we observed the girl.) The parents are sure there has never been any particular mental shock, and the mother has always felt that Janet was particularly free from contamination by bad children. At times she seems to realize her own bad behavior, and not long ago said she would become a nun, for in the tranquil life of the convent her tendency to lying would not be stimulated.

Further inquiry brought out the fact that it was true, as Janet stated, that in her high school course she became nervous to the extent of jerking and twitching, and that also for a time she stuttered. Their physician said, however, that there was no definite nervous disease.

As a young child the parents never thought this girl in any way different from the rest of the family. As she grew older she has been regarded as physically the most robust, but, as she stated to us, she has done the poorest intellectual work and that has often been a matter of family comment. The other children are careful truth tellers.

The type of Janet's lying has been not only in the form of falsifications about matters which directly concerned herself, but also involved extensive manufacture of long stories, phantasies. Meeting people she might give them extensive accounts of the wealth and importance of her own family. She once spread the report that her sister was married and living in a fine home close by, giving many elaborate details of the new household. Such stories naturally caused much family embarrassment. Then she worked up an imaginary entertainment and gave invitations to her brothers and sister at the request of a pretended hostess. Just before the event she, simulating the hostess, telephoned that an accident had taken place and the party would not be given. An extremely delicate situation arose because she alleged a certain young man wanted to marry her. The truth of her assertions in this matter never was investigated. The parents felt it quite impossible to go to the young man about the facts on account of the danger of exposing their daughter. They were long embarrassed by the extent to which she kept this affair going, but it finally was dropped without any social scandal occurring. In this and other affairs the family situation was at times unbearable because of the possibility that there might be some truth underlying the girl's statements. As the years went on Janet, of course, suffered from her loss of reputation, but still continued her practices of lying. In the two years before she left home she worked as a clerk.   Previously she had held two or three situations and was reported to give good satisfaction in her work, but something would always come up about money matters, or other things, which would finally give rise to trouble.   It is not known that she ever really took any money except the last time when she ran away and took a considerable sum from her parents.

A period of extensive untruthfulness and deception occurred before she left home.   Janet represented to her parents that she was working at a certain place after she had left. She got into some mix-up about money matters, the rights of which never were straightened out.   As usual, the affair was too complicated to be understood by anything short of a prolonged investigation.   After things had come to this pass and her parents hardly knew what to do with her, she took money from them and ran away.   She was readily traced because the ticket agent in her home town could give a description of her.   She had bought a ticket to an intermediate point and there stopped over night.   Her father followed her thus far.   It seems when she finally got to New York she hunted up the distant relatives who took her in and informed the mother.   The girl intended to earn her own living and soon found a good place.   She was always able to make a good presentation of herself, being a quiet and convincing conversationalist.

Out of the mess of lies surrounding her New York experience, it was finally found that she had met a young man in a boarding-house and had become infatuated with him.   He was an honest enough fellow, but fell in readily with her forwardness.   He took her to shows, and letters, intercepted by the mother, showed that between them there had been some premature love passages.   At that time Janet started making weekly payments on a gold watch to give to this young man at Christmas, a curious and quite unwarranted expenditure. Perhaps this was the fact around which some of her fabrications at that time centered. Perhaps it was this money which became now the amount she was paying to her father's pensioner, now what she had to send home to her mother, and, again, her payments upon an imaginary sewing machine. In this affair, as at other times, the lying was extremely childish, inasmuch as the truth, through receipts found in her room, proved to be readily ascertainable.

A good example of the character of Janet's falsifications was the story about the death of her lover, told to us at our last interview with her when she had come to us with the specific purpose of trying to get herself straightened out once and for all. She was not aware that her parents had given me any account of this young man, but she might well have supposed that I had inquired about him, or at least would inquire. Only a few minutes previously she had told about her lying and given a very definite account of its beginnings which was much in accord with what her parents had said. Mentioning her love affairs, she maintained that, unbeknown to her parents, she had been engaged to this man, but that he had proved to be a thief, stealing money and robbing the mails. She started off on a story of how another young man was accused, but no evidence was forthcoming about him, and soon afterward her lover died. Getting him safely buried for us, she was quite willing to go on to another topic.

The workings of Janet's mind in connection with her alterations of a story were sometimes most curious. We were interested to study a long letter quite coherently written to her mother a few days before we saw the young woman, and about the time when she first told her long story to the department manager. In the letter she spoke of the extraordinary opportunities she now had in this place of employment, exaggerating her salary to $14 a week. She stated she had already had a raise, and could get work for other members of her family at good salaries. She was about to start a bank account, and so on. But instead of making any remittances to her mother (such as she asserted at one time) she requested her parents to send her $5 to tide her over. We counted no less than nine definite falsehoods in this epistle. We were keen to know if Janet could remember her own prevarications and so asked her if she could recall what she had written to her mother. She trimmed her statements most curiously then, being aware we knew her salary to be $8 a week. She said she had told her mother her salary was $10, but in answer to our reply, "Oh, you said more than that," she blurted out, "Well, I said $14." It was quite evident she remembered this, as well as certain other exaggerated statements and figures in the letter.

We were fortunate enough to be able to analyze out much of the genesis of this girl's career as a pathological liar. After the immediate situation was somewhat cleared and Janet asserted she was anxious to make a new start in life, we began our inquiry into beginnings. Janet showed willingness to enter into the question of her mental antecedents and tendencies which she maintained she heartily deplored. To be sure we had evidence that even in her most sincere moments she was unable to refrain from occasional falsifying, but the main facts seemed self-evidently true, and some of them were corroborated at interviews with the parents.

After considering her own career with us for a time, she asserted that it now was clear to her just how and when she began lying. As a child of about 12 years it seems she was wont to meet with a certain group of girls on a hillside and they indulged in many conversations about sex matters. Evidently the circumstances surrounding this important introduction into affairs of sex life were indelibly impressed upon her mind. She was there instructed not only in the general facts, but also in methods of self-gratification. It is clear to her, she states, that it was exactly at this time that she first began deceiving her mother and telling lies. She explains these tendencies as the result of a guilty conscience. It comes out that the mother did not know this group of girls to be undesirable companions for Janet, but the latter's consciousness of their frailties always led her to state that she had been with other children when in reality she had been in this bad companionship. Through dwelling on their teachings she began sex practices by herself, and in order to carry this out she had to indulge in other deceptions. She remembers distinctly her willful repression of the facts, and states that the nervousness which she displayed for two or three years in her school work was undoubtedly due to this cause. In fact, she thought so at the time, but persisted in deceiving her mother and her physician in regard to the matter.

Her mental repressions and conflicts did not begin, however, at this period. By digging further into her memory Janet tells us about a girl in another town where they used to live, a girl who, when Janet was about 7 years old, wanted to show her about sex practices. Janet knew this girl to be bad by general reputation, and ran away when this offer was made, but it was too late — the mental impress had been formed. She thinks her mother would remember this girl. The things which this bad girl started to tell came frequently up in Janet's mind and she wondered much about them. No practices, however, were indulged in and even the thoughts were fought against until the time mentioned above when other sex ideas were implanted. Janet's mother had neither given nor received confidences on this subject, and indeed never throughout the daughter's life has there been anything except vague warnings on the part of the mother about the general dangers of sex immorality.

We gradually came to learn that Janet had been subject to much sex temptation from her own physical feelings. She never was a good sleeper, she thinks, and she often lies awake, or will wake up for a time in the middle of the night and think of sex affairs. She feels sure there has been considerable stress upon her on account of this temptation which she has felt should be combated. The occasional giving way to sex habits also resulted in mental stress and, as she expresses it, worry.

At the time of her failure to do well in school work her internal conflicts were especially acute. There was before her continually the success which the other members of her family had made, which she herself admired, and for which she was ambitious. She hid at that time the cause of her nervousness and failure; there was the danger of its being discovered. After thus reviewing her case with us, Janet reiterated that she was sure her tendency to prevaricate came on at the time when she first began her bad sex habits.

This girl was probably not much of a day-dreamer. She denies being so, saying she had always been too busy for such to be the case. We also obtained corroboration of this from others who had closely observed her. She says she had lived no specially imaginative life beyond occasionally thinking of herself as a well-to-do lady with many good clothes to wear, or sometimes lying in bed and imagining she had a lover there. Further inquiry into her imaginative life seemed futile because she was not trained in introspection and because even in her frankest moments we were always afraid that she might fall into her strongly formed habit of prevarication. We ascertained that in her home life special efforts had been made to keep her busy and she could not be regarded as a dreamer. Janet strongly denied the periodicity in her lying which her mother maintained, but the girl did state that her periods of sex temptation were mostly just preceding her menstrual period.

In giving the above account of what was ascertained by analysis with Janet we have offered such of her statements as are clearly probable or which are corroborated by the parents. Our many experiences with the young woman led us to be particularly careful in accepting as veracious any of her statements unless, as in what is given above, they clearly followed the type of fact which may be ascertained in the investigation of other instances of pathological lying where the individual's word is more reliable. The parents were able to corroborate many points. The mother remembers the older girl in the town where they lived when Janet was 7 years old and that this girl was notorious for her sex tendencies, although she was not in the least aware that Janet had been contaminated. Then she recollects that Janet used to tell her so particularly about going with a special crowd of girls (those which she now says were not her companions). Both parents considered the matter at great length in order to help my study of the case and both are very certain that it was just about this period when Janet says she was beginning her covert sex experiences that she began the lying, which was petty at first, but after a time expanded into the type of detailed falsifications we have enumerated above. Altogether there was little doubt in our minds that Janet was giving the truth in its main outlines. Undoubtedly it was merely her habit which always led her to alter somewhat the details.

We were interested to note that in her letters and in her ordinary conversation Janet took up the topics that a fairly well educated girl would naturally discuss. For instance, she would give us some account of her recent reading, or a visit to an art gallery, telling us with normal vivacity about a couple of pictures which had deeply impressed her. She spoke not only of their subjective influence, but discussed the details of composition and coloring. We might mention that in a characteristic way she interjected some remarks that she herself used to be very good at drawing and won several prizes at it. She stated that she thought of going farther in art, but that her parents could hardly afford to allow her to do this. These remarks were found later to be quite aside from the truth.

Telling us the story of her school career, Janet insists her memory had never been good for learning poems or for languages, particularly Latin, but anything in the way of a picture she could recall with ease. What she has read she often thinks of in the form of pictures. Concerning her lying she denied it was done particularly to cover up things, at least since the time when the habit was first formed. She feels that it really is a habit, a very bad one. She hardly knows she is going to prevaricate; the false statement comes out suddenly. In thinking about it all she harks back once more to that crowd of girls; everybody thought they were good, but she knew they were not.

After a time of quieting down in her behavior tendencies, although there was never complete cessation of the inclination to falsify, a new exacerbation of lying arose. This time it seemed to center about a clandestine love affair of a mild type. There was one trouble with this case which neither I nor any one else was able to clear for the parents. It was perfectly apparent that the girl might naturally be expected to marry at some time. Now, when an honest young man felt inspired to keep company with this vivacious, healthy, and generally attractive young woman, what were the parents to do? It was easy enough for them to decide that she must not go with a man of bad character, but were they bound in honor to inform any young man, before affairs

had gone too far, that the girl had this unfortunate tendency
and that she had had rather a shady career? It was perfectly clear to them that she herself would not tell him.
This was how the matter stood at the time we last heard of
the case, and while the parents were holding back, a young
man's affections and the girl's fabrications were growing
apace.

Janet had been suffering from a chronic inflammation of
the bladder, which, however, did not cause any acute symptoms. A chronic pelvic inflammation was discovered, for
which she was operated upon in her home town. The surgeon
reported to the parents that conditions were such that they
would naturally be highly irritative, although there had been
no previous complaint about them. The girl made an exceedingly rapid recovery. It was after this that her last
affair of the affections was causing the parental quandary
and distress.

Our final diagnosis of this case, after careful study of it,
was that it was a typical case of pathological lying, mythomania, or pseudologia phantastica. The girl could not be
called a defective in any ordinary sense. Her capabilities
were above the average. She showed good moral instincts
in many directions and was at times altogether penitent.
Nor could she be said to have a psychosis. The trouble was
confined to one form of conduct.

The lying, as in all these cases, seemed undertaken sometimes for the advantages which thereby might accrue. On
the other hand, at times the falsification seemed to have
no relation to personal advantages. Indeed, this girl had
experience, many times repeated, that her lying very quickly
resulted in suffering to her. There were aspects of her
falsifications which made it seem as if there was pleasure in
the mere manufacture of the stories themselves and in the
living, even for a short time, in the situations which she had

created out of her imagination and communicated to others. Frequently there seemed to be an unwillingness on her part to face the true facts of existence. In her representation of things as different from what they really were she seemed to show even the desire for self-deception. Another point: no student of cases of this kind should allow himself to forget the potency of habit formation. There can be little doubt but that a large share of this girl's conduct was the result of her well developed and long maintained tendency to trim the facts.

As far as we were able to determine, and we undoubtedly got at the essential facts, this girl's falsifying trait was based on the following: The fact that she came of neuropathic stock would make us think that she possibly inherited an unstable mental make-up. To be sure, the only evidence of it was in this anomalous characteristic of hers, namely, her pathological lying. She seemed sound in her nervous make-up. The idea that the grandmother passed on as inheritance her prevaricating traits is open to discussion, but we have seen that environmental influences from this source may have been the only effect, if there was any at all. Very important in this case, without any doubt, is the early sex teaching, its repression and the mental conflict about it for years, and then the reintroduction into the subject just before puberty. Probably this is the vital point of the girl's whole career. The success she early achieved in deceiving her mother, not by denials, but by the elaboration of imaginary situations, has been the chief determinant of her unfortunate behavior. Added to that was the formation of a habit and of an attitude towards life in which the stern realities were evaded by the interposition of unrealities. Even the affair of the imaginary social gathering can be conceived in this light, for evidently she and her family were not engaged then in social affairs and the preparation for a gay event would for a time be a source of excitement and pleasure. Her auto-eroticism may have helped towards the production of phantasies and the general tendency to evasion of the realities of life.

It was clear from first to last that the exploration of the genesis of the tendencies in such a case as this could be but one step towards a cure. What was also needed was prolonged disciplinary treatment under conditions which were well nigh impossible to be gained at her age. Willingness on the part of the individual to enter into any long period of discipline or education, such as an institution might offer, is not easily obtained.

Mental conflict: early and severe.	Case 6.
Early sex experiences and habits.	Girl, age 19 yrs.
Mental habit formation.	
Home conditions: defective understanding and control, although ordinarily good home. Early acquaintance with lying.	
Heredity: neuropathic tendencies on both sides.	
Delinquencies:	Mentality:
Excessive lying.	Ability well up to
Runaway.	the ordinary.

Case 7

Summary: A girl of 16 brought to us by her mother, who regards her as abnormal mentally because she is an excessive liar and delinquent in other minor ways, proved to be an habitual masturbator. Under direction, the mother succeeded in curing her of this habit, with the remarkable result that the young woman became in the course of a couple of years quite reliable.

We first saw this young woman of 16 with the mother who maintained that there must be something wrong with the girl's mentality because of her lying, recent running away from home, and some minor misconduct. There had been trouble with her since she was 7 years old. She was the twin of a child who died early and who never developed normally. Her mother said she seemed smart enough in some ways; she had reached 7th grade before she was 14, but even at that time she was a truant and would run off to moving-picture shows at every opportunity. Her father was a rascal and came of an immoral family. He had a criminal record, and that was another reason why the mother felt this girl was going to the bad. The mother herself was strong and healthy; she was remarried. The existence of feeble-mindedness, epilepsy, or insanity on either side was denied.

We quickly observed by the physical conditions of this girl that something was the matter. Expression sad and dull. Long thin face and compressed lips. Vision almost nil in one eye, but normal in the other. Hearing normal. Color only fair. Weight 115 lbs.; height 5 ft. 4 in. Most notable was her general listlessness. "I feel draggy and tired. I'm yawning all the time."

On the mental tests we found much irregularity. Tasks that were done without effort were done fairly well. The girl was a good reader and wrote a good hand. A long task in arithmetic was with difficulty done correctly. When she was able to get hold of herself she could do even our harder tests with accuracy. Her failures were apparently from lack of concentration and attention. Although she did some things well we felt obliged to call her dull from physical causes, feeling that if she were in better condition she might give a much better performance.

On the "Aussage," or Testimony Test, 11 items were given on free recital and 2 of these were wrong. Upon questioning, 17 more details were added and 4 of these were incorrect. 2 out of 5 suggestions definitely accepted.

Under observation it was just as the mother said.   The
girl was an extreme falsifier.   As one observer puts it, "she is
not malicious in her lies, but just lies all the time and seems
to try to make herself believe what she is saying."

"I was in the 7th grade.   Had a hundred jobs since then.
Can't keep them because I'm so draggy.   They want their
money's worth — they want a more live girl.   Sometimes
I don't mind my mother and I get spunky.   I feel lonesome
and get mad.   I feel tired.   I can't please my mother no
matter how hard I try.   I'd like to go in some little home
where I could have a chance."

After a few days we found this girl in a decidedly good
mood, wanting to be helped.   She willingly entered into the
analysis of her case with us and said she thought most of her
trouble came because she was a day-dreamer.   "Sometimes
I dream of things in the day time.   I'll sit and stare and stare
and think of different things.   I'll think I'm doing them.
I'll dream of things what I do and if I read a good play I'll
dream of that.   When I think of myself or somebody starts
looking at me I'll stop dreaming."

To another observer this girl gave a vivid description of
how she felt after seeing pictures in the nickel shows.   She
states that love-making scenes lead her to practice self-abuse.
This matter was taken up with her mother who stated that
when this child was 7 years old she and the father had
caught her at this habit and had severely reprimanded her
and had thought she had stopped it.   We were particularly
interested to hear this because it was exactly the time the
mother had specified as the beginning of her lying and
general bad behavior.   Going farther into the case with the
mother and the girl we ascertained that her bad sex habits
had been continued more or less during all these years, and
of late, particularly under the influence of picture shows, and
of what some other girls were doing in the way of delinquency,

the habit had become worse than ever. It was closely connected evidently with day-dreaming all these years and with the development of the fabricating tendency.

The mother who had been apparently so negligent of causes proved now to be a stalwart in this case and took the girl under her immediate charge. There was steady betterment. The girl went back and finished school and at the end of a year was reported as tremendously improved. There was no further complaint about her lying. We know that after this she long held a good position which any hint of untrustworthiness or lack of capacity would have lost her. Thus the cure of her sex habits brought about cessation of her extreme untruthfulness.

Bad sex habits long continued.   Case 7.

    Heredity. (?) Father immoral   Girl, age 16 yrs.
             and criminal.

        Home conditions.   Lack of understanding and
                      supervision.

Delinquencies: Mentality:
  Excessive lying.   Dull from physical
  Early truancy.   causes. (Later
  Running away.   quite normal.)

CASE 8

Summary: A thoroughly illustrative case of long continued, excessive pathological lying on the part of a very bright girl, now 17 years old. As this young woman has well known, her falsifications have many times militated against the fulfillment of her own desires and interests. In the face of clear apperception of her fault, the tendency to react to a situation by lying sometimes appears to be fairly imperative. The only ascertained bases of the tendency are her early reactions, unthwarted by

parental control, followed by habit formation; all in an environment peculiarly favorable to deception. The lying passed over
into swindling.

Gertrude S., who immigrated from England with her
parents ten years previously, was seen by us when she was 17,
after she had been engaged for months in a career of misrepresentation which had led her case into the hands of
several social agencies. Much difficulty was encountered
because repeatedly when people had tried to help her she
had led them astray in their investigations by telling ridic-
ulously unnecessary falsehoods. Her parents came to see
us and gradually we obtained a detailed and probably quite
reliable family and developmental history. About the
evolution of the young woman's mental life we have unfortunately had to rely much upon her own word. This has
made our studies rather more unsatisfactory than in other
cases where corroboration from parents was obtained.
However, there is much that rings true and is of interest even
in the unverifiable part of the study.

There is not much to be said about the physical examination; it was negative in most respects. She is of rather
slight type; weight 110 lbs., height 5 ft. 1 in. Delicate
features of mature type. Expression intelligent and decidedly refined for her social class. Gynecological examination made by a specialist revealed nothing abnormal and no
evidence of immorality. Menstruation said to have taken
place at 13 years and to be regular and not difficult.

In studying Gertrude's mental powers we gave a considerable range of tests and found her to be well up to the ordinary
in ability. She showed no remarkable ability in any direction, but gave an almost uniformly good performance on
tests. Concerning her other mental traits and especially
her range of information and reading more will be said later.
No signs of aberration were discovered by any one.

The record on the "Aussage" picture test is as follows: She gave 16 items on free recital with considerable reference to functional details and with side comments as to who the little girl might be, and what the dog wanted, and so on. So far, this was the performance of a rational, quick-minded person. On questioning, 28 more items were added, but no less than 12 of these were incorrect — she evidently supplied freely from her imagination. Of the 7 suggestions which were offered she took 5. Twice not only was the main suggestion accepted, but imaginary details were added. Naturally, this is a very unusual record from a normal person.

There is absolutely nothing of significance in the heredity, according to the accounts received by us. All the grand-parents are still alive in the old country. They are small townspeople of good reputation. Epilepsy, insanity, and feeblemindedness are stoutly denied and are probably absent in near relatives. The father is a staunch citizen who feels keenly the disgrace of the present situation. He is a hard working clerk. We early learned the mother was not to be relied upon. Our best evidence of this came from Gertrude. She told us she had always been accustomed to hearing lies in her own household. According to the father his wife's falsifications are merely to shield the children and she only shows the ordinary deceit of woman. We have no history of this woman ever having indulged in elaborate fabrications and, in general, she is of thoroughly good reputation. In delicacy of feature the girl is her mother over again.

Gertrude's birth was comparatively easy after a normal pregnancy. After a healthy first infancy she had an illness at 2 years which lasted for three or four months. The exact nature of this is not plain, but it was probably bronchitis with complications. There were no evidences of any involve-ment of the nervous system. She walked and talked early, at about 1 year of age. She has had no other serious illness

in all her life and has had no convulsions. None of the
children has suffered from convulsions. Gertrude is one of
five, all of whom are alive and well. In the last couple of
years she has complained a little of headaches and some
other minor troubles. It was typical of the family situation
that after Gertrude had told us of a series of fainting spells a
year previously, the mother corroborated her and, indeed,
made them out even worse. But when the reliable father
was consulted on the matter it turned out there had been no
such fainting attacks, nor could they be verified by communication with a doctor who is said to have attended
Gertrude. Unquestionably they never occurred. Gertrude
went to school at the usual age, but on account of poverty
and immigration missed many long periods. However, at
14 she had gone through the 6th grade.

About Gertrude's moral evolution we got very little aid
from the parents or indeed from any others. It was very
evident that from earliest childhood the girl had led a mental
life of which her relatives knew nothing. Naturally, the
mother gave us no account of the development of the tendency to lying; she merely glossed over her daughter's
deceptions. The father, who had been obliged to work away
from home much during Gertrude's early years, merely
knew that at about the time she left school, namely 14 years,
she began to lie excessively.

Anything like a complete account of Gertrude's prevarications, even as we know them, would require much space.
Some idea of their quantity and quality may be gained from
the facts which we have gleaned from several sources. As
might be supposed, Gertrude has established a reputation
for falsification among many of her acquaintances. One
friend tells how she represented herself as a half orphan,
living with a hard-hearted step-mother. Demanding prom-
ises of secrecy, Gertrude told this girl about a sum which

she had with much difficulty gradually saved from her earnings in order to buy needed clothes. She asked the friend to come and help her make a selection. (Now the $20 or so that was spent Gertrude had stolen. By following her strange impulse she, with danger to herself, related a complicated story to this other girl who needed to know nothing of any part of the affair.) We have knowledge of scores of other fabrications which were detected. They include her alleged attendance at a course of lectures, her possession of a certain library card, and her working in various places. For many of these stories not a shadow of a reason appeared — especially during the time we have known her she has had every incentive to tell the truth about everything.

When by virtue of our court work we first knew the case, her lying centered about her other delinquencies, but even so its peculiar characteristics stood out sharply.

Gertrude was held to the adult court in the matter of the forgery of a check, which had been presented in an envelope to a bank teller by her and cashed as in the regular line of business between the bank and the firm for which she worked. Finding the girl had lied about her age, she was held, after the preliminary hearing, to the proper court. There, in turn, she did not appear at the right time, it being stated that she was sick in a hospital. One officer knew better and further investigation showed that Gertrude herself had come to the court, represented herself as her sister, and made the false statement about the illness. A telephone call the same afternoon to her house Gertrude answered.

Months of difficulty with the case began now. Her employer and all concerned experienced much difficulty in getting at the truth of the forgery, particularly through her clever implication of a man who had no easy task in freeing himself. Even after the girl confessed herself a confirmed liar she told more untruths which were peculiarly hard to

unravel. Gertrude's firm bearing, her comparative refinement and her ability made every one unusually anxious to do
her justice, and to save her from her own self-damaging
tendencies.

During the continuance of the case, when all her interests
demanded her good behavior, Gertrude could not refrain
from what were almost orgies of lying and deceit. She well
realized how this would count against her and, indeed, wrote
letters of apology repeatedly for her misconduct.

"Let me come and tell you all. The time has come when
things must stop, therefore I feel that I must talk to someone. I have lived a lie from the day I was born until now."

After these letters she went on making false statements
which could readily be checked up. Nothing is any more
curious in Gertrude's case than the anomaly of her telling
several of us who tried to help her that up to the time of the
given interview she had not thoroughly realized how bad it
was to lie, and how she now felt keenly that she must cease,
while perhaps at the end of the very same interview a reaction
to a new situation would produce more fabrications. Per-
sonally I have seen nothing any more suggestive of the typical
toper's good resolutions and sudden falling from grace.

The story of the forged check was fancifully embellished
and ever more details were supplied at pleasure. While
this matter was under investigation Gertrude stayed away
from home several nights, two of which have never been
accounted for. She told fairly plausible stories about going
out of town, but she first should have studied time tables to
make them wholly convincing. The mother, too, told that
the girl had been out of town, but in this she was caught,
for it was found that Gertrude had been part of the time
with other relatives.

The main story of the check involved a man who worked
in the same office. She stated that he made an immoral

proposal to her on the basis of immunity from prosecution. After a couple of months Gertrude got round to confessing that she alone was responsible for the entire forgery and that her previous quite clever stories were not true. Her main confession was made in the form of a long letter written entirely aside from the influence of any one. In this she also stated that she had stolen money and jewelry, which was known to have been taken. There was no untrue self-accusation, except that she may have exaggerated her own tendency to falsify at a very early age. Naturally, in such a case as this, even the latest confession must always be taken *cum grano salis*.

Passing from the above probably sufficient account of Gertrude's falsifications as we knew them, we can take up her mental life and traits. We have had to rely on the girl herself, as we stated above, for many of these facts. She was brought up in poor circumstances in a manufacturing town in England where there had been many labor troubles. On two occasions when she was a child she had seen encounters on the street, and during one riot in their neighborhood her uncle was injured. She was considerably frightened, but, so far as we could learn, this was the only time in her life that she experienced any fear. Very early she found that stories told to frighten her were untrue, and what was said about the undesirability of certain children as playmates proved false when she came to know them. She early discovered that for self-satisfaction she would have to live a mental life of her own. There were many things which she could not discuss with her mother. In early childhood she was a great reader of novels and spent many hours lying on the bed living an imaginary life. She never discussed her ideas with any one. Later she took to more serious reading, and of recent years she has assailed many of the world's greatest problems. Particularly she tells of the influence of Tolstoi's "Kreutzer Sonata" upon her. During two years she has read it four times and it has convinced her of the shams of character and that people lead dual lives.

When she was about 9 or 10 years old she began talking with other girls about sex problems and up to the present time has never consulted any grown person about them. Her first information of this kind was obtained from a crowd of girls who used successfully to lie to their teachers and mothers to get out of school work. Going further into the question of this hidden knowledge of sex things, she tells us she has never worried much about the things she has heard, but she has wondered a great deal and they have often come up in her mind. She pursued the course of asking many girls what they knew about this subject and then, getting unsatisfactory answers, picked up what she could from ordinary literature. Gertrude maintains that all her dwelling upon sex affairs never aroused within her any specific desires. (Gertrude is anything but a sensuous type and it may be that her statement in this respect is true.) When she went to work she fell in with girls who talked excessively about boys and sex affairs, but at this time she had a mental world of her own and so did not pay much attention to them. Gertrude talked much to us of the possibility of her studying civil law, history, economics, and so on — it is very clear that she has really dwelt on the possibility of being a student of serious subjects.

Very willingly this young woman entered into the problem of solving the genesis of her own tendencies. She repeatedly said that she, of all things, wanted to break herself of this. She maintains she can perceive no beginnings. It seems to her as if she has always been that way. She spoke at first of this crowd of girls who successfully lied to their parents and talked to her about sex things, and we are inclined to believe that this really may have been the beginning, but later she affirms this was not the beginning and that her lying began in earlier childhood. All that she knows is that it has grown to be a habit and now "when I speak it comes right out." After she has told a lie she never thinks about it again one way or another. Her conscience does not trouble her in the matter. She does not tell lies for what she gets out of it, nor does it give her any particular pleasure to fool people. She does not invent her stories, but at the time of talking to people she simply says untrue things without any thought beforehand and without any consideration afterward. To one officer she flung the challenge, "Oh, I'm clever, you'll find that out." After months of effort and when it was clear that the girl for her own good must be given a course of training in an institution she quite acquiesced in the wisdom of such procedure, after a few hours' rebellion.

It has been noted by many that one of Gertrude's outstanding traits is her lack of emotion. She never cries and only rarely does the semblance of a blush tinge her cheeks. She neither loves nor hates strongly. She seems remarkably calm under conditions where others storm. She says she never is frightened, that she never worries, or is sorry. She is well aware of her own ego; that she may be trespassing upon the rights of others never seems to enter her head. Certain simulations of physical ailments, which at times she showed, we could only interpret as part of her general tendency to misrepresent.

Our summary of the causative factors in this case, made, unfortunately, partly on the basis of this unreliable girl's testimony, offers the following explanation of her remarkable tendencies:

(a) There was early development of an inner life which dealt vividly in imaginary situations. This grew into a mental existence hidden entirely from the members of her family.

(b) There was early experience with successful lying on the part of others, and this as a main episode probably occurred at the time when the emotion natural to first knowledge of sex life was present.

(c) There was frequent experience with the falsifications which were her mother's frailty.

(d) For her lying there were no parental disciplines or corrections at any time, so far as we have been able to learn.

(e) The young woman shows unusually little emotion, and only sporadically demonstrates conscience.

(f) There is unquestionably marked habit formation in the case.

Habit formation: Very strong.   Case 8.
    Lack of parental correction.   Girl, age 17 years.
        Early experience with lying.
            Development of inner life: Imaginative and
                                              hidden.
Delinquencies:
  Excessive lying and misrepresentation.
  False accusations.
  Forging.   Mentality:
  Stealing.   Good ability.

CASE 9

Summary: A girl of 14 had been notoriously untruthful for years. She had created much trouble by her petty false accusations, and her lying stood often in the way of her own satisfactions and advantages. Analysis of the case shows the girl's dual moral and social experiences and tendencies, her inner conflicts about the same, and her remarkably vivid mental imagery — all of which leads her to doubt sometimes concerning what is true and what is false.

A strange admixture of races, of religion, and of social and moral tendencies was brought out in the study of Amanda R. and of her family conditions. We were much helped in the study of this case, which has long been a source of many social difficulties, by the intelligence of certain relatives who knew well the family facts, and also by the good mental capacities of the girl herself.

Amanda is an orphan and has been living for years with relatives. She has caused them and others, even those who have tried to help her, extreme annoyance on account of her quite unnecessary lies, her accusations, and some other delinquent tendencies. The main trouble all concede to be her falsifications, which vary from direct denials to elaborate stories invented without any seeming reason whatever. Reports on her conduct have come from a number of different sources. Neighbors have complained that she has come to them and borrowed money with the statement that her family was hard up. At school she stated for a time that she had come unprovided with lunch because her people were so poor, but it was ascertained that she had thrown away her lunch each day. The lies which she told to the other school children were extraordinarily numerous and fertile; unfortunately they sometimes involved details about improper sex experiences. A long story was made up about one of her relatives having committed suicide and was told to the school teachers and others. She defamed the character of one of her aunts. To her pastor she told some outrageous falsehoods. A home for delinquent girls, where she was once placed on account of her general bad behavior, would not put up with her, so much trouble arose from her prevarications. She accused the very good people there of not treating her well because she was not of their race. All of the above is quite apart from the girl's own romantic stories which have been told in her family circle and have

done no especial harm. Of these we had the best account
from the girl herself.

An intelligent relative gave an account of the facts.
Amanda has been tried in a number of households, but has
been given up by everyone after a short period of trial. Her
word is found so unreliable that in general she is regarded as
thoroughly untrustworthy. This particular relative, who is
most interested in her, tells us she thinks the girl is mentally
peculiar. She states that in general her mind is both romantic and rambling. She constantly has the idea that her
beauty will bring her a wealthy husband. She lies about
other people to these relatives and about them to others.
They have a comfortable home and are very anxious for
Amanda to do well, and many times have had serious talks
with her, all to no purpose. They themselves have attempted
to analyze the nature of the girl's characteristics, and say it
is quite evident that the telling of untruths with this girl is
the result of quick reaction on her part. Fictions of all
kinds come up in her mind constantly and are uttered quickly.
It is doubtful whether she premeditates her stories. She has
threatened suicide. They think she is the biggest liar that
ever lived and can't understand how she can engage in such
unforesighted behavior unless she is somewhat abnormal.
Only once did they ever notice anything suggestive of a
mental peculiarity other than her lying. Then she did talk
quite incoherently and at random for a time (she is a great
talker anyhow), but later she said she realized what she had
done, and said not to mind her — she had just let her tongue
rattle on and did not mean anything by it.

On two or three occasions Amanda has started to school
in the morning and wandered off and kept going all day.
She had been immoral with boys, but not to any great extent.
She undertook to be religious for a time, but her sincerity
was always in question. She knows the character of her

own mother and threatens at times to follow in her tracks.

The racial heredity of this girl is a strange mixture. Her father was a Scandinavian and her mother colored. The maternal grandfather was colored, and the maternal grandmother was an alcoholic Irish woman and died in an insane hospital. It is possible, also, that there is Indian blood in the family. The mother kept an immoral resort and drank at times. The father is said, even by his wife's relative, to have died some years ago of a broken heart about her career. She died of tuberculosis a few years after him. Amanda was the only child. About the early developmental history we have no reliable information. The girl was taken by relatives before her mother died, but was allowed to visit her, and there was evidently real affection between mother and daughter. Long contention over religious affairs in the family led to some bickering about placing the girl.

We found Amanda to be rather a good looking girl with very slight evidences of colored blood. Quiet and normal in her attitude and expression. Slightly built — weight 93 lbs.; height 4 ft. 10 in. Vision R. 20/80, L. 20/25. Coarse tremor of outstretched hands. No evidence of specific disease. All other examination negative. The girl complains of occasional sick headaches with photophobia. Pelvic examination by a specialist negative.

On the mental side we quickly found we had to deal with a girl of decidedly good general ability. Tests were almost uniformly done well. Memory processes decidedly good — span for eight numbers auditorily and for seven numbers visually. No evidence whatever of aberration.

Results on the "Aussage" test: Amanda on free recital gave 12 details of the picture; on questioning she mentioned 32 more items, but a dozen of these were incorrect. Of 7

suggestions offered she accepted 6.   This was an exceptionally inaccurate performance.

   In the course of our study of this case we obtained from
Amanda a very good account of her own life, deeply tragic
in its details, and a probably correct analysis of her beginnings in lying.   It seems that she remembers well her mother,
particularly in the later visits which the relatives allowed.
These must have been when she was about 5 or 6 years old.
"I know a lot.   There isn't anything bad that I have not
seen and heard.   I try to forget it, but I can't.   What's the
use anyhow?   When I think of my mother it all comes up
again.   When I was very little I would sit in a room with
my mother and a crowd of her friends and they would say
everything in front of me.   I would see men and women go
into rooms and I kept wondering what they did in there.
I think I was quicker and sharper then than I am now.   I
think I was about 3 when I used to see them smoking and
drinking.   Then I used to think it was all right.   I thought
it was swell and that I would like to do it too.   I thought
about it a lot.   Mother, you see, would tell me to be good
one minute and the next would teach me how to swear.   I
remember once when I was about 7 they brought her home
drunk.   She looked terrible.   I can close my eyes and see her
just as plainly as if it is there before me.   A protective society
once found me and took me to their place.   Then I lived with
my grandfather.   Mother stole me from them and then my
uncle took me.   I lived around in lots of places.   I have done
lots of bad things. . . . .

   "I picture these things too — I can't help it.   The pictures come up in my mind as plain as can be — not just at
night, but in the daytime too.   The only thing I have ever
been really afraid of is the dark.   Then I imagine I hear
people talking.   I see things too.   I see whole shows that I
have been to.   But then, as I have said, I see them when I'm

awake and in the daytime. I dream about them also.
Sometimes they are so real I don't know whether I'm asleep
or awake. For instance, a long time ago I read Peck's Bad
Boy and I can see those pictures now just as plain as when I
read the book. It is always that way about what I read.
The things I read I always see in pictures. It's that way with
the love stories too. I used to read lots and lots of them.
I like to read about murders. I can see those too. When I
read about the R. murder in the papers lately I just felt like
I was there. I could see everything he did. I don't know
why I like to read such things so much. It was the same way
last winter. I read a story with suicide in it and someway
I just wanted to commit suicide myself. I did go to the
railroad tracks and stood around until the train came and
then walked away. . . . . .

"My aunt says that I am too attractive and that I stare
at the men. Well, when she was with me a man did stare at
me and I stared back at him. I could have turned my head
away, but I'm not that kind of a girl. I'm a bad girl. Everyone believes me so and I might just as well be. When I was
little in my mother's place I used to smoke and drink. I
dream every night — often about men doing bad things.
I wake up and sit up to see if men are there or if they are gone.
My dreams are always just that plain. If I read a book I
can sit down and imagine all the people are right before me.
I can get it just by reading. If anybody speaks to me I
jump, and it is all gone. When I go to the theatre or the
nickel show I can come home and see the whole show
over again. I have been that way ever since I could
understand things. When I was small and people would
tell me things I could imagine them right in front of me.
Even now I will be sitting still and I will imagine I see my
mother taking me up in the way she used to. When I came
to see her she would rock me to sleep, and I can plainly see

her lying in the coffin. Often I think I see my mother brought home drunk.

"If I have anything to recite in school I just think of it all the time. I dream a good deal about what that boy did and about these other things. I can sit and think of everything he did to me. I go to bed and I lie awake and think all these things and I can't get them off my mind and then I start to dreaming about them.

"There is always this trouble — my mother wasn't good and I can't be good. That's what people say, but, of course, that's not so. I know I start talking to girls about these things when they are talking to me. I sometimes think that things will come back — that the Chicago fire is coming back, and that slavery is coming back.

"About my lying? I don't know why I tell things like that about my aunt committing suicide — it just came into my head. Oh, I've got lots of things in my head. I never had any chance to forget. I can't forget at school. School does not interest me any more. That's why I want to go to work. Perhaps then I should be interested in something new.

"I used to tell lots of things that were not so out there at P. Sometimes I did it as a joke and sometimes I meant it. It is hard sometimes to tell just what is the truth, I imagine things so hard. I can remember lots that I've read."

Amanda in several interviews went on at great length in a very rational way, but altogether the gist of her view of her case is to be found in the above. She told that she was a masturbator, as might be supposed. She feels she can't help this and never felt it was so particularly bad. Apparently it is a part of her life of imagination at night. She insisted frequently on the vividness of her mental content, and indeed was anxious to talk about her peculiarities in this respect. It was very apparent that she showed real understanding of the forces which had influenced her. It should be noted that we felt sure that it is not only the strength of imagery, namely, of actually recollected material, but also of imagination which is characteristic of this girl's mental make-up. This was noticeable, as we have shown above, in the "Aussage" Test. In our notes on psychological findings we stated that the girl has both strong emotions and strong convictions, together with her other qualities. She expressed herself with considerable vehemence, and under observation we noted changes from pleasantness to extremely ugly looks when her relatives were mentioned. It was true that she had seen immorality in other households than that of her mother, and this, of course, rendered her even more skeptical about true values in life.

It seemed clear that this bright girl had experienced so many contradictions in life that she was much mixed about it all. We might venture to suggest that the delinquency involved in lying could seem very little compared to the actual deeds with which she had come in contact. No idea that falsification was wrong was expressed by her. She had used double sets of standards in behavior all through her life. What she was urged to be and to do seemed impossible in the light of her past and its connections. Even her apparent decency belied the reality underlying her career, she thought. With all this and her vivid imagery it is little wonder that her magnificent powers of imagination had full sway and that she said and half believed all sorts of things which were not true. Then, probably, habit-formation of indulging in day-dreams accentuated the falsifying tendency.

It is too early to report on further progress of this case. For some months she has been in a school for girls where discipline and education are both emphasized.

Mental traits: special powers of imagery   Case 9.
                and imagination.   Girl, age 14 years.
Early immoral experiences: much later conflict
                        about them.
Home conditions: unstable for many years.
        Heredity (?): mother immoral,
                    maternal grandmother al-
                    coholic and insane.
Delinquencies: Mentality:
    Excessive lying.   Good general ability,
    Sex.   special capacities.

CASE 10

Summary: A boy of 14, supernormal in ability, coming from family circumstances which form a remarkable antithesis to his intellectual interests, is found to be a wonderful fabricator. His continuous lying proves to be directly inimical to his own interests and, indeed, his own satisfactions are thwarted by the curious unreliability of his word. The case unfortunately was not followed far, but study of it clearly shows beginnings in the early obtaining of advantages by lying, and brings out the wonderful dramatic and imaginative traits of the boy and his formation of a habit of falsification.

This case in its showing of intrinsic characteristics and incidental facts is of great interest. Robert R. for about a year when he was 14 years old we knew intimately, but after that on account of the removal of the family we have no further history of him. Intellectually and in his family and home background he presented a remarkable phenomenon. His parents were old-country peasants who just before Robert was born came to the United States. The father had never been to school in his life and could not read or write. Here he was a laborer; before immigration he had been a goose-herd. The mother was said to have had a little schooling at home and could read and write a little in her native language. In 15 years in the United States she had failed to learn to speak English. It is needless to say that our knowledge of the forebears is almost nil. Inquiry about mental peculiarities in the family brought negative answers. These parents had had nine children, seven of whom had died in early infancy. Robert was the older of the two living. We did not learn that the other child displayed any abnormalities. The mother helped towards the support of the family by doing coarse sewing.

About the developmental history we had the assurance that it was entirely negative as regards serious diseases. Pregnancy and birth were said to have been normal. For long, Robert had been very nervous and frequently slept an unusually small number of hours. Sometimes he would go to bed very late and get up early. Although he was a very small boy he was accustomed to drinking six or seven cups of coffee a day. No suspicion from any source of other bad habits or of improper sex experiences. The boy's home was clean and decent. The father was accustomed to celebrate once a month or so by getting intoxicated, but otherwise was a well behaved man.

On physical examination we found the boy in fair general condition, although very small for his age. Weight 80 lbs.; height 4 ft. 7 in. Well shaped, normally sized head. No prematurity or other physical abnormality. Somewhat defective vision. No complaint of headaches. All other examination negative. Regular sharp features. Much vivacity of expression. A nervous, alert, responsive, apparently frank and humorous type. Speech notably rapid.

Our acquaintance with this boy on the intellectual side proved to be a great treat. He was only in the 4th grade. His retardation was the result of having been changed back and forth from foreign-speaking to English schools and having been sent away to an institution for truancy.   In spite of his backwardness Robert had a fund of remarkably accurate scientific and other information which a mature person might envy.   We found our regular series of tests were all done unusually well, except those which called for foresight and planfulness.   It was interesting to note that when a problem in concrete material was given that required continuous thoughtful effort he proceeded by a rapid trial and error method and without the application of the foresight that many a slower individual would show.   He consequently did not always make a good record.

It seems an important fact that on the "Aussage" Test this exceedingly bright lad gave a fairly good detailed narrative account of the picture and proved himself not in the least suggestible, but he added a number of items which were not seen.

It was in the field of general information, obtained from a really wide range of reading, that this young boy shone. We found that he remembered an unusual amount of history he had read, that he had a lot of knowledge picked up from the newspapers, and that he had digested considerable portions of scientific works.   He described correctly the main principles involved in the use of telescopic and other lenses, he knew well the first principles of electricity, and he could draw correctly diagrams of dynamos, locomotives, switchboards, etc.   We noted he had read books on physiology, astronomy, physics, mechanics, etc.

It seems that neither his school nor his home offering him much intellectual satisfaction, he had frequented the public library, sometimes being there when he was truant from school, and staying there in the evening when his mother supposed he was out in a street gang.   In regard to his selection of reading: he had perused novels and books on adventure, but "I wanted to read something that tells something so that when I got through I would know something." He copied plans and directions, and with a hatchet, hammer and saw attempted at home to make little things, some of which were said to have been broken up by the parents. The boy had much in mind the career of great men who had succeeded from small beginnings, and he spoke often of Benjamin Franklin, Morse, and Bell, all of whom had started in the small way he had read of in their biographies. Robert had not been content with book knowledge alone, but had sought power-houses and other places where he could see machinery in actual operation.

Our acquaintance with Robert began and continued on account of delinquencies other than lying. He had run away from home at one time, he had stolen some electrical apparatus from a barn and was found in the middle of the night with it flashing a light on the street. He also had taken money from his parents and had threatened his mother with a hatchet. After much encouragement and help he yet stole from people who were trying to give him a chance to use his special abilities, and he began various minor swindling operations which culminated in his attempt to arrest a man at night, showing a star and a small revolver. Before we lost sight of him Robert had gained the general reputation of being the most unreliable of individuals.

Given splendid chances to use his special capacities, his other qualities made it impossible for him to take advantage of them. His wonderful ability was demonstrated in the school to which he was sent; there the teacher said that if she had the opportunity she really believed she could put him through one grade a month. His mental grasp on all subjects was astonishing and he wrote most admirable essays, one of the best being on patriotism. But even under the stable conditions of this school for six or seven months the boy did not refrain from an extreme amount of falsification and was much disliked by the other boys on account of it.

Robert had continued his lying for years. At the time when we were studying his case his prevaricating tendencies were shown in the manufacture of long and complicated stories, in the center of which he himself posed as the chief actor. These phantasies were told to people, such as ourselves, who could easily ascertain their falsehood, and they were told after there had been a distinct understanding that anything which showed unreliability on his part would militate against his own strongly avowed desires and interests. After special chances had been given this boy with the understanding that all that was necessary for him to do was to alter his behavior in respect to lying, on more than one occasion new fabrications were evolved in the same interview that Robert had begged in fairly tragic fashion to be helped to cure himself of his inclination to falsify.

A great love of the dramatic was always displayed by this boy, which may largely account for the evolution of his lying into long and complicated stories. When truant one day he boldly visited the school for truants, and when under probation, after having fallen into the hands of the police two or three times, he impersonated a policeman. The latter was such a remarkable occurrence and led to such a peculiar situation that much notice of it was taken in the newspapers. The incongruity between apperception of his own faults and his continued lying, considering his good mental endowment, seemed very strange. One day he sobbed and clung to my arm and begged me to be a friend to him and help him from telling such lies. "I don't know what makes me do it. I can't help it." Over and over he asserted his desire to be a good man and a great man. This was at the same time when some of his most complicated fabrications were reiterated.

No help was to be had from his parents in getting at the genesis of this boy's troubles; we had to rely on what seemed to be the probable truth as told by the boy himself. It is only fair to say that in response to many inquiries we did receive reliable facts from the lad. My assistant also went into the question of beginnings and was told at an entirely different time the same story. Robert always maintained that his lying began when he was a very little boy, when he found out that by telling his grandmother that his mother was mean to him he could get things done for him which he wanted. Later it seems he used to lie because he was afraid of being punished or because he did not like to be scolded. We found there was no question about the fact that his parents never were in sympathy with his library reading and his attempts to learn and be somebody in the world. At first, then, there seemed to be a definite purpose in his lying. At one time he pretended to be hurt when taken in custody and thought because of this he would be allowed to go home.

On many occasions this boy made voluntary appeal to us, describing his lying as a habit which it was impossible for him to stop, and implored aid in the breaking of it. Up to the last that we knew of him he occasionally made the complaint to strangers of mistreatment by his family, which in the sense in which he put it was not true at all. The dramatic nature of his later stories seemed to fulfill the need which the boy felt of his being something which he was not, and very likely belonged to the same category of behavior he displayed when he attempted to impersonate a policeman in the middle of the night, and to pose as an amateur detective by telling stories of alleged exploits to newspaper reporters. A long story which he related even to us, involving his discovery of a suspicious man with a satchel and his use of a taxicab in search for him, was made up on the basis of his playing the part of a great man, a hero. When we ran down this untruth (it was long after he had told us what a liar he was) it seemed quite improbable that he had suddenly improvised this story. It was too elaborate and well sustained. Later, when the boy again tragically begged to be helped from making such falsifications, he said the incident had been thought out some days previously and it seemed an awful nice story about the things that he might do. Daydreaming thus masked as the truth.

Environmental maladjustment:	Case 10.
incongruity between	Boy, age 14 yrs.
supernormal ability and home	
conditions.	
Innate characteristics: nervous, active,	
dramatic type.	
Stimulants: excessive use of coffee.	
Mental habit-formation.	
Delinquencies:	Mentality:
Lying excessive.	Supernormal in ability.
Petty stealing.	

CASE 11

Summary: An orphan girl of 10 had been in several institutions and households, but was found everywhere impossible on account of her incorrigibility. The greatest difficulty was on account of her extreme lying which for years had included extensive fabrications and rapid self-contradictions, as well as defensive denials of delinquency.

We were asked to decide about this girl's mentality and to give recommendations for her treatment. We need take little space for describing the case because the facts of development and heredity and of earliest mental experiences are not known by us. The case is worthy of short description as exemplifying a type and as showing once more the frequent correlation of lying with other delinquency, and especially with sex immorality.

We found a girl in good physical condition, small for her age, but without sensory defect or important organic trouble. Hutchinsonian teeth. High forehead and well formed features. Expression old for her years and rather shrewd, and notably unabashed. No evidence of pelvic trouble. Clitoris large. All the other examination negative.

Mentally we found her rather precocious. Tests well done. Reads and does arithmetic well for her age, in spite of much changing about and other school disadvantages. No evidence whatever of aberration. The examiner noted that she seemed a queer, sophisticated child, laughing easily and talking fast and freely. Evidently tries to put her best foot forward. Coöperates well on tests.

On the "Aussage" test this little girl did remarkably well both as to the details and general ideas expressed in the picture. Absolutely no suggestibility shown. The examination was made before our later methods of scoring this test, and the inaccuracies were not counted, but even so the positive features are of interest, namely, the good memory and non-suggestibility.

We found this youngster all along to be evasive, shifting and self-contradictory, even on vital points. She glibly stated anything that came into her mind, and ideas came very rapidly. She told us stories that with a moment's thought she must have known we could discover were false.

This child was a foundling, and was adopted by people whose family was broken up by death when she was about 6 years old. By the time she was 8 years old she was expelled from school and was generally known as an habitual liar and a child who showed most premature sex tendencies. She then went much with little boys and was constantly in trouble for stealing as well. Occasionally good reports were made of her, but sometimes she was stated to have a perfect mania for taking things. A number of people who have tried to help her have spoken of the elaborateness of her verbal inventions. At one place she destroyed letters and took a check from the mail and tore it up. She talked freely of sex affairs to many people, particularly to women, and showed evidence of intense local feelings. At one time she expressed great desire to be spanked, probably from a sex impulse. One intelligent person reported her as being simply animal-like in her desires. In a country home a thoroughly intelligent woman was unable to cope with her and she was finally delivered into the hands of an institution.

Through dearth of reliable information about the antecedents in this case we were unable to make a card of causative factors. It is sure, however, that the pathological lying and other delinquencies sprang from a background of congenital defect, probably syphilitic in nature, of lack of early parental care, of precocious sex desires, and sex experiences.

In the school for girls, where this unfortunate child remained for four years, it is stated that her tendencies to prevarication were mitigated, but never entirely checked. Her school record was decidedly good ; she was regarded as a bright girl, and advanced rapidly to the eighth grade. She was tried again in the world midway in her adolescent period with the most untoward results. She found temptations offered by the opposite sex irresistible and began a career of misrepresentation concerning her own conduct. Through her lies, proper oversight was not given in the home which received her once more. Pregnancy ensued and again she had to receive institutional care.

CASE 12

Summary: An extremely interesting case showing strong development of a tendency to swindling on the part of a young man of curiously unequal mental abilities, a subnormal verbalist. Pathological lying in this case quite logically developed into swindling. The main behavior-tendencies of this individual closely follow the lines of least resistance, the paths of greatest success. As a matter of fact, the use merely of his general subnormal abilities would never have led to as much advancement as he has enjoyed. His special capabilities with language have brought him much satisfaction at times, even if they have also led him into trouble. An astonishingly long list of legal proceedings centers about this case, illustrating very well the urgent need for coöperation between courts.

Adolf von X., now just 21 years old, we, through most unusual circumstances, have had more or less under observation for a number of years. Correspondence with several public and social agencies has given us close acquaintance with his record during this time, and earlier. Our attention was first called to Adolf in New York, when he was a boy under arrest in the Tombs. A fine young lawyer, a casual acquaintance of Adolf's through court work, asked us to study the case because he felt that perhaps grave injustice was being done. Before his arrest the boy, who seemed to be most ambitious, had been about the court rooms looking into the details of cases as a student of practical law. He had attracted attention by his energy and push; he earned money at various odd jobs and studied law at night. At this time the boy was under arrest charged with disorderly conduct; he had beaten his sister in their home.

We found a nice looking and well spoken young fellow who said he was 17. Although he had been in this country only three years from Germany, he spoke English almost without an accent and did quite well with French also. He had been brought up in Hamburg. His statement added to that previously given by the lawyer aroused in us great interest concerning the constructive possibilities of the case. It seemed as if here was an immigrant boy for whom much should be done.

"I was taking up law suits, little law suits. There was a case on before Judge O. and I wanted a new suit of clothes to wear to go to court in. My sister said I could not take my brother's suit. He told me to take it and bring it home in good condition at night. My sister is supposed to be the plaintiff, but she did not make the complaint. The landlady came in and hit me three times in the head with a broom. My sister called her in and then she threw a piece of wood after me. Sister started crying, but she did not get hit. The landlady got hit. When I fell down I striked her with my head and hurt my head bad. I think I hit her with the left side of my head. The landlady made complaint in German to an Irish policeman. He could not understand. The officer did not do what the law tells because he took a complaint from a boy of the age of 6 years. He translated for her.

"The trouble started because I wanted to get my brother's suit because I wanted to appear before Judge O. to protect a party in the hearing of a case. I took a few lessons over in the Y.M.C.A. class and in a law office I read books through. I have books at home, rulings of every court. I know I got a good chance to work up because I know I have a good head for the law. My father he wont believe it, that's the trouble. I know I could stand my own expenses. I said, 'Officer, wait here a minute. I'll explain how this is.' He began stepping on me. He threw me on the floor. I wanted to go out the back way so nobody would see me. He kicked me down the front way. There was a big crowd there. Another rough officer pinched my arm. At the station when the officer said this boy hit his sister, my sister said, 'No, he did not hit me,' but she said it in German.

"I was in court awhile ago because father thought I would not work. I was paroled. I was trying to find a position. This man that had the rehearing said, 'You wont lose anything.' He made as much as a contract with me. He said to another person in my hearing, if that fellow wins my case I will pay him $10 for it. The first case I had was in X court. I was interpreter there. I want to make something out of myself. Labor is all right, but I like office work or law work better. I tell you, doctor, if I come up before the judge I will tell him just the same story I tell you. I can remember it just that way."

This young man told us he had graduated from intermediate school in Hamburg; in this country he had attended for about a year and a half and, in spite of the language handicap, he was in sixth grade. There is a brother a little older and an older sister. Mother has been dead for 5 years. His father is an artisan and makes a fair living.

We soon found means of getting more facts concerning this case. The first point of importance was concerning his age. It appeared that he at present was lying about this, probably for the purpose of concealing his previous record in the Juvenile Court and in other connections. There had been previously much trouble with him. He had been long complained of by his father because of the bickering and quarreling which he caused in the household and on account of his not working steadily. He had shown himself tremendously able in getting employment, having had at least twenty places in the last year and a half. He was known to lie and misrepresent; on one occasion when he was trying to get certain advantages for himself he falsely stated that he was employed by a certain legal concern, and once he tried to pass himself off for an officer of a court.

The father willingly came to see us and proved to be a somewhat excitable, but intelligent man of good reputation. We obtained a very good history before studying the boy himself. Mr. von X. began by informing us that we had a pretty difficult case on our hands, and when we spoke of the boy's ambition he became very sarcastic. He stated that up to the time when the boy left school in Hamburg he had only been able to get to the equivalent of our third grade. To be sure, it is true that Adolf had learned English quickly and much more readily than any one else in the family, and in the old country had picked up French, but "he hasn't got sense enough to be a lawyer."

Both the older children did very well in school, and the father and mother came from intelligent families. All the children are somewhat nervous, but the two older ones are altogether different from this boy. They are quiet and saving. A grandfather was said to have been a learned man and another member of the family very well-to-do. The mother has one cousin insane and the father one cousin who is feebleminded. All the other family history from this apparently reliable source was negative. Both the father and mother were still young at the birth of this child. The mother died of pneumonia, but prior to this sickness had been healthy.

The developmental history of Adolf runs as follows: His birth was preceded by two miscarriages. The pregnancy was quite normal; confinement easy. When he was a few days old he had some inflammation of the eyes which soon subsided. Never any convulsions. His infancy was normal. He walked and talked early. At three years he had diphtheria badly with delirium for a couple of weeks and paralysis of the palate for some months. After this his parents thought the boy not quite normal. He had slight fevers occasionally. At 9 years he was very ill with scarlet fever. Following that he had some trouble with the bones in his legs. Before he left Hamburg he had an operation on one leg for this trouble which had persisted. (It was quite significant that in our first interview Adolf had told us his leg had been injured by a rock falling on it, necessitating the operation.) Up to the age of 14 this boy, although apparently in good physical condition, used to wet the bed always at night, and sometimes during the day lost control of his bladder. Also lost control of his bowels occasionally after he was 10 years old. He sleeps well, is moderate in the use of tea and coffee, and does not smoke.

When young he played much by himself. After coming to this country his chief recreation was going to nickel shows. He was fond of music as a child. He had been a truant in Hamburg. As a young child he was regarded as destructive. The general statement concerning delinquency is that Adolf is the only one of the family who has given trouble and that the father was the first to complain of the boy to the authorities. Before he reported it there had long been trouble on account of frequent changing of employment and misrepresentations. The boy had forged letters to his family and others. In the office of a certain newspaper he once represented himself to be an orphan, and there a fund was raised for him and he was outfitted. The father insists that the boy, in general, is an excessive liar.

Further inquiry brought out that other people, too, regarded Adolf as an extreme falsifier. The principal of a school thought the boy made such queer statements that he could not be right in his head. In the office of a clerk of a court he represented himself to be employed by a certain legal institution and demanded file after file for reference. Everybody there was friendly to him at first, but later they all changed their attitude on account of his unscrupulous and constant lying.

Physically we found a very well nourished boy, rather short for his age. Weight 121 lbs.; height 5 ft. 1 in. Musculature decidedly flabby; this was especially noticeable in his handshake. Attitude heavy and slouchy for a boy. Expression quite pleasant; features regular; complexion decidedly good. A North European type. Eyes differ slightly in the color of the irides. Noticeable enlargement of breasts. Well shaped head of quite normal measurements; circumference 54.5, length 18, breadth 15 cm. No sensory defect, nor was anything else of particular interest found upon examination.

The mental study, particularly the testing for special abilities, has been of very great interest. Fortunately for the scientific understandings of the problems involved we have been able to see Adolf many times at intervals and to check up previous findings. Our first statement will be of the results obtained at the earliest study of the case.

When we first saw Adolf, although he talked so intelligently, we asked him to give us some evidence of his educational ability, and to our tremendous surprise he failed to be able to multiply simple numbers or even to do addition correctly. There was no evidence of emotional upset, but we waited for further testing until we had seen the father, that we might be sure of the school history. As mentioned above, we found that the boy had entirely misled us.

We then entered upon a systematic study of the boy's abilities and found some strange contrasts. Perceptions of form and color were normal. Given a very simple test which required some apperceptive ability, he did fairly well. Given simple "Construction Tests" which required the planful handling of concrete material, Adolf proceeded unintelligently. He showed no foresight, was rather slow, but by following out a trial and error procedure and with some repetition of irrational placing of the pieces he finally succeeded. Moderate ability to profit by trial and error was shown, but for his age the performance on this type of test was poor. On our "Puzzle-Box," which calls for the analysis of a concrete situation, a test that is done by boys of his age nearly always in four minutes or less, Adolf failed in ten minutes. He began in his typically aggressive fashion, but kept trying to solve the difficulty by the repetition of obviously futile movements. On a "Learning Test," where numerals are associated in meaningless relation with symbols, Adolf did the work promptly and with much self-confidence, but made a thoroughly irrational error, inasmuch as he associated the same numeral with two different symbols — and did not see his error. His ability to mentally represent and analyze a simple situation visually presented in our "Cross Line Tests" was very poor. In this he failed to analyze out the simple parts of a figure which he could well draw from memory. This seemed significant, for the test is practically always done correctly by normal individuals, at least on the second trial, by the time they are 10 or 12 years of age. A simple test for visual memory of form also brought poor results.

As an extreme contrast to the above results, the tests that had to do with language were remarkably well done. A visual verbal memory passage was given with unusual accuracy, also an auditory verbal passage was rendered almost perfectly. Considering that the former has 20 items and the latter 12 details, this performance was exceptionally good. Also, the so-called Antonym Test, where one is asked to give as quickly as possible the opposite to a word, the result, considering his foreign education, was decidedly good. Three out of twenty opposites were not given, apparently on account of the lack of knowledge. The average time was 2.3 seconds. If two of the other time-reactions were left out, which were probably slow from lack of knowledge, the average time would be 1.6 seconds for 15 opposites. This shows evidence of some good mental control on the language side. Motor control was fair. He was able to tap 75 of our squares with 2 errors in 30 seconds, just a medium performance. A letter written on this date contains quite a few mis-spelled short words: "My father Send me to This Court for The troubels I had with my sister," etc.

While awaiting trial Adolf, stating that he was desirous of doing so, was given ample opportunity to study arithmetic. After a few days he told us unhesitatingly that he now could do long division, but he utterly failed, and, indeed, made many errors in a sum in addition. He had acquired part of the multiplication table.

Study of his range of information brought out some curious points. He told of some comparative merits of law schools, had some books on home-taught law, and was a great reader of the newspapers. In the latter he chiefly perused reports of court cases. He was quite familiar with the names of various attorneys and judges. He could give the names in contemporary politics, and knew about sporting items. His knowledge of the history of this country was absolutely deficient, but he does not hesitate to give such statements as the following: "The Fourth of July is to remember a great battle between President Lincoln and the English country." Again he makes a bluff to give scientific items, although he has the shallowest information. When it comes to athletics, much to our surprise, we hear that our flabby boy is a champion. Of course, he knows some of the rulers in Europe and by what route he came to New York, but he informs us that Paris is the largest country in Europe.

Adolf says he plays a very good game of checkers, that he had played much, but on trial he shows a very poor game, once moving backwards. When purposely given chances to take men he did not perceive the opportunities.

We asked him to analyze out for us a couple of moral situations, one being about a man who stole to give to a starving family. He tells us in one way the man did right and in another way wrong. It never is right to steal, because if caught he would be sent to the penitentiary and would have to pay more than the things are worth, and, then, if he was not caught, a thief would never get along in the world. The other was the story of Indians surrounding a settlement who asked the captain of a village to give up a man. Adolf thought if he were a chief he would say to give battle if the man had done no wrong, but on further consideration states that he would rather give up one man than risk the lives of many, and if he were a captain he would surely rather give this man up than put his own life in it. He thinks certainly this is the way the question should be answered.

On our "Aussage" or Testimony Test Adolf gave volubly many details, dramatically expressing himself and putting in interpretations that were not warranted by the picture. Indeed, he made the characters actually say things. On the other hand, he did not recall at all one of the three persons present in the picture. He accepted three out of six suggestions and was quite willing to fill in imaginary details, besides perverting some of the facts. This was unusually unreliable testimony.

Our impressions as dictated at this time state that we had to do with a young man in good general physical condition, of unusually flabby musculature, who showed a couple of signs that might possibly be regarded as stigmata of inferiority. Mentally, the main showing was irregularity of abilities; in some things he was distinctly subnormal, in others mediocre, but in language ability he was surprisingly good. No evidence of mental aberration was discovered. The diagnosis could be made, in short, that the boy was a subnormal verbalist. His character traits might be enumerated in part by saying that he was aggressive, unscrupulous, boastful, ambitious, and a continual and excessive liar. In the exercise of these he was strikingly lacking in foresight. This latter characteristic also was shown in his test work. The abilities in which he was overbalanced gave him special feelings of the possibility of his being a success and led him to become a pathological liar. From the family history the main suggestion of the causation of the mental abnormality is in illness during developmental life, but neither ante-natal nor hereditary conditions are quite free from suspicion.

At the time of this first trial Adolf maintained a very smart attitude and tried to show off. He had succeeded in having two witnesses subpœnaed in order to prove that he did not hit his sister, but on the stand it came out that one of them was not there at all, and the other, who was a little girl, stated that she saw Adolf hit some one. Just why the boy had these witnesses brought in was difficult to explain. Perhaps he had the idea that some one ought to be called in every case, or perhaps he thought they would be willing to tell an untruth for him. His statement in court did not agree with what he had told us and was utterly different from what his sister stated. It came out that he had struck her on a number of previous occasions. It was shown clearly that the boy was a tremendous liar. The case was transferred to the Juvenile Court and from there the boy was sent away to an institution for a few months. After the trial his father said in broken English, "To me he never told the truth."

Just after his release the family moved to Chicago and Adolf soon put himself in touch with certain social agencies. He found out where I was and came to see me, bright, smiling, and well. He had gained eight pounds during his incarceration. He wanted to tell all about his life in the institution and because we were busy said he would come the next day. He did not do this, but a few months later came running up to me on the street with a package in his hands, saying he was already at work in a downtown office and was doing well and going to night school. Five years more would see him quite through his law course. A few months after this he applied at a certain agency for work as an interpreter and there, strangely enough, some one who knew him in New York recognized him. He, however, denied ever having been in court and produced a list of twenty or twenty-five places where he worked and gave them as references. It is to be remembered that at this time he had already been brought up in court at least three times, that he had been on probation, and been sent away to an institution.

During the last four years we have received much information concerning the career of Adolf, although his activities have carried him to Milwaukee, Cleveland, St. Louis, and other towns, in several of which he has been in trouble. He has very repeatedly been to see us and we have had many opportunities of gauging his mental as well as his social development.

His family continued to live in one of the most populous suburbs of Chicago and Adolf maintains that his residence is there, an important point for his political activities which are mentioned later.

What we discovered in our further studies of Adolf's mental condition can be told in short. We have retested him over and over. (When he has been hard up we have given him money to induce him to do his very best.) There are no contradictions in our findings at different times. Once, in another city, in connection with his appearance in court, Adolf was seen by a psychiatrist who suggested that he was a case of dementia precox, but nothing in our long observation of him warrants us in such an opinion. His mental conditions and qualities seem quite unchanged in type during all the time we have known him, and instead of any deterioration there has been gradual betterment in capacities, certainly along the line of adjustment to environment. His wonderful ability to get out of trouble is evidence of these powers of adjustment, as is also, perhaps, his keen sensing of the utility of the shadier sides of politics and criminal procedure.

In work with numbers Adolf is still very poor. He is unable to do long division or multiplication, and cannot add together simple fractions. Addition he does much better, but even at his best he makes errors in columns where he has to add five numerals. He now can do simple subtraction such as is required in making change, but fails on such a problem as how much change he should get from $20 after buying goods costing $11.37. His memory span is only six numerals, and these he cannot get correctly every time.

After numerous attempts to mentally analyze our simple "Cross Line Test," with much urging and extreme slowness he finally succeeded at one time in getting it correctly. As stated above, this is a test that is done with ease usually by normal individuals 12 years of age. On our "Code Test," requiring much the same order of ability, but more effort, he entirely failed. For one thing, he has never known the order of the alphabet either in English, German, or French. Our "Pictorial Completion Test," which gauges simple apperceptive abilities, he failed to do correctly, making three illogical errors.

The result on the Binet tests are most interesting. From years of experience with them we ourselves have no faith in their offering sound criteria for age levels above 10 years. Adolf goes up through all of the 12-year tests (1911 series) except the first, where he shows suggestibility in his judgment of the lengths of lines. In the 15-year tests he fails on the first, but does the three following ones correctly. Two out of the adult series are done well — those where the definition of a word is required and the statement of political ideas. Two or three of his specific answers are worth noting : "Honor is when a person is very honest. It means he will never do what is wrong even if he can make money by it." "Pleasure is when everything is pleasant, when you are enjoying yourself." Adolf tells us that the king is head of a monarchy, he has not the power to veto, and he acquires his position by royal birth. In contrast to this he says the president is the presiding executive of a republic, he has the power to veto, and he gains his position by election. It is perfectly clear in this case, as in many others, that the Binet tests show very little wherein lies the nature of a special defect or ability. Adolf's capacity for handling language has grown steadily. He has been reading law and knows by heart a great deal of its terminology. In a short conversation he talks well and is coherent. The aggressiveness which is ever with him leads him to stick to the point. He has had very little instruction, his pronunciation is often defective and he does not know the meaning of many of the longer terms with which any lawyer should be acquainted. He speaks fluently and has now long posed, among other things, as an interpreter.

Our final diagnosis after all these mental tests is, that while he could by no means be called a feebleminded person, still Adolf is essentially subnormal in many abilities — we still regard him as a subnormal verbalist. Probably what he lacks in powers of mental analysis has much relation to the lack of foresight which he continually shows in his social career. His lying and swindling have led him almost nowhere except into difficulties.

Adolf has been steadily gaining weight, although he has grown only an inch and a half in these years. He is stout and sleek-looking and as flabby as ever. He has not been seriously ill during this time. Whereas before he used to be untidy in dress he now gets himself up more carefully.

The following are examples of Adolf's conversation and show many of his characteristics: (Soon after he came to Chicago we spoke to him of his progress.)

"The other day I met a fellow and he says, 'How long have you been in this country?' and when I says four years he says, 'You're a liar. There never was a fellow I ever heard of who got hold of the language and was doing as well as you are in four years.'" A few months later he tells us he is selling goods on commission and descants on how much he can make: "That's 'Get-rich-quick-Wallingford' for you. There's Mr. A. and Congressman X., they started out from little beginnings just the same as me. I'm going along their line.

"Do you know I got sued by the Evening Star for libbel. That's what I got for testifying in that case. I tell you what I would like and that's vice investigation work."

At another time: "Well, doctor, I am general manager for my brother's business now. He's got a bottle business. There's money in that, ain't there? I was down in court to-day. I tell you, there was a fellow who got what was coming to him. It was a case before Judge H. — assault and battery. He was fined $10 and costs — all amounted to about $30. Well, I had a little dog and I tell you I have a heart for animals just the same as persons. He kicked the dog and I told him not to do it and he says, 'You're a liar,' and then he ran down stairs and pushed me along the stones over there. I called the police and they did not come for about three quarters of an hour.

"I'm studying law. Taking a correspondence course. They give you an L.L.B. It's a two years work and you get all the volumes separately," etc. "Then we have a slander suit. A neighbor called my sister dirty names. I am going to file a $5000 slander suit. I would not let that man call names like that, and then he's got about $5000 in property.

"Some people are down on me, but I tell you I have been a leader of boys. We got the Illinois championship — you know, the boy scout examinations. There was an examination on leaves. I was their leader. I had 9 boys up and there were 117 leaves and every boy knew every leaf. Of course I told them or they would not have known. Some people are down on me for what I do for the boys, but I tell you I've been in court and I've made up my mind I will help other kids. Sometimes kids can be helped by talking to. Then there is me. I won the boxing championship this year." (At this period I enquire about his prowess and the recent encounter with the young boy who dragged him over the stones. With a blush he says he never was any good at real boxing or real fighting.) "I'm this kind of a fellow. If they let me alone I'm all right, but if they start monkeying with me something is going to happen. When you start a thing don't start it until you can carry it through. These people that started with me were not able to do that."

Later it came out that the alleged fighting with the boy is all in Adolf's mind. He tells us, without noticing any discrepancy, that no complaint against this boy, who he said had been already tried and fined, would be received by the police authorities, nor will they issue a warrant.

Within the last year or two there has been almost complete cessation of Adolf's attempt to become a lawyer. At an earlier time he came to us with a speech written out in a book. He was going to recite it when a certain case came up in the Municipal Court. As a matter of fact we heard that the boy said nothing on the occasion. At various times we have heard of his getting mixed up in different ways in a number of cases. Once he succeeded in giving testimony in a notorious trial. His own account of his interest in the case is shown in the following:

"Doctor, you remember that X. boy and that Y. boy.

Judge B. is going to try them. They are down in the S Station and they are going to stay there unless they sign a jury waiver and they can't do that. They are only 15 years old — I got their ages — it cost me $1 to get their ages and I am going to be there when they are being tried." (The statement of the ages is untrue.) "It ain't right to keep these boys down there. They look pale. They don't give them anything but black coffee. I'm going to represent them boys. You know, doctor, I'm working in three places now — holding three jobs. Two days in the week I work for the A's, two for Mr. B. — he ain't exactly my boss — and then for myself. The A's pay me $6, Mr. B. pays $3, and then I make $7 or $8 myself interpreting. I'm saving it up to go to law school. In three years I graduate. They are going to hold it up against them boys, their records, and I am going to deny it. It ain't right. I was talking to the detective that arrested X. and I says to him, 'Look here, you took the knife. What right have they got to take in one fellow without the little fellow?' I want to represent this case myself."

Adolf has worked for law firms and aided at times as an investigator of criminal and vice situations. Occasionally he has been much worried about his own court record. He did not want it to stand against him. He thought he could get his sister to swear that he never quarreled at home. Shortly afterwards he served a short sentence for stealing from a law firm. Later he came in and said he had a job in the legal department of a large concern and that he had changed his name because he believed his old name was ruined. "I'm determined to be a lawyer. Ever since a little fellow I have wanted to be — ever since I have had an understanding of what the law means. I used to play court with the other little ones and talk about law." At this time he wanted a little loan. He had become particularly interested in philanthropic work and thought he could do something on the side about that — perhaps become a leader of boys, or help the unprotected in some way. Adolf was really employed now to investigate cases by some lawyer. About this time he had been wearing a badge, impersonating an officer of a certain philanthropic society.

For long this young man was concocting all sorts of schemes how he might work in at the edge of legal affairs, as an interpreter, a "next friend," an investigator, etc. More recent activities have taken Adolf away from the field of his first ambitions and he has tried to use his talents in all sorts of adventuresome ways. The accounts of his lying and impostures belong logically together, as follows.

During all our acquaintance with Adolf we have known his word to be absolutely untrustworthy. Many times he has descended upon his friends with quite unnecessary stories, leading to nothing but a lowering of their opinion of him. Repeatedly his concoctions have been without ascertainable purpose. His prevaricating nearly always centers about himself as some sort of a hero and represents him to be a particularly good-hearted and even definitely philanthropic person — one who loves all creatures and does much for others. Pages might be taken in recounting his falsehoods. Most of them, even when long drawn out, were fairly coherent. I remember one instance as showing how particularly uncalled for his prevarications were. After hearing one of his tales, we started downtown together, but missed a car. Adolf walked to the middle of the street and said he could see one coming just a few blocks away. Being doubtful, I a minute later went to look and no car even yet was in sight. Adolf sheepishly stared in a shop window. He never took any pleasure in his record of misdeeds. He was never boastful about them and indeed seemed to have quite normal moral feeling. But so far, none of his perceptions or apperceptions has led him to see the astonishing futility of his own lying and other misrepresentations.

Already this young man's court experiences we know to be very numerous and possibly we are not acquainted with all of them. Early we knew of his forging letters and telegrams and engaging in minor misrepresentations which were really swindling operations. Later his transactions have been spread about in different cities, as we have already stated. The young man borrowed small sums frequently on false pretenses. He has found the outskirts of legal practice a fruitful field for misrepresentations galore. For instance, at one time he stood outside the door of a concern which deals with small legal business and represented to the prospective patrons that he as a student of the law could transact their business with more individual care and for a less sum. He really succeeded in getting hold of the beginnings of a number of legal actions in this way. In one city he posed as the officer of a certain protective agency and posted himself where he would be likely to meet people who knew of this organization, in order to obtain petty business from them. We have heard that he has been a witness in a number of legal cases and has earned fees thereby. In Cleveland Adolf succeeded in starting a secret service agency and obtained contracts, among them the detective work for a newly started store of considerable size. This was a great tribute to his push and energy, but his agency soon failed. In St. Louis, where he stayed long enough to become acquainted with not a few members of the legal fraternity, he forged a legal document. A great deal was made of the case by the papers because of its flagrancy and amusing details. It seems Adolf had become enamored of a certain woman who was not living with her husband. The account runs that he urged his suit, but she refused because she was not legally free. Adolf replied that he would make that all right and in a week or two produced papers of divorce. These were made out in legal form, but it seems that he over-stepped the mark. The alleged decree stated that the fair divorcee must be remarried inside of a week. This seems to have aroused her suspicion, as had also some violence which Adolf had prematurely displayed. The young man was duly sentenced for the fraud.

Concerning punishments we can say that in the five years since he left New York he has served at least four terms in penal institutions and has been held to trial on one other occasion. This latter event concerned itself with Adolf's impersonating a federal officer. He made his way into a home under these conditions, just why we do not know. The case was difficult to adjust and was dismissed because no statute exactly covered it.

Perhaps nothing in his remarkable history shows Adolf's aggressiveness and peculiar tendencies any more than his political career. He had been voting long before he was of age and had even succeeded in getting a nomination for a certain party position during his minority, polling a considerable vote at the primaries. Following his defeat at election, which was at the time when the new party showed marked weakness, Adolf told us that he, after all, was only in the Progressive Party to wreck it. He felt that the leaders belonged back in the Republican ranks, and he thought he could help to get them there.

Mentality: Subnormal verbalist type.	Case 12.
	Man, 21 years.
Developmental: Early illness with involvement of nervous system.	
Delinquencies:	
Lying excessive. Swindling. Stealing.	

CHAPTER IV

CASES OF PATHOLOGICAL ACCUSATION

WE include in this chapter pathological self-accusation as well as incrimination of others. In court work one sees many cases of false accusation, but few belong to the pathological variety. We have not considered those based upon vindictiveness, or self-defense, or where any other even slight, recognizable, normal gratification was at the bottom. We have tried to hold strictly to our definition. Selection of the cases for this chapter has been easier than discriminating those who are merely pathological liars in general. It is simpler to distinguish those who accuse others for the purpose of injury or self-protection, or those who make self-accusation under the influence of delusional conditions, than it is to decide upon similar distinctions in cases of mere pathological lying. Several authors, such as Gross, have noted false accusations made during a short period of early adolescence, or in connection with menstrual disturbance. Our cases corroborate these facts, but show also that extreme false accusations may be made by girls *before* puberty. Satisfactory knowledge of such cases is not gained by learning merely that the accuser is under temporary physical stress — it is to be noted that our material clearly shows that there is always more in the background.

The many cases observed by us of false accusations made, rarely, by the feebleminded and, more often, by those suffering from a psychosis, need not be mentioned here — they are obvious in their abnormality and have little bearing upon our immediate problem.

For the sake of illustration of the fact of pathological accusation Case 17 is given in this chapter, but in its mental aspects it belongs more properly under the head of border-line cases. In our final deductions this has not been counted as a mentally normal case.

CASE 13

Summary: An exceedingly important case from a legal standpoint. A girl of 15 years persistently, but falsely accused her own mother and her step-father of the murder of the youngest child of the family. Some apparent physical corroboration was found. The woman and her spouse were held from the inquest to the grand jury and later were indicted. They were in jail for four months until the case was finally tried, when they were discharged.

We studied Libby S. as a delinquent some eight months after her mother and step-father had been acquitted of murder. These unfortunate people had been held and tried almost entirely upon the testimony given by this girl. It goes without saying that they were very poor and not ordinarily self-assertive, and so did not obtain competent legal advice. We were naturally interested in this remarkable affair and were glad to be able to get at the truth of the matter and bring about forgiveness and reconciliation within the family circle.

Libby was now under arrest for stealing and for prostitution. Her statement to us was that she had been immoral and wanted to be sent away to an institution where she would be kept out of trouble. She had been working in a factory. Her mother and step-father were temperate and the latter was always good to her and to her brother. She told about being extremely nervous when she got to thinking about different things, and maintained that she worried so much at times that she did not know what she was doing. Later we learned from her of her little sister's death, of the fact that the child was not really her sister, and that her mother had not been married to her present husband until the time of the trial, although for long they had been living together. She added that she had been a witness five times in court against her mother and step-father. A younger brother had also testified against them to some minor extent. "We had to tell what we saw — we told enough lies as it was."

Following the latter remark as a clew we went as thoroughly as we could into the details of the whole case. No report of the court proceedings being available we obtained what we could from the newspaper accounts. Obviously, however, much of these was impressionistic and unreliable. The coroner's physician testified to many bruises being on the body, and to the bottom of the feet being blistered. The report of what the police said at the inquest made anything but conclusive testimony. Even from that, the murder seemed highly improbable. It was shown that a physician was called to the child before she died, but did not respond. Libby testified at the inquest and later against her mother, stating that the child had been beaten and tortured in various ways. We also learned from other than newspaper sources that when Libby was waiting to testify, with her mother suffering imprisonment in the same building, the girl was nonchalantly singing ragtime songs in the court-house corridors.

The facts about the alleged murder of the five year old child as we could finally summarize them from various accounts, and after hearing the confession of Libby, are as follows. This child was an epileptic and had frequent attacks of falling, when she injured herself, once having fallen in this way against a hot stove. The little child engaged in extremely bad sex habits. Indeed, Libby herself had been somewhat involved with her in these. Once when she was ill hot bricks had been placed in the bed, and, while unconscious, her feet had been blistered. The child had also suffered from various other ailments, including a skin disease which left sore places and scars. When she died Libby first told a neighbor that the parents were responsible and this person referred her to the police. The false testimony began there and continued at the inquest, before the grand jury, and at the trial. Upon thorough final sifting of the evidence in court nothing was found in the least indicating that the child had died from mistreatment. The younger brother had been told by Libby to testify against the mother. There was no question but that Libby started and continued the whole trouble, but the unnatural fact that she was willing to make sworn statements jeopardizing her mother made her testimony have all the earmarks of antecedent probability.

The mother herself, in whom we gradually came to have full confidence, informed us that the dead child had an epileptic attack and was unconscious for several hours before she died. They lived on the outskirts of the city and it was bad weather, and although they sent twice for doctors, no one appeared. The child had been mildly whipped at times in an attempt to cure her of her bad sex habits. She had many sores from her skin trouble and these were by some interpreted as caused by beatings.

When under our observation, and during our attempt to analyze her career, Libby underwent a change of attitude and confessed thoroughly and definitely that the story about the murder was lies all the way through. For the sake of the poor little mother we had the girl make a sworn statement to this effect. It was of some little interest to us to note that the police account given in the newspapers about the little child being beaten with a rubber hose was derived from the story told by Libby. It was a wonderfully dramatic and pathetic scene when this woman met her daughter and the latter confessed to her lies and asked forgiveness. All the mother could say was, "Oh, the suffering she has caused me ! But I do want her to be a good girl."

From the girl's long stories to us we may derive the following points of interest. Before her confession she was very emotional on the subject of her little sister. She dwelled much upon her dreams of the child, but proved self-contradictory about the matter of her death, as well as about her own history. Even then she began telling us what a bad girl she herself was in various ways. She said, "I did not see Laura die, but I guess they did burn her up because her finger tips were all gone and her hands were all swollen up. Ma said she would burn her up if she did not quit wetting the bed. Yes, I used to worry about Laura awful. She always had been the trouble. I would have been a good girl if it had not been for her. I used to worry so fierce that I could not help from stealing and then when I stole I was scared to go back to my jobs. I had to have money and so I made good money by going with these fellows. I used to feel fierce about the money I took from my mother and used to put it back and then would say, 'No, I just must have it.'"

This girl had been working at different factories and homes since her mother's trial. She confessed to thieving from stores. The stealing she had done at home was, it seems, long before the death of the little child. Libby made much of her mental states and of her dream-life in talking to us.

"I like to go to nickel shows.   I saw a sad piece once and if I feel sad now I think about it and it makes me want to go to my mother.   I have a funny feeling about going home. I don't know what it is.   At night I dream about it and something keeps telling me to go home.   I want to go to an institution now and learn to do fancy work and to be good, and then I want to go home."

Libby told us enough about her first father for us to know he had had a terrifically bad influence upon her.   She also long associated with bad companions who instructed her thoroughly in the ways of immorality.   She described attacks in which she felt weak and thought she was going to fall, but never did.   (The young child in the family who had epilepsy was no relation whatever to her.)   She knew that her mother had long been living with her step-father in common-law relationship, but insisted on what was undoubtedly the truth, namely, that they were temperate and very respectable people.   Libby never gave us any explanation for her testimony against her mother, but acknowledged that she herself had been delinquent earlier.

The physical examination showed a normally developed girl: weight 108 lbs.; height 5 ft. 3 in.   Well shaped head and rather delicate features.   Her teeth showed a defective line in the enamel near the gums on the incisors and the cuspids.   Bites her finger nails.   Slight irregularity of the left pupil.   Careful examination of the eyes in other ways entirely negative.   Prompt reaction of pupils to light. No sensory defect of importance.   Knee jerks active.   Heart sounds normal, and all other examination failed to show defect.   Complained of frequent headaches, but these were not of great severity.   After information from the mother we felt that Libby's feelings of weakness and tremblings were probably of the hysterical variety.

During the period in which we had Libby under observation she showed more or less emotional disturbance, but even so we were able to assure ourselves that her mental ability was fair. We did not expect good results from formal education because in her case it had been very irregular. Many of our ability tests, however, were done well, but she failed where she was asked to demonstrate good powers of concentration and attention. We noted that she showed a very eager attitude toward her work, but was nervous about it. Always pleasant demeanor.

Most significant results were obtained on the "Aussage" or testimony test. After viewing our standard picture she volunteered only 8 details in free recital. On cross-examination she gave 21 more, but no less than 7 of these were incorrectly stated. Then she accepted the 4 suggestions which were given her. This result from a girl of her age and ability was exceedingly poor.

We never found any evidence whatever of aberrational mental conditions. Our final diagnosis was "fair in mental ability with poor educational advantages."

It should be definitely understood in considering this case that even to the time of our last interview with Libby, after she had acknowledged her own extensive prevarications, we had evidences of the unreliability of her word. In giving details she never made any special effort to tell the truth, whether it was in regard to the date of her father's death or any other immaterial detail. We were inclined to classify her as a pathological liar, as well as a case of pathological false accusation. Her traits as a liar and a generally difficult case have, we learn, been maintained during her stay up to the present time in an institution for delinquent girls.

From the fairly intelligent mother, who coöperated well with us, we obtained a carefully stated developmental history. During pregnancy with Libby the mother was run over by a bicycle, but was not much injured. The child was born at full term and was of normal size and vitality. Instruments were used, but no damage was known to have been done. Libby walked and talked early. A couple of times when she was an infant she had convulsions, but never after that. From 7 weeks until she was 3 years old there was constant trouble on account of some form of indigestion. For a time at that age she was in the hospital, but the mother was never told exactly what the trouble was. Her stomach was large. As an older child she was subject to fits of anger when she could not have her way. She never had anything that was suggestive of epilepsy. Twice she fainted, but once was when she came home half frozen one winter's day. At 11 years she had pneumonia. She menstruated at 14 years.

The heredity and family history in this case is of great interest. Libby's mother went to work for her first husband's family in the old country. At about that time this man's first wife died, but he had previously left her. He came of a good family, he was himself, however, a harddrinking man. He left two children by his first wife with his parents and came to this country with Libby's mother. Here they lived in a common-law marriage relationship for many years, and two children (one of them Libby) were born to them. The man continued to be a terrible drunkard and was probably insane at times. He once bought a rifle to kill his family. He was notorious for his great changeableness of disposition. Sometimes he would be very pleasant, and then quickly be seized by some impulse when he would grind his teeth, become very angry, and use vile language. Even when sober he would go along talking to himself and people would follow him on the street to hear what he was saying. He threatened often to kill his wife. He deserted her at times for months together. He only partially supported his family and his wife worked as a washerwoman. She left him once, but later went back to him.

In evidence of the character of this man and his wife we have seen several statements from reliable people. The man's son by his first wife came to this country and lived with them. He found his own father impossible — a terribly bad man who was continually fighting at home. He himself urged his step-mother to break up the home on account of the way in which she was abused. He made a statement of this fact under oath. (It is only fair to say in this whole connection that these people all came from a part of Europe where what we call a common-law marriage is an ordinary relationship.) It was from the language of her father that Libby first gained acquaintance with bad sex ideas, we are assured by the mother. After a terrific time of stress Libby's mother was rescued from her miserable conditions by the man who later lived with her and finally married her, and who has supported her and been true to her ever since. He is a sympathetic man of good reputation.

Libby's maternal grandparents died early and her mother had to begin very young to support herself. All that we know of the mother's developmental history is that she had some sort of illness with convulsions once as a child and is said to have been laid away for dead. She has brothers and sisters who are said to be quite normal. She knows her own relatives and her first husband's, also, and feels very sure there has been no case of insanity, feeblemindedness, or epilepsy among them.

Libby's moral history is of great import. She became definitely delinquent very early in life. At 13 years she had already been in an institution for delinquent girls in an eastern State and the superintendent writes that she was notorious for disobedience, lying, and stealing. She was placed there twice, besides having been returned once after an escape. When she was 6 or 7 years of age she began thieving. She took things from her mother's trunk and pawned them. The child stole from the people's rooms where her mother worked as janitress. Later she was truant and associated with immoral girls. In Chicago she stole a bracelet and a ring from a down-town store, wearing the bracelet later. She took $15 from a neighbor's house. She went to saloons in company with an immoral woman, and at least on one occasion she had been drinking. At 12 or 13 she was known to be "crazy about boys," but probably was not immoral then. The mother insists that the girl, resembling her father in this, is most changeable in disposition. Long before the trial for murder her pastor had urged the mother to put the girl away in an institution, but the mother's heart was too soft. (It seems strange that all this evidence of the girl's own bad character and unreliability, which was readily obtained by us, was not utilized at the time when she first made the charges of murder.)

The mother's explanation of Libby's behavior is that it was spite work. However, that is, of course, unsatisfactory. The mother not long previously earnestly had warned the girl against pursuing her downward path and had stated she must be sent away again if she did not do better. Libby then was doing pretty much as she pleased, for the mother, who was all along a frail woman, sick much of the time, had really no control over her daughter. Another feature of the case that is interesting came out in the fact that Libby herself had neglected the little epileptic girl who died. When the mother was ill in bed Libby had refused to properly care for the child. To some extent she also engaged in bad sex practices with the little girl. Libby never gave us the slightest indication that her false testimony was incited by spite.

Anyhow, she involved the step-father, who she always insisted had been very good to her. The motive undoubtedly is not so simply explained. A really deep analysis of the behavior could not be undertaken.

Mental conflicts: About sex experiences and own misbehavior.	Case 13. Girl, 16 yrs.
Bad companions: Including father.	
Home conditions: Notoriously bad in early life.	
Heredity: Father alcoholic, brutal, and perhaps insane.	
Delinquencies:	Mentality:
False accusations. (Extreme case.) Stealing. Sex immorality, etc.	Fair ability.

Case 14

Summary: A girl of 13 during the last year or more had been lying excessively and in uncalled-for ways. She also obtained money by misrepresentations and had made false charges of sex assault against a stranger. To be thought of as causative factors were defects of environment and possibly heredity, markedly imperfect vision, improperly obtained sex knowledge, and a distinct mental conflict.

We were asked to study this Emma X. on account of the various social issues involved in her case. Her family found her beyond control; she had been expelled from school; by her false accusations she had created much trouble for the police in her home town; officials of a public welfare agency found her altogether difficult to understand. We obtained an account of the case from several sources, including the mother.

The trouble with her had begun about a year previously.

She had been notoriously untruthful, and had forged a relative's name to the extent of obtaining $40 — in small sums. Emma remained out late in the evening sometimes, and on three occasions stayed out all night. The first time this happened she came home scratched and untidy and told a sensational story which led to much newspaper notoriety. She said a man took her to the woods — this was in the summertime — and kept her there all night. A loafer in the town, who was arrested the next day, she positively identified as the one who had assaulted her. This man was later discharged in the police court, however, because he abundantly proved an alibi, and because by this time the girl's story had become so twisted that even the mother did not believe it. A physician's examination also tended to prove that no assault had been attempted.

After this Emma was known to sleep one night in a cellar coal-bin. In stealing and general lying she became worse until with a change of residence to an uncle's home she improved for a time. It was after a little backsliding that we saw her.

The mother frankly tells us that the girl's mind must be affected; otherwise how could she act as she does. Emma has complained frequently of headaches and of a little dizziness. She has lately been lonely for a sister who went away. For the last two years Emma has not seemed altogether well; she has been nervous. A time ago she had for a friend a girl who spoke too freely with men, and her mother stopped the companionship. This other girl has a sister in the Industrial School. Emma's mother does not know of any definite harm done by the companionship.

During the pregnancy with Emma the mother had a rather hard time for a while on account of the severe illness of another child. The pregnancy began when the mother was still nursing a baby. However, when Emma was born she

proved to be a healthy and normal child.   Birth was normal.
No convulsions.   First walked and talked at the usual age.
She was a fat child until 8 years, and then, after an attack of
pneumonia, she began to ail somewhat.   At 10 years tonsils
and adenoids were removed.   The mother had no knowledge of Emma's defective vision.   Emma started to school
at 7 years, but at 13 had reached only the 5th grade.

There are 8 living children in the family; one died in
infancy.   There has never been much illness among them.
Most of them did well in school.   The family physician says
the boys show a "queer streak," but nothing, evidently, at
all well defined as compared with the career of Emma, whom
he characterizes as a "moral pervert."   The mother is a
well-meaning, hard-working, moderately intelligent woman
of about 45.   She is said to be somewhat slack in her household, but perfectly honest.   The father is desperately
alcoholic and peculiar at times.   It is not known that his
aberrations are ever shown apart from his drinking.   Years
ago he was in a hospital for the insane for several months as
an alcoholic patient.   The trouble with this girl is said to
have led him to drink again.   Both parents were from immigrant families.   It is positively denied that there are any
cases of insanity, feeblemindedness, or epilepsy on either
side.   Some other members of the family are known to have
better homes.

On the physical side we found a small child for her age;
weight 81 lbs., height 4 ft. 9 in.   Nutrition and color fairly
good.   Vision about 20/80 R. and 20/60 L.; never had
glasses.   Crowded teeth.   High Gothic palate.   Regular features.   Expression peculiarly stiff with eyes wide open.   Flushes
readily.   With encouragement smiles occasionally.   Other
examination negative.   Tonsils, and probably adenoids,
removed three years previously; formerly had trouble with
breathing through the nose.   Complains much of frequent

frontal headaches.   Says she gets dizzy often in the school-room.

Our "psychological impressions," dictated by Dr. Bronner, state that at first we found Emma very quiet and diffident, possibly somewhat shy and timid.   At best she did not talk freely, only in monosyllables as a rule.   She appears rather nervous.   She says she thinks of lots of things she does not speak of.   Emma smiles in friendly enough fashion, and later became more at ease, and more talkative.   She was rather deliberate in work with tests.   With concrete material she did better than with tasks more purely mental.   She succeeds eventually with nearly everything, but is slow. She seems anxious to do well, but acts as if unable to rouse herself to any great effort.   She is quite inaccurate in arithmetic, and only fair in other school studies.   Emotions normal.   In many ways appears normally childish.   Her interest in fairy tales and in the type of make-believe plays in which she engages with her younger sisters seems mixed with her wonderment in regard to sex life.   There is a distinct tendency to day-dreaming.

In reviewing the results of tests the only peculiarities to be noted are a definite weakness displayed in the powers of mental representation and analysis (she failed on Test X, usually readily done at 12 years), and a rather undue amount of suggestibility and inaccuracy in response to the "Aussage" test (Test VI).   The latter, naturally-to-be-supposed important test in a case where lying was a characteristic, showed a result that belonged to the imaginative, inaccurate, and partially suggestible type.   Many details of the picture were recalled correctly, but a few were manufactured to order, and 4 out of 7 suggestions were accepted.

About the general diagnosis of mentality there could be no doubt; the girl had fair ability, but there had been poor educational advantages on account of extremely defective vision. No signs of mental aberration were discovered.

Our attempt to try to help Emma decide why she got into so much difficulty resulted in a most convincing discovery of beginnings. We found a keynote to the situation in asking her about the companionship which the mother had said she had broken up. It seems that Emma had for a year, quite clandestinely, been familiar with this family. She apparently now desired to reveal the results of the acquaintance. Long ago the older sister, at present in a Reform School, boasted of her escapades with boys. Emma states that she herself never talked of these topics with her mother, who had said that girls who don't do such things should not talk about them. But Tessie, the younger sister of the delinquent girl, says many bad words about boys. These words and ideas about them bother Emma much. They come up in her mind, "sometimes at night and sometimes in the day." She even dreams much about them and about boys. "I seen the girls do bad things with boys. It is in the dream, it was in the house, in the front room on the floor." Emma says she never saw it in reality, but Tessie had boys in their front room when she went there, and then came running out when she heard Emma coming. She wonders just what Tessie does. Boys never bother Emma, but all these ideas bother her. "Then I think that the boys are going to do it to me." In school she cannot study for this reason. "Sure, when I start to study it comes up. I just think about what she tells me, Tessie. She tells me she liked to do these things with boys."

This little girl in the couple of interviews we had with her gave vent to much expression of all this which had perplexed her, and she really seemed to want help. She was very willing to have her mother told. She went on finally to say that the delinquent girl had taught her long

ago about masturbation and that she thinks of it every
night in bed. She can give no explanation of why she runs
away and why she falsely accused the man. She says it
was not true at àll what she said about him. She thinks she
would behave better if she were less bothered about the
things which those girls taught her. Emma says she questioned a young woman relative who did not tell her any more
than her mother did.

Regarding her diversions Emma says that she likes reading, especially fairy tales. She reads mostly Andersen's
Fairy Tales. She enjoys dressing up as a grown lady and
playing make-believe. She particularly likes to go to bed
early and lie and imagine things. She imagines sometimes
that she is grown up and married and has her own home and
children.

The neglect, through ignorance, of the several genetic
features of Emma's case was quite clear. The mother was
made acquainted with the facts, which her little daughter
then affirmed to her, and she promised to alter conditions.
We insisted on attention to Emma's eyes and general
physical conditions, on removal from neighborhood association with these old companions, on the necessity for
motherly confidences, on watchfulness to break up sex
habits, and on the development of better mental interests.
Through relatives in the home town it seemed there was
some chance to get these remedial measures undertaken.

A year and a half later we can state that a certain number
of our suggestions were followed out. The mother gained
a better understanding of the case and there were some,
although not enough, environmental changes. The father's
mental condition has been much better, perhaps because he
has largely refrained from drink, and consequently family
affairs are more stable. The girl herself is said not to be
doing perfectly either in school or home life, but to be vastly

improved. We have obtained no definite statement concerning whether she now lies at all or not, but it is sure that Emma has engaged in no more egregious types of prevarications and in no more false accusations. Competent observers think the case is fairly promising in its general moral aspects if environmental conditions continue to improve.

Mental conflict.	Case 14.
Improper sex teachings.	Girl, age 13.
Bad companions.	
Home conditions: Lack of understanding and control. Father alcoholic, insane (?)	
Defective vision.	
Delinquencies:	Mentality:
False accusations.	Ability fair.
Runaway.	
Obtaining money by false representations.	

Case 15

Summary: Girl of 16, over a period of some weeks made extreme accusations against several members of her family. She gave detailed account of sex immorality, alleged drunkenness and thieving, and an attack on her own life. She had herself, it was found, begun delinquent tendencies. The family circumstances and her clearly detailed account gave the color of possibility to her accusations, but investigation proved some of them false, and all of a sudden, after maintaining for long a most convincing demeanor, she withdrew her allegations. Both before and since this episode she has given no marked evidence of being a falsifier.

We were asked to study this case by police officials who thought perhaps the girl was the victim of some delusional state. She appeared at the police station and informed them her adult brother had been thieving from the place where he worked. She lived with him. Investigation by detectives on the strength of her convincingly given details proved his innocence. When the brother appeared on the scene he said he had been intending to report her on account of her being away from home. She herself was then held in custody.

We found a girl in very good general physical condition. Well developed in sex characteristics and a very mature type of face. Outside of a somewhat enlarged thyroid and moderately defective vision, we found nothing abnormal. Weight 114 lbs.; height 5 ft. Notable was her strong features, deep set eyes, high, broad forehead and sharp chin.

Our study of her on the mental side led us to denominate her as having fair general ability. She had had poor educational advantages. We noted much irregularity on work on tests. She did comparatively poorly on anything that called for careful attention and concentration. This was especially notable when she was dealing with abstractions or situations to be mentally represented. Although she could do arithmetic up to simple division she made a bad failure in the continued process of subtraction as given in the Kraepelin test of taking 8's from 100. In the work on the Code, Test XI, she found it altogether impossible to keep her mind concentrated. In tests where perceptions were largely brought into play she did very well. We noticed that she was possessed of a very dramatic manner. She sighed frequently as she worked. She was very nervous, continually moving her hands and tapping the table. She was quite satisfied with her superficial efforts. It was very curious that we, as well as others, were able to note her apparent sincere belief in her own statements about her family. As she made them she looked the interviewer straight in the eyes; there was not a hint of evasiveness.

Her result on the "Aussage" (Test VI) was very meager. She only recalled 10 details of the picture. On cross-examination she gave correctly 14 more items and was wrong on 3 of them. She accepted only 2 out of 5 suggestions offered and these were the most probable ones.

A full family history was never to be obtained. The best that we came ultimately to know was that her father and mother had been long dead and she had lived in institutions for years, then with a relative who was not at all a good person, and then with her brother and sister, whom she bitterly accused. These were people in decidedly poor circumstances and living in very congested quarters. Indeed, we were inclined to believe, finally, that crowded housing conditions with the necessary unfortunate familiarity with sex affairs and the like was largely responsible for her trouble. A few months prior to these events she had become acquainted with a girl who had drawn her into running away from home a few nights. During her unsettled home life she had seen a good deal of immorality in other houses, but had not been immoral herself. Conditions of squalor surrounded the whole situation.

Her accusations against her family as told to others, and reiterated to us, involved the drunkenness of her own father and mother. (We were never able to verify whether this charge against her mother was true or not.) Then she went on to allege extreme immorality on the part of her three sisters. She gave these in the utmost detail. (There is little doubt but that one of her sisters was rather free living before she was married.) She constantly maintained that she was the only virtuous one in the family and had withstood all advances. She then recounted much personal abuse and cruel treatment, and accused the brother and his wife of an attempt to poison her because they wanted her out of the way.

Her story was told in such detail, was so well remembered from time to time, and she presented such outward form of sincerity that experienced people were led to believe there must be much in what she said. On one occasion, under observation, she cried nearly all of two days because one good woman would not believe her statements. At least she said this was the reason of her tears. Her general behavior during this period of observation was perfect.

We found her hazy and somewhat incoherent about a number of the details of her life, but she had lived under such varied circumstances that this alone was not convincing of her insincerity. When we met her brother we were very sure that at least a part of her story was false. He seemed to be a very decent fellow and was really interested in her. Several months earlier he had trouble with her on account of her staying out late at night, and had threatened her. Then there was no more difficulty until her recent acquaintance with this other girl. He stated that he had been obliged to scold her very severely, and then finally she stayed away for five nights and wound up by going to the police station and making the accusations against him and the other members of the family. When the case came up in court she stated she wished to go back to live with this brother and admitted having continued misrepresentations about him and the others in the family since her acquaintance with this girl. It really was all false. She was placed under probation and the case has been, except for environmental circumstances, entirely successful. She is now a young married woman, and has had no further delinquent record against her.

Our investigation of the causation showed perhaps self-protection from punishment for her own behavior, but there was apparently much mental conflict about sex affairs and she had a very unfortunate acquaintance with such details, resulting partly, as she acknowledged, from her peeping through keyholes and so on. On account of her peculiar unreliability of statement and many quiet and staring periods, seen while she was under observation, we questioned whether she was not verging on psychotic conditions. However, all this tendency seems to have passed away.

Adolescent instability.   Case 15.

Girl, 16 years.

Home conditions: Defective through poverty and congestion.

Early sex experiences and mental conflict about them.

Reaction to own delinquencies, self protection phenomenon.

Heredity.   Mentality:

Delinquencies: Fair ability, poor

False accusations.   advantages.

Case 16

Summary: A motherless girl of $9\frac{1}{2}$ years, following her complaint of local symptoms, which proved to be due to vulvitis, accused her father and brother of incest. She was a bright child and normally affectionate, even towards these relatives. Her father and brother were held in jail for several weeks, but were dismissed at the trial because of the ascertained untruth of the charges.

As causative factors of her false accusations our study showed (a) her local irritation, (b) for which her father had treated her, (c) prior crowded housing conditions with her father and brother, (d) her lack of mother's control, (e) early and intimate acquaintance with atrocious sex knowledge and sex habits, and (f) recently becoming the center of interest in a group of friends made through her statement of the vileness of family conditions.

We were requested to study this case by the judge of the court in which the father and brother of Bessie M. were to be tried for the crime of incest with her. At a preliminary hearing the judge had felt that the remarkable statements of the little girl savored of untruth, and that the character sustained by the brother, in particular, was quite out of keeping with the grave accusations against him. The girl's charges, so clearly detailed, together with her local ailment, had proved thoroughly convincing to a group of women who had become interested in her. Bessie was evidently quite normal mentally and apparently affectionately regarded her only near relatives — this father and brother. Her story appeared thus entirely credible. The judge stated that he had been approached outside of court by these women, who in their righteous indignation were insistent upon the need of dire punishment of the outrageous conduct of Bessie's natural protectors.

We found a rather poorly developed little girl. Weight 64 lbs.; height 4 ft. 4 in. Bright, pleasant, vivacious expression. Attitude normal. High, prominent, narrow forehead. Head: length 19 cm., breadth 13 cm. Slightly asymmetrical frontal bosses. Snub nose; eyes fairly bright; ears asymmetrical in size — .6 cm. difference in greatest length. Thyroid palpable. Tonsils enlarged moderately. No sensory defect of importance. Strength good for size. Color only fairly good. (Results of gynecologic examination later.)

Bessie was given a wide range of mental tests, with the result that we classified her as being well up to the ordinary in ability. Indeed, considering her poor school advantages through frequent changes of residence she did very well in the subjects covered by formal education. Her memory processes and ability to testify correctly — in which we were naturally most interested — seemed, so far as we were able to test them, quite normal. Of a standard passage about a fire (Test XII), which she read once to herself, she recalled

17 out of the 20 items. A passage containing 12 main details (Test XIII), which was read to her in the usual way four times, she recalled with 2 details omitted. The "Aussage" test (Test VI) was done very well indeed, with 17 items of the picture given correctly on free recital, and 5 rejections out of the 7 suggestions proffered. Bessie's conversation was fluent and coherent, her range of information was good. She showed fondness for the dramatic statement.

Her mother died in the old country when she was about four years old, and her father had immediately come to America, but had never established a home of his own. For the last nine months Bessie had been living with a woman, Mrs. S., who was deeply interested in her. Previously to this she roomed for about six months with her father and brother, and prior to that time she had been placed about in different homes by her father. After some months with Mrs. S. she complained of local pain and irritation. When taken to a physician, she said her father was accustomed to touch her, and her story involved incest by both her father and brother. After others had become interested in her case, the matter was turned into the hands of the police. It was notable that during this period Bessie's love of the dramatic was being fostered by her newly found woman friend, who was providing her with lessons in dramatic reading and taking her extremely frequently to moving picture shows and theatres.

When first seen by us, Bessie reiterated her story of sexual relations with her father and brother. As she had done with others, and with the judge, she went into almost convincing details. Her knowledge of such relationships was apparently complete. She informed us that she had caught "an awful disease" from her father. She said that while rooming with them her sexual relations with her father and brother were nightly occurrences. They all slept in one bed.

A careful inquiry into Bessie's earlier knowledge of such things brought forth the most astounding account. One may say that this little girl had the most extensive acquaintance with many kinds of pervert sex practices that one has ever known in a young individual. She now said that the last ones who engaged in such things with her were her father and brother. Her experiences began at 5 years with a boy and a girl, and, she maintained, they had been very frequent ever since, up to within the last 9 months. A number of boys and girls were involved, as well as the men in two households where she had been placed. The practices she had engaged in were many, running all the way from self use of pieces of broom to normal intercourse, and both active and passive forms of pervert practices. It is unnecessary, even in this medical case, to go into details or to give her actual phraseology. It is sufficient to say that she frankly stated her early discovery of the pleasures of local stimulation and how she asked others to give it to her in various ways. Then she performed different perversions on boys and men. She told about observing sex relations between husband and wife in households where she had lived. She now says she had a disease before she came home to her father — a doctor had told other people previously. The men in two homes frequently had complete intercourse with her, she maintains, and gives description of it.

The credible substance of Bessie's long story elaborately told upon inquiry into her life history was that she certainly had had many sex experiences. When, in the light of these, it finally came to the question of the charges against her father and brother she said that it was really she who had been the instigator. When in bed she had begun playing with them. She described her method, learned before. She now says they did not have real intercourse with her, but the other men did.

The account of local physical conditions as obtained from several sources is as follows.   Bessie was taken to a physician for vulvitis, etc., by some people before she came back to her father.   During the period she roomed with her father he regularly treated her locally with a salve and a wash.   The physician who later examined her for Mrs. S. found the parts so swollen that he could make no diagnosis of ruptured hymen, but took it for granted.   After the father and brother had been in jail for some weeks the inflammation had subsided.   (It is only fair to say that the father had clamored for a specialist's examination, which, he contended, would prove his innocence.   Of course he was not aware of her earlier experiences or he would not have been so sure.) Then a competent gynecologist found that coitus had never taken place.   The hymen was intact.   This was at the time we studied the case.   On the day of the trial, I with two other physicians examined the girl.   It was found that a cotton swab about $\frac{3}{8}$ of an inch in diameter could with difficulty penetrate the vaginal orifice.   There was not the slightest evidence of any rupture of the hymen or of any vaginitis.   So far as the "awful disease" was concerned, repeated bacteriological tests over a considerable period failed to show the extensive vulvitis to be due to gonorrhea. It seemed much more likely that it was due to nonspecific infection following traumatism from the use of the various foreign objects which the girl told she had used.   Perhaps it was partly the result of the perversions which, judging by her knowledge of them, had been practiced by others on her.

We were informed later that much indignation at our report to the judge was expressed by the crowd in attendance at the trial.   The girl's first story was so well told that many had been irrevocably convinced of the utter guilt of the father.

The father himself, who was brought to us in the course

of our study of the case, was rather a low type in appearance. He was a poor earner, evidently had earlier been alcoholic, a small whining figure with tears in his eyes. His appearance would prejudice against him. The brother, on the contrary, made an unusually good impression. He had the best of recommendations. His sister's first charges ought not to have been believed on the basis of his qualifications. There had been 5 children, 3 died in infancy. No history of any significance was obtained except that the development of Bessie had apparently been normal in all ways. Her mother was said to be normal. Both parents were evidently representative products of the underfeeding and generally poor hygienic conditions of the laboring classes in a large Irish city. There was unquestionably a great feeling of affection between the three. Indeed, Mrs. S. stated that it was the excessive kissing of the child by the father which made her suspicious. Bessie always maintained that both father and brother treated her very well and that she loved them much.

It seemed clear to us that Bessie never knew in the least the significance of the charges she so glibly made at first. Her mind had long been so full of these things, and their social import seemed so slight, that it meant no vindictiveness towards her loved ones to say what she did about them. She asserted to us later that she really did not know what she said to the judge at the first hearing. The case illustrated well the fallibility of a young girl's accusations coming even from the lips of a normally bright and affectionate daughter or sister.

For her own protection Bessie was given a trial in an institutional school. From there it was reported after a few months that her mind was found to be so continually upon sex subjects that it would be most advisable for her to remain long under the quietest conditions and closest supervision.

Physical conditions: Local irritation.	Case 16. Girl, age 9½.
Housing conditions: Crowded.	
Early sex experiences: Excessive and pervert.	
Parental control failure: No home, no mother.	
Delinquencies: Serious false accusations.	**Mentality:** Good ability.

CASE 17

Summary: Boy of 16 years, not living at home, made false accusations of excessive immorality against his own family. These involved sex perversions, and he implicated even his own sister and brother, and alleged the connivance of his mother. The main complaint was against the step-father, who he also said was a professional thief. The improbability of such stories being told without good foundation led to much time being spent on investigating the case.

As possible causative factors of the unmitigated lying we found (a) defective heredity leading to (b) typical constitutional inferiority with the peculiar states of mind characteristic of the latter, (c) poor developmental conditions through early illnesses; (d) excessive bad sex practices on the part of the boy himself. Vindictive reaction to charges of delinquency against himself might be considered a factor if his false accusations had not been made without any such stimulus a long time previously.

(According to another classification this case belongs in our chapter on Border-line Types. It is retained here because it so well illustrates pathological accusation.)

John S., an undersized boy of 16, a pitiable specimen, when under arrest for vagrancy told such a heartrending story of home conditions, with assertions against family morality, that the judge and others were moved to indignation and an investigation was started. The general feeling was that no one who was not insane could make such statements about their nearest of kin without foundation in fact.

We found a poorly developed, but fairly nourished young fellow; weight 112 lbs., height 5 ft. 2 in.; good strength for his size. Stigmata: slight facial asymmetry, ears very long and narrow, dentition very irregular — one upper canine having erupted behind the central incisors. Tattooing on the chest. Vision defective, but how much so was impossible to estimate on account of corneal ulcer and general gonorrheal ophthalmia. Gait and attitude very slouchy. In contrast to general poor development, has already full sex development and much hair over body for his age.

On the mental side we found an excitable and talkative fellow, quite coherent, and giving in no way any indication of aberration by the form or trend of his conversation. He tells us he reached the 6th grade. He willingly works on tests and we note the general result as follows: Learning and memory processes, both for logical verbal and for meaningless associations, quite good. Perception of form, normal. Power of analysis of situations mentally represented, only mediocre. Associative processes, verbal, not normally accurate. Writes good hand. Simple spelling correct. Arithmetic correct for 4th grade. Tests for several other points hardly fair to register on account of defective eyesight. On one he failed because of not knowing the alphabet in order. Suggestibility extreme, as evidenced by testimony test. In giving report on the "Aussage" picture, Test VI, he enumerated 12 items, 11 of them correct, on free recital. Then he gave 11 more details, all correct, on cross-examination, but he accepted no less than 7 out of 8 suggestions offered.

Information on current events is good, but on points

said to have been learned at school is much mixed up. In giving responses to questions, he seized on any slight suggestion and adopted the idea. For instance, he said he had read the life of Napoleon, but could not remember to which country he belonged. When England was suggested he agreed to it. He then told various wrong incidents of Napoleon's life and death, also as suggested by the examiner. It finally came out that Bonaparte was an English nobleman who fought against France and Waterloo, was never defeated, and got sick in England. Then in the same way we get the information that this country gained its freedom from France, that Lincoln was president directly after Washington, and so on. John has read books from the library and various magazines, a considerable assortment. He knows almost nothing of even simple scientific facts, but is well acquainted with items gained from the newspapers and the theatres.

Going into his story, as we were requested, we heard at once about the cruel conditions at home. The boy's own father had been dead for ten years and up to within three years he had lived with a relative. While he was there letters indicated that queer things were going on at home, and the step-father was cruel to the other children. The mother was afraid to tell the whole story. When the boy came home the step-father at once began pervert sex practices with him, horrible things, and John found this man had been doing deeds of the same kind with an older sister and a younger brother. It seems the step-father also beats the children and has put this older girl out of the house. Recently he has left his wife.

When we go into John's own record, with which we had already made ourselves acquainted, he tells us he does not know what gets into him, but he has run away from home no less than eleven times. He works for a while, takes his wages and then stays at a hotel. He says he has been arrested several times on this account. His mother always telephones to the police about him and that is why he is under detention now. He wishes he were at home. The next day we went into more of the details which had been liberally sketched to the judge and other officials. We now learn that the step-father is a professional thief and that stolen goods he has taken are to be found in their home. He often leaves home and perhaps takes his wife's wages — she has to work out — and just now is again living at a hotel. The family have been informed by a physician that he is probably crazy.

On a later occasion the boy told my assistant that he wished to relate the whole story of his family. He then describes how the step-father even blackens the eyes of the sister and that he has long been immoral with her. It now appears that perversions began between this man and John some two months ago, never before that. The mother is there in the house all the time and knows about and permits the step-father's immorality with daughter and son. Cross-questioned afterward, the boy (evidently remembering what he said before) states these practices with him began the night he came home three years ago, but they had been going on with his sister before that. He knows this because his mother wrote and told him about it. His uncle wrote and told her to put a stop to it, but the step-father intimidates her with a revolver.

Our notes state that one afternoon when tests were being given him, John seemed to be in an excited state and often interrupted the procedure with talking. Seen in the hallway soon afterwards he waved his hand and insisted on telling more about home conditions and about what the officers would find if they went up there. On still another occasion he reiterated the same things, giving many details.

It was about this time that John was found to give strangely fantastic and childish accounts of circumstances with which he had been connected. We transcribe his story of a celebration at a school — it is a good example of his tales.

"They had it on Lincoln's birthday and on the 4th of July, too. The teacher did not believe that Abraham Lincoln freed the slaves. The children said, oh yes, he did. But they did not believe it. The children all hollered and said yes, he did. Then they all run up on the platform and got to fighting about it. The teachers would not believe that Lincoln freed the slaves till an old soldier came up there and told them yes, he did do it." I questioned him about this matter whether it was only a play they had, or were they in earnest. "Oh, all in earnest and they had a fight about it. The teachers would not believe that Abraham Lincoln freed the slaves and the children all run up on the platform and had a fight about it."

Home conditions were next looked up by a court investigator and we came to know the mother and sister. Much to our surprise we found them to be quite self-respecting, entirely credible people of good reputation in the neighborhood. The mother is an honest hard-working woman and is exceedingly depressed about the career of this boy. The sister is a modest and unquestionably good, self-supporting, young woman. Not a word was heard against them in any way. In their distress they gave us the full story.

The parents were immigrants when young. The father died through an accident some ten years previously. The mother has kept track of the members of both families fairly well. She had a sister insane, said to have become so as the result of the menopause. The father himself had occasional attacks of epilepsy, but they were never frequent enough to hinder him working as an artisan. He was a very moderate user of alcohol. The mother has always been fairly healthy. Thinks she now has a cancer. There are no other significant points in heredity that she knows. There are three living children; a number of miscarriages came after John was born.

The pregnancy and birth were normal. John walked and talked very early. Never any convulsions. At about two years of age he was very low with a complication of diseases. He was sick at that time for three months. Later he was operated on for rupture. The trouble with his eyes is of recent origin. When he was a young boy in school a teacher once told her she did not consider him right mentally.

There has been an exceeding amount of trouble with this boy. He was a great truant and reached only the 4th grade. When he was living with the uncle he caused much trouble, and the uncle warned her. He has run away from home twelve times, stays away perhaps two weeks at a time, and comes home ragged and filthy. He has had many jobs, but stays only a day or two at work. He steals in petty ways, takes money from home when he runs away. He is very lazy, but a great reader, especially of cheap novels.

Among the troubles with this boy is his extremely filthy talk. He has even lost one position on account of this. An aunt caught the boy in bad sex practices several years ago and told the mother. Neighbors, and earlier the school people, warned the mother that this was what was the matter with the boy. About a year ago John was found in a room with a man and other boys engaged in bad practices. The man was sentenced to a long term in the penitentiary on account of it.

Worst of all, the mother says the boy is the most malicious liar she has ever heard of. They have had a frightful time with him on account of this. For over two years John has been telling bad stories about the step-father. Recently he could not stand it any longer and left the mother. He was a good and rather strict man who took much interest in the children. He tried rewards with John, but this was of no avail. The boy has destroyed the home life, but she thought it her duty to try further with her own flesh and blood. The sister is in utter despair about what John has said concerning her. The younger brother also feels great humiliation. The boy has told his worst stories about them even in their own neighborhood.

After our investigation the boy was sent to an institution for delinquents where he could have the best of treatment for his ailments. The report from there after a few months was that he proved to be an exceedingly weak and vacillating type. He was notorious for being a boy that would do anything that was suggested to him. An outlook was kept for signs of insanity, but none was noted.

Over three years later we hear that John's character has not shown any radical change as demonstrated by his mode of living. He has served at least one term in a penal institution for adults. We do not know anything further about lying or false accusations in the case.

Constitutional inferiority: Stigmata.   Case 17.
                     Mentality.   Boy, age 16.
   Heredity: Father epileptic.
         Maternal aunt insane.
    Masturbation plus.
     Pervert sex experiences.
       Developmental: Much early illness.

Delinquencies:	Mentality:
False accusations excessive.	Dull from physical
Running away repeatedly.	causes (?).
Stealing.	Beginning psychosis (?).
Sex perversions.	Pathological liar (?).
Vagrancy.	

CASE 18

Summary: Little girl of 7 makes false charges of sex assault against boy in the same institution. She is later found to be an excessive liar and to steal.

Causative factors: (a) Atrociously immoral home environment, (b) early sex experiences, (c) local irritation from active gonorrhea.

This case illustrates the fact that a young girl, who has had unfortunate sex experiences, especially if her mind is kept dwelling on sexual subjects through bodily irritation, is apt to take advantage of the stir which she knows she can make by her statements, and glibly make false accusations. The case offered no difficulties for study and can be presented in short as typical of a number of similar cases seen by us.

We were asked to see this girl a few days after she had been taken from very bad home conditions and temporarily placed in a good institution for dependent children. While there she had much upset the high-minded superintendent and her helpers by stating that an older boy in the place had sex relations with her.

She was a small, bright-eyed, vivacious child. General physical conditions decidedly good. No sensory defect. Well shaped head. Weight 55 lbs.; height 4 ft. Active gonorrheal vulvovaginitis.

On the mental side we found, although she spoke in somewhat broken English, an ardent conversationalist. With her many ideas about many subjects, she appeared decidedly precocious. We noted her also to be very defiant and self-assertive, and her tendency to lie without rhyme or reason was soon discovered. Her exact age never was ascertained, but undoubtedly it was about 7. She was in the 2d grade. At times when doing the Binet tests inhibitions would appear and she would give no answer at all even to some easy ques-

tions. Her positive responses graded her as $6\frac{2}{5}$ years, but
undoubtedly she could have done much better had she so
wished.

In her talkative way she used English very graphically,
but with curious misuse of pronouns and a few other words.
Considering the fact that her family spoke a foreign language at home and she had been but a short time in school
this was not strange. Her lack of veracity was shown even
in her assertions about her inability to understand English.
At the first approach she denied her ability to do so, but later
showed that she understood very well. This behavior was
of a piece with her attitude shown in doing the Binet tests.

"Police bringed me. Don't know why. Cause my
father run away, she don't want to stay with my mother.
My father Austrian. Sometime my father talk Italian.
Then God make him sick cause she talk Italian. My neck
is sick. I go to Italian church and I talk Italian and God
makes me sick.

"They bringed me home to-day, then they bringed me
back here, then I stay here all along." (What is the matter
with you?) "A big boy — up in school — upstairs — don't
know his name. I came Saturday. She came Saturday.
She came Sunday, too. When we come to listen to music
then she gave to me that disease.

"Papa is bad. She run away. She run away. She take
from my mama $12 — all the clothes. She got another
lady. Is that your lady? Why do you write? I could
write better than you because I go to school all the time.
I never take money. I Catholic and Catholic can't tell
lie. Well, I going to tell the truth now. I found it in bed,
in paper inside. Then I give it to teacher and then I give
it to nurse. I never tell lies."

Before we had seen her this child had given some sort of
description of a big boy in the institution who she said had

assaulted her. There was no such person there, but her vehement statements caused much disturbance. Later she denied this to us and accused somebody at her own home. She came from miserable environment, as may be surmised from the fact that her father was a deserter and probably immoral. On account of her unreliability nothing could be done in the way of prosecuting the offender. We always felt it a possibility that some member of her own family was guilty and that was the reason she had told so many different tales about it. An owner was not found for the money which she had stolen. The person from whom she said she had taken it had not lost it. She took it under conditions when she had no chance to spend it. Her excessive lying was a continual source of trouble as long as she was kept in this institution. She was long treated in a public hospital for her gonorrhea. Since then she has been lost track of. It is interesting in this case to note that the child maintained that she belonged to a church, which made it impossible for her to tell lies. We have heard almost exactly this same assertion on numerous occasions. It is clearly made by way of affirmation when the offender covertly feels the need of bolstering up false statements.

Early sex experiences.	Case 18.
Bad companions.	Girl, age 7.
Physical conditions: Local irritation.	
Home conditions: Father immoral and deserter.	
Heredity(?): Father as above.	
Delinquencies:	Mentality:
Stealing.	Fair ability.
Sex.	
Lying.	
False accusations.	

Case 19

Summary: Girl of 18 made accusations to officials that a lawyer for whom she worked had been immoral with her. About the same time it was found that she herself had been stealing and lying about other matters. Later, when there was reiteration of the charges, a physician's examination showed that she had not been immoral. Some months afterward she went to other officials and insisted she ought to go to a reform school. A year still later she did have sex experiences and contracted venereal disease. Her succeeding record is totally different. For several years now she has been a young woman of thoroughly good character.

In its progress, after extended exhibition of exceedingly erratic conduct, to complete stability now long observed, this case is of considerable interest. It was after some months of effort on the case by experienced social workers that we were asked to study this girl. We found no difficulty in rapidly becoming intimately acquainted with her conditions and troubles.

Physically she was a normally developed young woman of distinctly good strength, but slouchy attitude. In expression rather dull and pleasant; laughs much in rather childish way for her age. Weight, 110 lbs.; height, 5 ft. 2½ in. No sensory defect. Good color.

Mentally we gave her a wide variety of tests with the result, in general, that she did well on them. She had left school at 14 years when in the 7th grade, but had not forgotten what she had learned. Her arithmetic was done very well indeed and she wrote a very good hand. The tests, which brought her abilities in many directions into play, were done almost uniformly well. Her memory processes were distinctly good and showed her capacity by her remembering logical connections as well as details. Her casuistic responses which were asked for in two moral situations, verbally presented, Test XXI, were rather vacillating, but evidently sound. It was easy for her to appreciate the intricacy of the situation.

On the "Aussage" experiment, Test VI, out of 15 details given as remembered from the picture just seen two were imaginary, and of 9 more items given on cross-examination two were erroneous. Her account as given was functional, not at all enumerative as in the usual childish fashion. Out of 6 suggestions proffered she accepted 4. This was a poor result for a person of her age. Her range of information was normal. Her interests while at home had been very simple; for instance, she had not been allowed to read novels nor go to theatres. In all our work on tests and in our several interviews with her we never discovered any signs of aberrational tendencies. Her social conduct furnished the only evidence of erraticism.

This young woman's mother, who is said to have been a normal person, died a few months before we knew her daughter. She had long been ill and consequently had had very imperfect control over her daughter all through adolescence. The father had been dead for several years previously; he was a storekeeper in a small way, fairly educated and non-alcoholic. No other family history of importance was ever forthcoming. There was only one other child in the family, a younger brother, who was quite normal. Outside of bronchitis during infancy it was said this girl had never had any serious disease. In the last few months there had been much complaint about suffering at the menstrual period. Menstruation began at 13 years of age and was said to have been regular until seven months or so prior to the time when we first saw her. However, this latter statement was made by the girl herself and at this stage her word was not particularly reliable.

When we began study of this case we were put in possession of the following notes made by an unusually competent social worker, extending over the previous nine months. Attention was first drawn to her when she was living with someone who had offered to give her a home while her mother was mortally ill in a hospital. She then had clothing and trinkets the possession of which she could not satisfactorily explain. It was discovered that she was lying. It was about this time that the girl told her friends that she had been immoral, and accused a man for whom she had worked of being responsible for her downfall. She had also been flirting with a married man who had been talking to her about eloping with him. It was learned that she stayed all one night at a downtown hotel, but probably alone. Further investigation showed she had stolen a considerable sum of money from an acquaintance and also a watch. Then a physical examination was made and a certificate given that the girl had not been immoral.

Much trouble was taken about the case in the ensuing year, the notes naïvely say, "object being to see if the girl could not be reclaimed." She was given an unusually good opportunity with a sterling family. She made much trouble for them and others who were interested in her. Her mother died early in the period. On a number of occasions she left her place and stayed away all night, sometimes walking the streets. On one occasion she is reported to have gone to a certain agency, looking as if she had been recently intoxicated, and appealed to be sent to a reform school. She was taken in by the police on one occasion. We first saw her after she had been living in this good home for several months.

At the same time we studied her physical and mental conditions we attempted to make some analysis of her self-orientation. She maintained then that her main trouble was because she had got mixed up with this married man. She declared he threatened her. (This was very likely from what was discovered about his character.) She had very good words for the officials who had helped her so much. She told us how she had stolen a matter of $100 or so. When we questioned her about her early accusations she said that she did tell a lot of lies when her case first was looked into. "I thought they were too inquisitive. I thought if I told them a few lies they would leave me alone. Everybody has to know everything. I forget half of what I'm to say. I don't know why I stole that watch. I would have brought it back home if he had not taken it on me. I never told anybody that I wanted to go to the reform school. I was afraid to go home because I was afraid I would get a good scolding. I think I have told all the truth to the officers since the first. I was ashamed to tell it, that's the whole truth. That's the truth, there was no one with me this other night. I did not meet a soul I knew. I went out to the South Park. I had never been there before. Where I have been living they would not let me go out anywhere. I had to stay there Sundays and all the time. When I got out I was worse than a wild calf. Maybe if I went out oftener I would not be so bad. I am here now because I went to the police station and told them I would not go home. It was late and I was afraid to go home. I had stayed out on the street all night. One night I went home and it was all dark and I was afraid to ring and I stayed on the street all night. I was on the street all the next day too. I went to the cemetery. Late that afternoon I met a young man and stayed talking to him and a detective came along and told us we shouldn't stand there. I never did anything bad with any man. I never said so. A visiting nurse told me the dangers of life. My mother told me I should be careful. Oh, I worked for that lawyer before my mother died. I worked for him about two weeks and he did not pay me what he owed me. No, he never did me any harm.

A man came along with a lady from that office and he asked me some questions and I was so scared because I thought they were going to lock me up. I guess that was the question maybe and I said, yes, but I did not know just what it was."

It was after this that the girl gave much trouble because of queer little trickery concerning some insurance papers, and about losing some money. Her friends wasted much time in the endeavor to get these matters adjusted. The family she was with thought she was very childish for her age.

Our opinion as dictated at this time was that the girl was physically and mentally all right, but that she showed a decidedly childish reaction towards the world and was very suggestible and unreliable. We knew many more facts about her which proved these points. Our judgment set down was that she was an unstable adolescent with possibility of showing very different characteristics inside of a year or two. We noted she had a weak type of face.

She was seen four months later, after a period of having run away twice for several days at a time. On inquiry she maintains she was impelled to do it by her own feelings of restlessness and general dissatisfaction. She thought the people with whom she lived were very nice and only strict as they should be. There was some question raised about this time about the periodicity of her impulsions, but except for her own statement that it was just before her menstrual time, nothing definite was proved. On the last occasion she did pick up with a young man and was immoral with him. She stayed out in a hallway all night. A venereal disease was then acquired. This was speedily treated in a hospital and the girl was found another place. Three years have elapsed, and during the time this girl has continued under the observation of one of her old friends. She has remained steady and trustworthy, and shows no tendency whatever towards untruthfulness or evasiveness. She has lived in one good home for two years and the people are deeply attached to her.

Adolescent impulses: Lack of self-control.	Case 19.
Sex temptations, resisted.	Girl, age 18.
Lack of parental care.	
Deficient interests: Both mental and re-	
creational.	
Delinquencies:	Mentality:
False accusations.	Good ability.
Stealing.	
General lying.	
Staying away from home.	

CASE 20

Summary: A girl of almost 16 years, of attractive and innocent appearance, alleged that she had been leading an immoral life and frequenting houses of assignation. She told the story to the people of her church, who were naturally horrified and demanded a thorough investigation of the social vice problems involved. This was undertaken by the police authorities, but they failed to get any satisfactory evidence from the girl. It was later found that the story was all a myth and the girl had not been in the least immoral. Her first statements followed directly after her attendance at an emotional revival meeting where these topics had been preached about. Afterward this girl was in court many times for various reasons. She is a mild psychoneurotic type, exhibiting under stress unusual mental phenomena. She and her family have created an astonishing amount of trouble in law courts as both defendants and complainants, because their peculiar unreliabilities have not been understood.

This case has long been under observation and we have much information concerning it. It was found difficult

to understand by pastors and others who had given considerable attention to various aspects of it. Annie F. was first
seen by us when under custody because of her own statement
that she had been leading an immoral life. We have seen
her and members of her family many times since. The
account of the case can best be given, not by commencing
with the cross-section study as obtained at first, but by
going at once into its whole connections and evolution.
At first it was merely learned that we had to do with an
unstable, adolescent girl who had engaged for apparently
no purpose whatever in false self-accusations which would
naturally blight her career.

On the physical side we found a rather slight girl, however,
of normal development. Weight 102 lbs.; height 5 ft. 3 in.
No organic defect was ever discovered. Neurological examination showed as follows: No tremors. Tendon reflexes
normal. Conjunctival and palatal reflexes absent. The
sense of pain to pin pricks was almost nil on the arms, and
diminished on the face. Strength poor in the arms even
when there was evidently great effort made. (Several
of these functional findings, however, have varied from time
to time in the ensuing years.) Hearing normal. Ocular
examination showed hypermetropia 1.5 D. R. and L. with
marked astigmatism. Fields and color vision normal. Left
pupil about twice the size of the right. (A competent
oculist could find no evidence of organic affection of the
nervous system correlated with this.) Shape of head normal.
Bowels regular. Appetite capricious. When first seen
was anemic, but later color was very good. Temperature
was taken regularly, but no significant observations made.
Petite, pretty features, and unusually beautiful eyes. Complaint of frontal dull headaches, soreness of scalp, cold hands
and pain "about the heart." Menstruated at 15 years,
then much irregularity for two years. Several badly cari-

ous teeth and great crowding in a narrow upper dental arch.

This girl was several times observed during a period of about 5 years. She developed into an unusually attractive young woman, showing at times various mild nervous disturbances as well as character difficulties. Only occasionally has she worn the glasses which corrected her errors of refraction. During this time she has not been severely ill. She has a palpable thyroid which has hardly increased in size. When last seen she was notable for a very clear skin, good color, and bright eyes. Conjunctival and corneal reflexes much diminished. Palatopharyngeal reflexes quite absent. The headaches are said to have persisted during all the time we have known her.

We have repeatedly attempted to summarize the mental status and functionings of this young woman, but our findings on tests and otherwise have been irregular and diverse. She reached 6th grade at 14 years, but had been absent much on account of sickness. When first seen we found that she was already fond of Lytton, Scott, and Dickens, and that she was a great reader of the daily newspapers, dwelling much on accidents and tragedies. What we say about her ability must be based upon the best that she has demonstrated. Often when seen she has been in some mental state which has prevented her from doing, or being willing to do, the best that is in her. She writes a good hand, does long division promptly, and reads well. Her association and memory processes have been proved normal, but given a task to do she is prone to show inhibitory pauses and other phenomena which interfere much with a satisfactory result. She has some little reputation of being able to give long, almost verbatim accounts of sermons which she has heard, but the auracccy of her report we have not been able to verify. She gave the antonyms of twenty words in average time of 1.4″, which is a good record. There was one failure, but that was quite typical. At the end of 20″, which is beyond the time of failure, she gave "unhappy" as the opposite of "happy," adding that she had thought of that before, only she did not speak it out. Her tests for psychomotor control were miserably done. She was rapid in movement, but absolutely inaccurate and did not follow instructions. However, we felt that even this did not indicate her full ability, for she had capably held a position in a millinery establishment where she was required to show manipulative dexterity. Perhaps the best statement of her performances is that she demonstrated great irregularities from time to time, and even at the same examination in her work on different tests.

On account of her peculiar testimony against herself, her memory processes and especially her performance on the "Aussage" test the case seemed of great interest. We found, as we stated above, in various ways that her abilities to remember, when at her best, were normal, but using the "Aussage" picture we obtained only 6 details in free recital; she was sure that was all she saw in the picture. Then on cross-questioning she mentioned 9 more items correctly, and gave 8 others much altered from the truth. No other item was added, but her report on these was almost illusional in its incorrectness. Of 5 suggestions offered she accepted 2 of the least important, refusing the others entirely. This was a remarkably poor result for a girl of her age, but may not be indicative of her best abilities even on this type of work. Our final opinion was that she was not clearly subnormal in native ability.

Annie has grown somewhat more stable as the years have gone on. Following our first acquaintance with her we have known this girl to make serious false accusations against others (*vide infra*) and to again damage her own reputation by alleging herself to be pregnant when she was not. Her word in other matters all along has been found somewhat unreliable, but there has been no extensive weaving of romances such as those indulged in by typical pathological liars. Our original diagnosis of this as a case of pathological accusation upon the basis of mild hysteria we have seen no reason to change. Both Annie and other members of her family are representatives of a most important type for court officials and all other social workers to understand. A great deal of trouble has been caused in several religious congregations by the unusual character of the behavior of these people. Also the number of times they have been in courts for various reasons is astonishing.

The history of physical and mental development merges closely with the story of evolution in the moral sphere, and all can be given together. On account of the mother having long been dead and the father being the peculiar man that he is there is some question about the truth of some of the details which have been given us, but we have reason to believe that the main facts are true because they have been held to be the truth in the family circle generally and were not merely given to us. Verification of details would be very difficult because the family are distributed between Europe and America, and no relatives outside the immediate family are at hand. The mother was in excessively poor condition at the birth of Annie. She had miscarriages preceding and following. It is stated that the diagnosis of malaria was made and that the mother had convulsions both before and after confinement. At the birth the prolonged labor and instrumentation were not known to have done any damage. As an infant Annie is said to have been frail, but not to have had any definite sickness or any convulsions.

However, at about Annie's fifth year there began a long list of illnesses. She had scarlet fever severely and also a number of other children's diseases. At 8 years she had an attack of muscular jerking, and then had a number of successive attacks until she was 14 years. At one time she was in a public hospital for three weeks on account of this. It was stated that this was chorea, but of course we can not be sure on this point. Annie was always regarded as a very nervous child; she was frequently a somnambulist until she was about 12. She is very nervous before the onset of menstruation. Of recent years she has been an excessive user of tea — at times before we first saw her she is said to have had 12 cups of tea in a day. At times she was then suffering from sleeplessness, and was wont to feel tired in the morning. As a young child she had severe night fears, seeing terrifying shadows upon the wall.

On account of her illnesses and her general nervous condition, Annie was very irregular in her school attendance. However, she reached 6th grade. As to the family opinion of her mentality we hear that they have regarded her as being an odd type, not lazy, but irritable, hateful, and moody by spells. Her memory is said to be most irregular, sometimes exceedingly good. The other children find it difficult to get along with her because she slaps them so much. At times she swears. At the time of the revival meeting, shortly before we saw her, she is said to have come home from church in an hysterical state. When in custody she was in rather a dazed condition. Where she was detained they say she acted as if she were stunned. Her memory did not seem at all clear, nor has it ever seemed other than confused about the events immediately surrounding the main episode of her career. She maintained she could not remember just exactly what she had said, and her account of it contradicted that of her father.

As we afterwards learned from the church people, it is undoubtedly a fact that her notions of self-accusation came from a Sunday School session in which her teacher repeated what had been talked about in the revival meeting concerning the scarlet woman. A day or two afterward the girl told that she herself was "a scarlet woman." She told it first to the teacher, was then taken to the pastor, when she reiterated the story, and the police authorities were called in. Of course her story implied lack of home guardianship and consequently the whole affair was handled for some days by the police alone, after the girl had given a very detailed description of her immoral life. By the time we saw the father it had been ascertained that this girl had never been away from home a single night in her life and probably had never been in the least immoral sexually.

It is necessary to have knowledge of the heredity and environmental background to understand this case. Almost nothing is known of the maternal family. After losing his first wife, the father was twice remarried, and even the third wife has divorced him. He had a brother who, after going insane and killing two laborers, committed suicide. His grandmother, and probably also a cousin, were insane. Two of his sisters were of a nervous and hysterical type and said to have attacks of aphonia. A child by his second wife is epileptic. This man gives us a long account of his own defective heredity and of his own physical ailments. He does not recognize the fact, however, that he also is mentally below par. We have seen him on numerous occasions and known of his great activity in the courts, and have attempted to size him up. He is undoubtedly a constitutional inferior, in poor general physical condition and subject to episodic mental states. One would be inclined to call him a semi-responsible individual with mild delusions, defective reasoning ability, great energy in self-assertion, and of combative disposition. This latter shows itself in his voluble emphasis on the alleged ill treatment of himself and family, even by his wives. He is never physically violent. On account of false accusations, whether delusional or not, he got at least one pastor into a peck of trouble, and, strangely enough, his wives have been involved in some other church embroilments when his own character was called severely into question. On one occasion we were interested to enumerate an astonishing list of people and organizations which, he stated, had treated him and his family unfairly. It seemed to us that during the last two or three years he must largely have lived in the courts to carry on his transactions there. His concern for his daughter seemed genuine and her delinquency led him to seek the law more than ever. Some of the good people who have become interested in his affairs tell us that his is the strangest story they have ever heard. His veracity is often in question. On more than one occasion with us he has dwelled on his nervous states, and on the fact that he is subject to times of mental confusion, but he defends his own judgment and actions on all occasions with great vigor.

This most erratic father has nearly always sided with Annie and offered excuses for her under all circumstances. However, she has stated that he was most difficult to live with on account of his quarreling at home and general bad management of the household. We know that at times he has been a seeker of newspaper notoriety. From his conversations with us and with others we know that his mind dwells much on sex affairs and these things are frequently discussed in the home. There has been much turmoil and quarreling in the family circle, at least with the last two wives. On several occasions the family have had to appeal for aid from the charities because none of them succeeded in making a living. Annie alleged she was taught shop-lifting by the second wife — we regard this as being possibly true on account of the woman's general reputation, the fact that they were desperately poor, and that she drank at times.

The father has the ability to make a very good presentation of himself, to use the best of language and he has had musical training enough to be able to give lessons. Annie herself has taken many lessons in music.

The after-history of this case is instructive. Almost none of our suggestions were taken when our first diagnosis was made. Two years after we first saw Annie she was placed in an institution for delinquents, then having run away from home, " picked up " a man on the street and stayed all night in a hotel with him. At the institution the girl became very nervous and behaved badly and the authorities decided it was a poor place for her. The father, who at first wanted her placed there, very soon decided that she should be removed. It is very likely his attitude had something to do with her behavior there.

About this time Annie worked in a millinery shop where she proved herself quick and skilful. There she told stories again defaming herself. She said she had had a baby and went into complete details, such as giving the name of the nurse who had taken care of her, and so on. On account of this she was discharged. Later she told us she related these stories to get even with her father, for if there was ever a hell on earth it was living with him.

About three years after our first study of Annie, the father himself brought a complaint against her of untruthfulness and general unreliability. This was at one of the times when he was complaining bitterly of other people. It seems he had lately tried to restrain her from leaving the house and she had cut his head open with an umbrella. It was evident she had started downhill again, and she was placed in a Rescue Home. She now repeatedly told people she was pregnant and made charges against some man, but these soon fell through because a little detective work showed she was corresponding with a boy and had very likely been immoral with him and others. She was then making an attempt to lead a dual life, maintaining she wanted to save some of the unfortunates with whom she was placed, while at the same time entering into various escapades with them and others. At this period a suicidal attempt was reported, but we never had satisfactory proof of the genuineness of this. Annie was now regarded as being excessively delinquent.

A few months afterwards, when the young woman was in one of her better moods and wished to do well, we made a few vocational tests on her. We found her quite unfit for the position of telephone operator which had been suggested for her. Psychomotor control appeared then decidedly defective. However, there was great improvement on work done on intellectual tests two or three years previously. Although she had developed physically (she now was a particularly good looking young woman) we felt she was quite unfit for work which demanded steady effort. One trouble all along was the fact that she did not wear her glasses. We advised then, as we had advised at first, a quiet country life for Annie and the other members of the family. The constant stimulus of city conditions was too much for them.

Again our advice was not taken and some months later the father came to us with the story of extreme poverty, some recent attacks of unconsciousness on his part, separation from his third wife, and the information that Annie was about to become a chorus girl.

Even a final consideration of the general diagnosis in this case which has been so long observed by us does not seem to justify our including it among our border-line mental types. Application of the term constitutional inferiority seems *a priori* warranted by the family history and yet we have no proof that her physical and mental conditions as enumerated above are not the result of her many early illnesses and the excessively erratic environmental conditions, rather than of causes which existed at birth.

On account of the peculiar inhibitory phases which arose nearly always during observation, we never relied merely on the results of laboratory tests for our judgment, and her success in some social situations has proved the wisdom of this.   Our earliest feeling that we had to do with a temporary and mild psychosis was perhaps justified, but further observation of her has led us to see clearly that she is not to be considered as a deeply aberrational type.   Could she ever have been free from the extraordinarily upsetting home conditions one could have gauged much more accurately her mental capabilities.   As time went on, the moral difficulties, which were largely induced by family conditions, led to mental as well as moral upsets which could be considered as little else than normal reactions to the situation.   Her conduct lapses, under the circumstances, are no indication of any mental breakdown.   On the contrary, it is clear by our own examinations and the accounts of other observers that she gradually has showed greater mental stability.

(Since writing the above, we have had, by chance, the opportunity of getting some important information about this case from an entirely new source.   A person who knew the family many years ago corroborates the father's remarkable story of antecedents.   The father himself remains in about the same state of social incapacity.   Annie, now married to a young man with a long criminal record, has a child.   Her word has recently been found absolutely unreliable, and testimony lately given by her in court concerning her husband was grossly false when it would seem that her interests and welfare demanded her testifying the truth concerning his non-support.)

Mentality: Psychoneurotic.	Case 20.
Heredity: Extremely defective.	Girl, age 16.

Developmental conditions: Defective antenatal conditions. Difficult birth. Earlier neurosis.

Physical conditions: Earlier dental defects. Defective vision, usually uncorrected. Stigmata of eyes.

Stimulants: Excessive use of tea.

Home conditions: Highly erratic and unstable. Many bad influences there.

Excitement and suggestion from revival.

Delinquencies:	Mentality:
Self-accusations.	Abilities irregular,
Running away.	and as above.
Sex affairs.	

CASE 21

Summary: This case illustrates the fact that pathological lying and accusation may arise first during a period of special stress. A young woman of 19, after illegitimately becoming pregnant, was found home after home by a charitable organization. In each place she made false accusations of immoral proposals against some one in the family or neighborhood. This created much trouble and lost her several good homes. Her lies persisted after an abortion had been secretly produced, but it is to be noted that she now, as a sequel to the operation, suffered from irritative pelvic conditions.

A short statement of this case will suffice to bring out the point that during a period of social and mental upset pathological lying and accusation may be first indulged in. We studied the case of a young woman of 19 who had been the source of much trouble in a certain locality on account of her false accusations. She was taken in hand by a charitable organization and found a home, after she had become pregnant at a wedding feast where alcoholic stimulants flowed freely. There was then no one to look after her but an invalid father. She was placed with an estimable family. In a short time she made the shocking announcement to the wife, and to others, that the husband had made immoral advances to her. He was a man of excellent character and of course this could not be believed. She was then placed on a farm, where she showed erotic tendencies and insisted that one of the helpers about the place wanted to take liberties with her. She was observed flirting and making advances to thrashers and others. She had to be found a new home, and this time it was in a city, where new accusations were made against a delivery boy. After this the young woman made off and shifted for herself for a time, and succeeded in getting some shady character to produce an abortion on her. Later, she again came to the official attention of the social agency by reason of making new accusations. From the date of her impregnation to the time we first studied her, a period of about 10 months, she had made serious accusations against many. When her lies were told in a new environment they, of course, always made new trouble. Each time, however, the girl herself was the loser. Her real partner at the wedding feast had early deposited several hundred dollars for the expected infant.

We found a strong, normally developed young woman of rather attractive appearance for the grade in society from which she came. No sensory defect. Diseased tonsils. Complained of constant suffering from pelvic conditions, perhaps induced by the abortion. However, being such a strong type she has been able to get about well and do her daily work. When we saw her she was employed in a factory.

The question put to us was concerning her mentality. She came of a Slavic peasant family, had been in this country only 6 years, and her relatives spoke only Slavic. She had been to school but a very short time, either in the old country or here. Because of the language difficulty, the giving of many tests, such as those in the upper years of the Binet system, could be regarded as most unfair. However, the simpler language tests she did fairly well, especially those where she could understand the commonsense questions. In regard to her acquirement of English, she has done better than her relatives, who continue to live in a neighborhood where their own Slavic dialect is spoken. When it came to dealing reasoningly with concrete situations, such as those presented by our performance tests, this young woman did comparatively well — quite above the grade of the feebleminded. Our diagnosis, then, was that she could best be regarded as poor in ability or possibly subnormal as compared with our general population, but as correlated with her peasant type she was probably normal.

From the standpoint of aberration one could find no evidences of anything but eroticism and a constant tendency to deviate from the truth. About the affair of the abortion she showed herself unexpectedly shrewd, maintaining that she had had to work very hard carrying stones when a new silo was being built on the farm, and at her next menstrual period she had flowed for a week or so, and that was all there was to it, except that she had been suffering from pains continually since. (The charitable organization knew she had visited the office of a notorious abortionist.) She smiled much in a silly way when in the company of men; she proved herself easily led. Taking it altogether, there was no reason for considering her insane, or as being in any way a psychopathic personality. She showed no stigmata of degeneracy.

There was no opportunity to get a satisfactory family history. Many of the relatives were still in the old country. A sister and brothers have been known in the neighborhood where this girl lived, and are said to appear quite normal in their simple ways of living. They are of the peasant type and good laborers, but given to occasional indulgence in feasting with alcoholic embellishments. From the sister we learned that this girl had passed through a sickly childhood and had been most irregularly brought up on account of the illnesses of her mother. She was not known as a liar when younger. Her short school record showed nothing of value for diagnosis. What happened to this girl was no great exception; among these people, we know from their own accounts, free and easy sex relationships are common. We are advised that it was long ago known that this girl was going with bad companions.

In this case we advised gynecological and other medical treatment and segregation in a reformatory or industrial school. The young woman could be regarded as nothing else than a dangerous person in any community. Even when being brought to us she had endeavored to flirt with a conductor on the train. A fair diagnosis could only be that she was, for the present at least, morally irresponsible.

This case has been only recently studied and no further report can be given. It is cited in illustration of the fact that was not clearly brought out by our other cases, namely, that a period of stress may be very definitely the exciting factor in developing pathological lying and accusation. This stands out particularly clearly in this case because the young woman had, prior to the wedding feast, been a good worker and had given no trouble in the community.

CHAPTER V

CASES OF PATHOLOGICAL LYING IN BORDER-LINE MENTAL TYPES

WE could load our pages with histories of cases where the statement of delusions, unrecognized as such, has created much trouble in courts and out, but this type of case is too well known to need any illustration. Text books of psychiatry deal with the falsifications of paranoia and other insanities. That the really insane also sometimes lie pathologically, that is, tell for no normal purpose what they adequately know to be untrue, is a fact not so well understood. But even that we need not be especially concerned with in our case histories. It has been well brought out in the previous literature on pathological lying, as witness in our Chapter II. In the present chapter we do not include the out-and-out insane, nor the definitively feeble-minded, nor the recognizably epileptic.

Much more difficult of understanding and much less easily recognized because of the mildness of many of the symptoms, or their variations from time to time, are the types which we enumerate. Several of these offer no complete picture of insanity — even Case 25, although clearly aberrational, extremely defective in self-control, and markedly criminalistic, did not show

to some psychiatrists who observed him a sufficiently
clear correspondence to any form of insanity as laid
down in the old-school text-books to be practically
regarded as insane and in need of long segregation.
In considering this whole matter we must never forget
that there is no wall of demarcation between those
whose conduct clearly betokens insanity and those who
are not insane.   There are plenty of instances where the
easily passable border between the two is permanently
occupied or is at times approached.

We keep our border-line cases separate in order to
emphasize that pathological lying by an insane person
does not make a pathological liar in the true sense.
We should hesitate, however, to give in legal form
a verdict of insanity in several of these border-line
cases we cite — they are very difficult to classify, and
the question of responsibility called for sometimes in
court work is unanswerable.   Keeping even these mild
cases away from our others serves, however, to lessen
confusion; we need in this subject to conserve all the
clearness possible by holding to fundamental classifications and showing up vagueness of definition where it
does exist.

Perhaps we are over-particular in keeping such a case
as No. 22 in this chapter.   The commonsense observer
would hardly regard this girl as at all lacking, even
in self-control.   On the other hand, for the purpose
of illustrating the subject of pathological accusation
we have kept Case 17 in the previous chapter
when it clearly shows great resemblance to Case 26
and is in reality a border-line type.   Then, too,
the swindler, Case 12, in some respects belongs in
this chapter.

We are hardly called on in this work to discuss the

lying of drug habitués, although they so frequently in their mental conditions represent border-line types. They are often on the verge of a psychosis as the result of their intoxications. Their lying is mostly done for a purpose, to be sure, and hence much would not come under the head of pathological lying, but occasionally veracity is so much interfered with that there seems to be a tendency to aimless lying. This class of cases, however, is sufficiently discussed in special literature pertaining to the subject.[1]

CASE 22

Summary: A girl of 14, a most vigorous and vivacious personality, had for a couple of years pursued a curiously active career of misrepresentation, of obtaining goods under false pretenses and running away from home even to distant places. Her conversational ability was above normal; her lies were evolved for the purpose of adapting herself to the peculiar circumstances in which she frequently found herself. Her general conduct combined with her abnormal psychomotor activity gave ground for the diagnosis of constitutional excitement — hypomania.

Birdie M., 14 years old, we saw after some clever detective work had proved her to be the girl who in another town had repeatedly swindled shop-keepers. It seems she had been accustomed to take the train for localities where she had no connections whatever, and there enter shops and make away with whatever she could. An astounding incident was when she returned some goods she had stolen and persuaded the manager to "refund" her the money on the same. This was regarded by the authorities as extremely clever.

[1] *Vide*, " Morphinism and Narcomanias From Other Drugs," by *T. D. Crothers*. Philadelphia, Saunders and Co., 1902. Also Chapter V, Stimulants and Narcotics, in " The Individual Delinquent," by *William Healy*. Boston, Little, Brown, and Co., 1915.

We found Birdie very small for her age. Weight 76 lbs.; height 4 ft. 8 in. Tonsils very large. Teeth excessively crowded. No sensory defect. Not yet menstruated. A very nervous type; quick physical and mental reactions; exceedingly active, restless manner.

Our psychological impressions state that Birdie did all her tests brilliantly and quickly, but very often with less accuracy than would have been the case had she taken the time to think quietly rather than work rapidly. She was very keen to make the best possible record. "I am proud of being quick; nothing is hard for me; it was not hard at school." It was found by steadying her that she gave a more accurate performance. We diagnosed her ability as good, but her school advantages had been poor. Otherwise we noted she was a pert, talkative, responsive child, of a distinctly nervous and somewhat unreliable type. Her ideas came tumbling, one on top of another. Under close supervision she was able to control her mental processes fairly well. For instance, on the antonym test, where opposites to twenty stimulus words are called for, Birdie gave them in the remarkably rapid average time of .8 of a second, with only one failure and one error. This is an exceptional record. From this and her unexpected powers of self-control exhibited on some other tests we were obliged to conclude that her aberrational tendencies were not very deep-set. Her mental traits seemed to conform most nearly to the type designated as constitutional excitement, or hypomania. Further observation of the case confirmed us in this first view of it.

On the "Aussage" or Testimony Test she gave 13 items, all correct, upon free recital. On questioning, 14 more details were added, but 6 of these were incorrect. Of the 6 suggestions offered she accepted none.

Birdie immigrated from Austria with her family when she

was 10 years of age. She came of a healthy family; all of her grandparents and many of her uncles and aunts are living. We get no history of any insanity, epilepsy, or feeblemindedness on either side. She is one of 7 children, several of whom have had nervous troubles. Two of the children had convulsions in infancy, but then only. One brother at 10 years old is an excessive stammerer and extremely nervous.

Birdie was born after a pregnancy during which the mother was much worried and in poor health. The father, too, was sickly at that time. The family conditions were defective on account of poverty and illness during a large share of the period when the children were born. Birdie at birth was very small and there was difficulty in resuscitation. She, however, was never seriously ill until she was 7 years of age, when she had something like peritonitis. No spasms or convulsions at any time. She was a very small child during her infancy, but walked at 8 months and talked very well indeed when she was only one year old. Developmental history otherwise negative, but all along there has been poor family control on account of ill health and the slight earning capacity of the father.

During the several months we knew Birdie she was always a most unreliable person. She repeatedly ran away from home and was lost track of. On one occasion she got as far as Omaha. By the use of elaborate, but plausible stories she always succeeded in winning the friendship of reputable people. Once she was found, after she had been away several weeks, residing in a good home in another State where the people thought of adopting her on account of her brightness. Many times she wandered about her home city and in the most active and sly fashion purloined anything she cared for. Several times when she was taken by the police she invented clever stories, without the least faltering, that seemed entirely fitted to the occasion. As the investigator said, she talked incessantly with not the slightest hesitation and was always airy and sure. No one to whom she had gone with her misrepresentations questioned her veracity — she always came out with a clearly connected and plausible story. We noted that her parents in comparison seemed quite stupid.

Of course Birdie passed under various names. Once we recognized her picture in the newspaper representing a weary, disheartened girl who was tired walking all day long from one employment bureau to another. She stated to the reporter it was her ambition to become a model servant. When in Omaha her mental peculiarities were recognized and she was studied by a competent alienist who, however, was not willing to render a verdict of *non compos mentis* to the police. This was when she had run away from Chicago and had told a lot of stories all of which had turned out to be untrue. The trouble which she created in various communities by reason of her hyperactive delinquencies has not been small.

With much merriment and an excessive amount of facial expression this little girl held forth to us. It is hardly necessary to say that the account varied somewhat from day to day. She did not like it at home and did not propose to go back there. There were too many in the family. As soon as the floor was scrubbed one of the children would get it all dirty again. She had started for New York, but the old gatekeeper at the station was mean and she could not slip by him. She got along all right in Omaha, but finally she gave herself up to the police there. She thinks perhaps she might go up to the people in Wisconsin who wanted to adopt her. In any case, she can do a great deal better than Viola B. who ran away from New York and got caught, and was so much talked about in the newspapers.

Thus her story would run along at great length, Birdie in the meanwhile chuckling with the thought of her own escapades.

We never recommended institution life because it seemed as if better things might be done for this girl. We felt that if she were built up from a physical standpoint her tendency towards nervous excitement might grow less. Her tonsils were removed. Every one felt that the girl's good mental abilities should be conserved to the utmost. Attempts at management in a different environment gave some hope of success, and after a time her parents moved to a smaller town, when we lost oversight of the girl. Following our acquaintance with the case it had been managed in the light of her characteristics, and her falsifying tendencies were constantly discounted by those in charge. We felt that her tendency was to grow more stable.

Three years later: We have just gained further information concerning Birdie. The family is still in straitened circumstances, the father having proved too weak a character to support them. He posed as somewhat of a gentleman and made off to another country. Birdie is said to

---

Mental conditions: Constitutional excitement.   Case 22.
Girl, age 14 years.
Developmental conditions: Defective pregnancy.
Early impaction of teeth.
Poor general physical conditions.
Home conditions: Poverty.
Irritability of father and mother.

Delinquencies:	Mentality:
Running away.	Ability good;
Stealing.	Constitutional
Lying.	excitement.

have worked steadily for months at a time, but over a year ago suddenly left home once more, this time going with a stage company.   Although the police in several cities have been appealed to, no trace has been obtained as yet of our young friend.   Whether her lying was continued at home we cannot satisfactorily learn, nor do we know accurately about any continuance of her state of excitement, but without doubt Birdie in her present wandering is fabricating anew, and is what she was before, namely, a young adventuress.

Case 23

Summary: A girl of 15 having been out all of one night, re-lated a story to the police of having been led off, and incidentally made the statement that she had been repeatedly immoral, once with a relative.   She dictated and signed a detailed account of the affairs, giving times and places.   This was used in inves-tigating and led to much fruitless effort even on the part of experienced people — her story was quite untrue.   When studied she proved to be a mild case of chorea, exhibiting the typical psychotic tendencies of that disease, such as we have observed in court work a number of times.

Nellie M., when brought to us by her grandmother, fol-lowing the girl's experience with the police who had been told by her of immoralities practiced, was found to be rather a nice looking and gentle girl, pleasant and responsive with us.

On the physical side we found her to be poorly developed and nourished.   Weight 93 lbs.;   height 4 ft. 9 in.   Vision about $\frac{20}{40}$ in each eye, but wears glasses which correct this.   Rather poor color.   Complains somewhat of headaches.   Marked tremor of outstretched hands.   Moderate amount of choreic movements in arms and legs, exaggerated when attention distracted.   Knee jerks exaggerated.   Conjunctival and palatal reflexes almost absent. Small regular features. Well shaped head. Said to drink at least 4 cups of tea a day. Heart sounds negative.

Mentally, she seemed to be fairly normal in ability, but was undoubtedly in a peculiar psychical condition. She had reached 7th grade in spite of much moving about, even to different cities. We found evidence of lack of good apperceptive powers and the history of the case led us to see clearly that she had been just recently in a very unstable, if not quite confusional mental condition.

The "Aussage" or Testimony Test was not given in this case.

The history of heredity and development shows many points of importance. The mother died when Nellie was a very little girl. She was terribly abused by a husband who was excessively alcoholic and in general a tremendous brute. They lived in a roadhouse where drunken fights were not uncommon. Nellie has been brought up since her mother's death by other relatives. Outside of alcoholism on the father's side there is said to be no family peculiarities. The mother came from a very reputable family. Nellie suffered early from several severe illnesses. When only six weeks old she is said to have been in a comatose condition with scarlet fever and diphtheria. Later she had measles, whooping cough and other mild ailments, and at one time suffered extremely from constipation. Walked and talked early. No convulsions. Menstruated first several months ago. Sometimes complains of severe headaches. One observer reported that the girl had been subject to slight melancholia within the last year. Choreic movements have been present off and on for about a year, but have not been marked until a little while previous to the incident which brought her to us. The diagnosis had been made that it was a case of mild St. Vitus dance. During all the year Nellie had been regarded as in general unreliable, but nothing of importance had happened prior to the above episode.

Nellie's story as told to us seemed coherent enough. Apparently she had entire memory of her past actions and, in general, of what she had said. Her own statements convinced us as much as anything else of her unreliability at times. It seems she had run away and gone to a picture show and had fallen asleep there. When she got out it was very late, but it was election night and people were about on the street. She finally was accosted by a woman who took her home. After her story of being led off by a man the police were called into the case and she gave them her remarkable statement. Nellie told us of picking up with a man, too, who lured her to a theatre, but who left her there. There was no way of corroborating this. She fully acknowledged to us the lies which had created so much trouble. "Well, I was telling the first lies and then when I was going to tell him that I knew that I was telling wrong he acted so cranky and said such things to me. He said he knew somebody had done bad things to me and so I thought I had to give the name of somebody and so I gave those names.

"The girls around in the schools I used to go to talked about these things. I never went with them. I was always by myself. None of the boys said bad things. The police were so cranky I did not know what else to say. They said someone must have done it to me when I was younger and I said it was my cousin because he always used to want to. He said he would give me a pair of skates if I would. He was 13. I never asked my grandmother or anyone about these things. No one ever explained it to me. Just the girls are the ones who told me about these things. They told me themselves how they had been out at night with the boys. I never did do it with anybody."

Examination by a gynecologist about this time showed

positively that there had been no immoral relations, and after our findings the case became a closed incident so far as prosecuting anybody was concerned. Nellie was taken in hand by the family physician and no further delinquencies or false accusations have been complained of during the succeeding two years.

Outside of the girl's general frank bearing, undoubtedly a point rather indicating to the police possible truth in her statements, was the detail in which the alleged events were given. The signed statement coming from an apparently naïve girl of 15 would seem in its clearness and coherency to bear the earmarks of truth. We always regarded this case as one of our interesting examples showing the unreliability of girl witnesses, especially those who have had unfortunate experiences, even though merely mental, with sex affairs.

Mentality: Mild choreic psychosis.   Case 23.

                                       Girl, age 15 years.

     Early clandestine sex teachings.

Delinquencies:	Mentality:
Running away.	Normal ability,
False accusations.	temporary aberration.

CASE 24

Summary: A girl of 16 whose general conditions won ready sympathy created much trouble. She repeatedly made serious accusations against a man and her attempt at suicide made her statement seem convincing. Further study showed the absolute falsity of her charges. It was a case of hysteria which had developed largely upon a basis of injury — there was a traumatic psychoneurosis. Under good treatment she made a fine recovery; there being no more indulgence in pathological accusations, although her nervous symptoms recurred for a short time after a couple of years.

At the time when we first saw Georgia B. she was somewhat over 16 years old and had been only 5 years in this country. We saw her because she had run away from home and attempted suicide. From the latter she had been rescued, and then had accused a neighbor of raping her. The case proved to be very troublesome until the nature of the whole affair was understood.

We found a thin and anemic girl, not at all prepossessing in appearance, dull in expression, suffering from a chronic suppurating otitis media.

On the mental side we had much trouble in conducting an examination because she was greatly given to tears. She did work for us on a few tests and her efforts would have been graded as those of a feebleminded person if her emotional state had been left out of account. Even our physical examination was largely hindered through her crying. However, her story was told in a straightforward way and with that show of emotion which had previously convinced others that grave injustice had been done her. Distinct proof of hysteria was present; for instance, on one occasion in the middle of a test Georgia apparently became unconscious. Her head dropped to the table, but her lips were red, her face did not change color, she resisted having her head moved, and in a moment or two lifted it herself to a more comfortable position. The diagnosis from such symptoms as these and from her history was not difficult to make.

The "Aussage" test, for obvious reasons, was not given.

Georgia told her story with surprising coherency; in outline, it was as follows: She ran away from home, and then was put under protection of the police authorities by a man who caught her.   She said she was caught when standing by a drug store where she had been to get medicine, just ten cents worth of peroxide.   When asked by us if it were not really carbolic acid she called for, she said yes, it was and that she intended to take it.   She wanted to get rid of her life.   What could she do in the way of living?   Her father and mother were both sick and they could not live long and then how could she get along taking care of three little children?   When asked if her parents would not be terribly affected by her suicide she said that it would not be the first time they had buried a child.   At this time she would go no further into her history.

On the next day she talked straight to the point, but with a remarkably dull expression on her face.   She said that about five weeks ago, she cannot tell the exact date, she went to a neighbor's house.   A man there wanted her to come and look at some pictures.   He finally got her to go to a bedroom and then held her so she could not scream, and raped her.   She is sure of it.   He later choked and beat her and kicked her out of the house.   At first she was afraid to tell her people.   A couple of weeks afterward she went back and asked why he did that, and he swore at her and accused her of being bad, and she and he talked back and forth for some time.   "He says, 'I'll kill you.   I did not touch you at all.' I says, 'You did.   You're a liar and you can kill me now if you want to.   You have already killed me.   See, I grow large like this.'"   He then set upon her and beat her again. She has not seen him since.   After telling this Georgia began to cry very hard and said that she really is killed now and is done for.   The whole story was told in a straightforward way with a full show of emotion.

A complicating feature of this case, resultant upon lack of understanding of the characteristic vagaries of this type, was the action of a vigorous knight errant. He was the one who rescued her. Hearing her ask in the drug store for the carbolic acid, which she did not get, he thought she was desperate and questioned her, but she tearfully refused to answer. He quietly followed her until she got to the river, and then, when she had her foot on the rail of the bridge and was about to jump off, he seized her. She fought and kicked him so that she badly hurt one of his legs. She told him she had reason to commit suicide. He got her to some house and there she fainted. When she came to she described her situation to him, naming a man who boarded with a neighbor as having raped her. She told him this was the reason she had tried to commit suicide.

This young man visited Georgia's family, found them strangely indifferent and not inclined to believe the girl, so he set out to see that justice was done. With his well-intended efforts he succeeded in getting several agencies to work on the case, the parents meanwhile partly resenting his interference. They said they knew what kind of a girl she was.

We never felt thoroughly satisfied with the family history on account of the comparative ignorance of the parents, our only source of information, although they were honest enough people. All points in heredity seemed negative, nor could we learn that there had been anything significant in developmental conditions. The girl had only recently menstruated. Her people felt that of late her word was quite unreliable. She went as far as the 4th grade. On account of the short time in school in this country this was considered doing fairly well.

Ten months prior she had fallen off a street car; it was not known she was damaged seriously. A jury had given a verdict of several hundred dollars against the company, but on account of an appeal having been taken the case was still unsettled. Since the accident a number of fainting attacks had occurred and Georgia had lost one position on account of them, a place where she had worked for 2 years. She was said to have been quite healthy before the accident. Some 5 weeks before we saw her, the girl had become hysterical and announced that she had not menstruated the week before and the cause was that she had been raped. Her behavior was so peculiar in regard to this that her parents did not believe her statements and did nothing about it. The girl evidently was accustomed to telling falsehoods, although we could get no specific account of them. The parents were very anxious to avoid a scandal, for though they were poor they made much of their respectability.

Georgia was examined after a later reiteration of her charges; the physician said that she had not been raped. After we saw her the parents thought it was best to go to another physician with the young man who had become so interested. Once more the report was that there had been no rape, but it now appeared that there had been some manipulation of the parts. After this the case quieted down, but Georgia had run away again just before this second examination. When by our recommendation she was now placed in a convalescent home she repeated the same stories and announced that she was pregnant. Of course more trouble was created by this and a third examination had to be made to convince these good people who had been recently asked to interest themselves in her.

After her stay in the convalescent home Georgia returned to her parents, and, appearing to be recovered, went to work again. Her record for two years was unexpectedly satisfactory. When the above episode had blown over she regained control of herself, adapted herself to family conditions, and worked steadily. On one occasion her nervous symptoms have returned with much depression and again an attempt at suicide. She was now carefully studied in a hospital for signs of insanity, but again it was determined that she was not of unsound mind. She made a speedy recovery, adjusted herself once more to her surroundings, and after a few months became married. During the last year or so there has been no further trouble. A settlement of the law suit for injuries was made before her more recent period of depression. At the time of even her last attack we can learn of no more false accusations having been made. The family attitude about her has, all along, not been what it should have been to have gained the proper results, but the problem of poverty was always with them.

Mentality: Traumatic psychoneurosis.	Case 24.
	Girl, age 16 years.
Accident, with law suit following.	
General physical conditions:	Anemia, poor nutrition, otitis media.
Delinquencies:	Mentality:
Running away.	Poor ability;
Attempted suicide.	temporary
False accusations.	aberration.

CASE 25

Summary: Case of a young man of 19, with already a long record of criminalism, who created much trouble for a court where a judge was keenly anxious to do justice. The fellow implicated himself in a sensational murder, but investigation proved this to be untrue. In other ways his word was found most unreliable. The question concerning his sanity could only be answered by stating that he was an aberrational type peculiarly inclined to criminalism, and therefore needed segregation,

and that he was also given to pathological lying and self-accusation. From the legal and social standpoints it is important to note that the case represents a type, unquestionably abnormal, although the mental pathology could not be subsumed under the head of any one of the designated mental diseases.

The case of John B. was studied at the request of a judge who had continued the trial because of the manifest mental peculiarities of the defendant. We were told that his behavior varied much, that one day he would cry and apologize, and on another would show stupid bravado. As the judge stated, John had long been in disciplinary institutions and this had failed to do any good. The immediately peculiar features of the case were that while he was being held for vagrancy and robbery, John made a strong attempt to implicate himself in a murder case. In other words he was a self-accuser.

We found a strong young man of 19 years; weight 157 lbs., height 5 ft. 5 in. Very broad shouldered and deep chested, but slouchy attitude. Good color. Eyes bright. Varicocele. Somewhat defective vision in one eye. Well-shaped head — circumference 56.5, length 18.5 and breadth 16 cm. Thick, heavy voice. Appears dull and depressed, but energizes under encouragement. Other physical examination negative. Complains merely of headaches in left frontal region, but says he has had these only since last year when he was struck there by a beer bottle. Recently an excessive user of tobacco.

In the mental examination we found much of interest. When first seen he gave every appearance of being a mental defective, but by judicious stimulation he could be waked up to do comparatively good work in several directions. On the Binet tests, 1911 series, he passed all but one of the 12 year set; in that he followed the suggestion offered. On the 15 year old tests he did three out of five. The failures were on the memory span of figures and in the repetition of a sentence of 26 syllables.

By our other tests we also found him defective in verbal memory processes, even when he read the passage to be remembered. In working with our so-called construction tests, where his success depended not only upon planning with concrete material, but even more on the ability to profit by his failures, he did decidedly poorly. In handling the puzzle box, where above everything is required perception of the relationship of one step to another, he succeeded very rapidly. With the cross-line tests, which require mental representation of an easily remembered figure and analysis of its parts, he did very poorly, succeeding only after the third attempt in each of the two simple tests. This is a type of work that is especially easy for the normal person.

In our "Aussage" or Testimony Test we got a decidedly poor result. At first enumeration he gave only 8 items, and on cross questioning gave only 6 more. He denied seeing other objects plain in the picture, but contradicted himself somewhat on this. It is interesting that he took only one out of four suggestions, notwithstanding his suggestibility on the Binet test.

On school work he does altogether much better. He writes a good hand, reads fairly well, and promptly does a sum in long division. He claims to have reached the 6th grade. One difficulty in testing him was his prevailing lethargy. We constantly had to fight this by encouragement. Once he insisted he must give up the work because he had not had a smoke for an hour or so. Altogether, including his irregularities, we could not call him lower than poor in ability, possibly subnormal. He did not come within the limits of the feebleminded group. Just where to place him would depend upon what he perhaps could do under other more favorable conditions. So much for the tests of ability.

In studying him for aberrational tendencies there were positive indications. Most significant it was when, in the Binet tests, he came to the word "justice" and turned to the examiner, saying feelingly, "I don't know what that is," and then burst into tears. Yet this was from a fellow who had offered to get himself into even worse trouble with the courts. He made much of his worrying about not having any home and not being the child of his so-called parents. His attitude was of sorrow and hopelessness about his whole situation in life. As seen again about two weeks later, still more evidences of aberration were found. He contradicted himself then in regard to his previous stories, in regard to his home life, denied he had made self-accusations, and very clearly did not remember at all accurately what he had previously told me. In fact, he evidently was not quite clear just who I was, although he had before been brought across town under the charge of a couple of officers to see me — an important break in his incarceration. He also told a different story from one he had told before to a certain official who now was present. He seemed rather mixed on a number of points, and this is all the more significant because he had been heartily afraid of being adjudged insane. Our diagnosis at this time was purely tentative as far as exact diagnosis was concerned. We stated that in our opinion he was an aberrational type and the practical point was that he should neither be allowed to go out in the community, nor be sent to a penitentiary, but rather to an institution for observation and perhaps for long detention. The jury found it necessary, as usual in such cases, to declare him insane.

The history of John runs as follows: From an evidently conscientious parent we learn of nothing significant in the family history. At birth he was said to be bright and healthy. He had diphtheria severely at 4 years. At 6 he started to school. He always got along well in his classes, but was very troublesome. At 11 years he began to run away from home. His father spent much time and money in going to various parts of the country for him, and at 13 years of age he was placed in an industrial school. He is the only child. He came home after 2 years, remained there for 3 or 4 months and then ran away once more to California. (His home was in the middle West.) He was returned by the police, sent to the industrial school for another year, and then again returned home. He stayed only 2 weeks before running away to New York. Coming back he got into some trouble and was sent for the third time to the industrial school. There he stayed until 6 months before we saw him. He was released once more on parole, stayed at home a week, and again ran away. It is reported that during his early time at the industrial school he was rather melancholy by spells, and at one time tried to poison himself. His relatives say he has a bad temper. He had typhoid fever at 14, but made a good recovery.

John has been known for years as a great liar, having told miserable stories about his parents, all of which were quite untrue. He has frequently mortified his father and mother by denying his parentage. The last time John was on parole he wrote more than one letter to police authorities in his home State, informing them he had been implicated in a serious crime. An officer at the reformatory institution had a letter from him purporting to be written from a penitentiary, stating he was sentenced there on a charge of robbery. When he was held in our city on a minor charge, he informed the police officials that he was connected with a certain notorious murder of which the papers had been full just previously. He was sent out with a couple of detectives who soon found he knew nothing about the actual facts, and that his alleged accomplices were innocent men.

In jail it is reported that he seems childish. He has to be locked up alone at times and then begs and teases to get out, but in ten minutes or so will repeat the bad behavior. He has stolen little things from others in custody and has attempted to dispose of his own clothes for a few cents. It is definitely reported that he has shown evidences of poor memory. From the institution where he previously had been so long, word comes that he was regarded there as not quite normal. John had been held in another city on a charge of rape, but without much evidence, for he was allowed to go. We could not find out whether he made self-accusations in that case.

In his story to us he complains bitterly about his treatment at the old institution, maintains he was head laundry man there, tells about his excessive smoking of late, denies his parentage, says the only friend he has is a certain church worker, maintains he did not have any home to go to from the industrial school, intimates he will commit suicide if there is any question of his being declared insane, says that he had earlier stolen things from home, tells of having spells when things get black in front of his eyes and can't see for a little while, says he wants to be sent to the penitentiary and wants to start right now serving his term.

All told, there was nothing so striking about this whole case as the extravagant tendencies towards prevarication. For years he has been lying to no purpose, although he has never been previously regarded as insane. Now he appears as an extreme self-accuser and as a fellow whose word can't be trusted from hour to hour. The lying, regarded as an aberrational tendency, is out of proportion to our findings of abnormality in any other sphere of mental activity, except perhaps the evidences of defective memory processes. One trouble in gauging his memory is, of course, the boy's prevarications, but one might argue that if his memory

processes were as good as his other abilities he would make
equal use of them.

Following our study and recommendation in the case
John was found not guilty, but insane. Then being resident
of another State, and, indeed, being on parole from a reformatory institution there, he was held over to the jurisdic-
tion of that State, and placed in a hospital for the criminal
insane. We have a full report from the latter place which is
exceedingly illuminating. It appears that despite his first
terror of being sent to an asylum he adapted himself to his
new surroundings very readily. It is stated that he assisted
with the ward work and spent his leisure time in reading
and playing cards. He asked for work outside on the
grounds and was regarded as a very courteous and genial
patient. No evidence of delusional or hallucinatory trends
could be obtained. He always seemed to be well oriented
and conscious of everything going on about him. Emotionally he appeared somewhat subnormal inasmuch as he did
not worry about his own condition, but said he was perfectly
contented. (The latter, of course, to a psychiatrist would
be significant.) He was a great talker and his stories were
well listened to. John said that when he was indicted for
robbery his lawyer advised him to feign insanity and as a
result he had been sent to that hospital. (It is to be remembered that with us he made great effort to show off his mental
powers at their best and evidently did somewhat better work
than when later in the hospital.) He gave them a history of
being somewhat of a cocainist and morphinist, of being a slick
"pickpocket," and of associating with prominent criminals,
particularly "auto" bandits. He was boastful of his experiences, but sometimes admitted that he prevaricated.
It is most interesting to note that he told a story of having
concealed in Chicago some plunder — jewels, money, and
so on — and was really taken to Chicago by one of the

Board of Visitors of the hospital to find the booty. It is hardly necessary to say it was not located. The last of the hospital report states, "Inasmuch as we were unable to prove that he had any form of insanity he was discharged."

It is of no small importance for discussion of the relation between insanity and criminalism to know that there are such cases as this where the individual is unquestionably aberrational and yet does not conform in mental symptoms to any one of the definitive "forms of insanity." They may be lacking in normal social control and in ability to reason, impulsively inclined to anti-social deeds and therefore social menaces, but, notwithstanding this, may not be classified under the head of any of the ordinary text-book types of mental diseases.

It is clear that for the protection of society a different notion of what constitutes mental aberration or insanity should prevail, so that these unusually dangerous types might be permanently segregated. It would really seem that just the findings which the hospital statement enumerates would convince one of this individual's marked abnormality from a social point of view and that his being at large was a grave undesirability.

The latest information concerning this young man is that he was being held in a Western city for burglary.

We should hesitate to make out a card of causative factors in this case. It is clear that the major cause in his delinquency was his aberrational mentality. What there was by way of causation back of this, our history, although obtained from an apparently conscientious parent, is too meagre for explanation.

Case 26

Summary: Boy of 16 had for 6 years caused a great amount of trouble by his general unreliability and excessive lying. He had been tried away from his own people in private homes and in institutions without success. His lying was excessive and often showed no purpose and no foresight. His peculiar delinquencies demonstrated weakness of will. Although in good general physical condition he simulated illnesses. Mental and physical characteristics rendered certain the diagnosis of constitutional inferiority.

We saw¦William S. first when he was over 16 years of age, after he had been arrested for stealing. He had already been in three institutions for delinquents. From his father and others we gained a long story of the case.

William was in fairly good physical condition. No sensory defect. Weight 125 lbs.; height 5 ft. 3 in. Although well enough developed in other ways he was a marked case of delayed puberty; as yet no pubescence. Strength only fair; for his age, muscles decidedly flabby. A high, broad forehead. Large nose. Peculiar curl of the upper lip. Small, weak chin. These features give him a peculiar appearance — readily interpretable as showing weakness of character. Cranium notably large. With small amount of hair measurements were: circumference 57.8; length 19.6; breadth 15.5 cm. (Head same size as father's.) Expression downcast. Voice high pitched. "Under dog" attitude. Slouchy. No analgesia or other signs of hysteria.

The performance on tests was peculiarly irregular. In this monograph we have omitted discussion of the results of separate tests, but the citation of the summary as dictated when the case was first studied will prove instructive: The work done on our tests was very irregular, peculiarly so. Perceptions good and most phases of the memory processes fair, but in reasoning ability and especially in tests which require the application of some foresight the results are poor indeed. The failure is remarkable in proportion to what he could do in school work and to his abilities in some other ways. He reads fluently, writes a very good hand, and in arithmetic is able to do long division, but showed no grasp of good method. When at his best he sticks at a job well enough, but does it with no intelligence and does not save himself in the least by thoughtful procedures. We were interested to note that in a game which he said he had played a great deal, namely checkers, he made the most foolish and shortsighted moves. It is only fair to say that this boy varied in his performance from time to time; his emotional condition largely controlled his performance.

On the "Aussage" or Testimony Test he gave a functional account upon free recital, with 15 details. On questioning he gave 13 more items. Out of the entire number only 3 minor errors. Of 5 suggestions proffered none was accepted.

There was a great deal more to be said about this boy's mental peculiarities than what was evidenced by the giving of tests. Our observations of him made at intervals over a period of several months corroborated entirely the statements of several others, including members of his own family. The boy was remarkably unstable in his ideas and purposes. What he apparently sincerely wanted to do and be at one time was entirely different at another. His changeableness was shown in many ways. When he had been found apparently suitable employment or a new home he often would stay only a few days. The father's first statement that the boy was a craven was borne out by all that we saw. He was too cowardly to be "tough," but he was a persistent runaway and vagrant. He sometimes used an assumed name. In general demeanor he was good natured, but always restless. Not the least of his peculiarities was his ready weeping. It was amazing to see so large a fellow draw down his chin and sob like a young child. He was easily frightened at night. Under observation he had peculiar episodes of behavior. Once in a school-room, without any known provocation, he suddenly began to cry and scream, picked up a chair and soon had the entire room cleared out. A moment afterwards he was found sobbing and bewailing his lot because he "never had a fair chance." On another occasion his legs strangely gave out and he had to be carried to bed by his fellows. The next morning a physician found him with his legs drawn up and apparently very sensitive over his back and other parts of his body, but with a little encouragement all his symptoms soon disappeared. He gave a history of having had convulsions, but this was found to be untrue. He was a "bluffer" among boys; when met valiantly showed always great cowardice.

We felt much inclined at first to denominate him a case of abulia, but his stubbornness in recalcitrancy led us to change our opinion. From the above physical signs and mental phenomena he was clearly a constitutional inferior.

Some facts we obtained on the family history were most significant. The mother of William suffered from attacks which were undoubtedly epileptic. Her mother, in turn, had convulsions at least during one pregnancy. We did not learn whether or not she had them at other times. No other points of significance in that family are known. The father himself was brought up, as he says, strictly, but he was inclined to be wild, and he has indulged for many years altogether too much in tobacco and alcohol. He is distinctly a weak type and the poorest specimen of his family. William is the only child. There was nothing peculiar in developmental history until he was $2\frac{1}{2}$ years old when he suffered from "brain fever and spinal meningitis." This was said to have left him with a stiff right arm and to account for his being left handed. (We could discover no difference in the reflexes.) Then at another period he was sick in bed for 6 months with some unknown, but not very serious illness. The mother has been dead for years and so we were unable to get accurate details about this. At a very early age William sought the pleasures of tobacco, even when a child of 6 or 7 he used his pennies for that purpose. He was brought up in an environment defective on account of his father being a poor earner and weak in discipline. But still his parent took for years a great deal of interest in him and it was not until the boy had proven himself most difficult that his father proclaimed himself unable to manage his son.

At about 10 years of age William began running away from home and manufacturing untrue stories. One of his favorite statements was that his father had been killed in an accident. It is notable that all these years he has been attempting to gain sympathy for this or that assumed condition, whether it be his own alleged physical ailments, or fictitious family difficulties. As a matter of fact, during this time he has been in some good homes, failing each time to comport himself so that he could be retained there. It was typical that he reiterated, "I have no friends; there is no one to stick up for me." Besides being in three institutions before he was 16 years old, William had been in homes which he had found when he had run away, or in which he had been placed by his father or by social agencies, the services of which had been evoked. His stealing was often done with an extraordinary lack of foresight. For instance, in one good position that had been found for him he took a box of cigars, when, of course, as the newcomer he would have been suspected, and even after his employers made it clear to him that they knew of the theft he took another box the next day. His lying under all occasions was nothing short of astonishing. To even his best friends he offered all sorts of fabulous tales which one iota of forethought would have made him realize would redound to his disadvantage. Almost his only show of common sense in this was when he gave an assumed name while getting a new position, and even this performance could hardly be considered deeply rational. It is hardly necessary to give lengthy specimens of his falsifications; they always pervaded his stories about himself, but strangely enough he acknowledged many of his delinquencies. A good example of the latter was when he collected a little money for a new employer and on the way back, looking in a shop window, saw an electrical toy and immediately bought it. He then went home, not even returning to the office to get the wages which were due him. An example of his lying is his responses to questions about his schooling. He maintained that he only reached the third grade. (In reality he could do sixth grade work at least.) He said, "I know long division by about 13 and about 5 figures. I don't know it by any other numbers." William maintained these same characteristics over the 6 years during which we have good data about him. We know he continued the same kind of a career for a year or so afterwards.

Three years later we have direct information from his family concerning William. His habits of prevarication have been kept up steadily, so it is stated. He has been in and out of institutions and at present is serving a sentence for larceny. He all along has been unwilling to face realities and has lied against his own interests continually. For instance, we are told that if he lost a place, instead of obtaining the help his family would have been willing to give him in gaining another, he would steadily pretend to be holding the former position. He is still considered utterly unreliable and a thoroughly weak character with a tendency to meet a situation as readily by a lie as another person would tend to react by speaking the truth. People who have known him of late speak of him as being at 21 "just the same fellow," which probably indicates that he is thoroughly a victim of habit formation as well as of innate tendencies.

Mentality. (Typical constitutional inferior.) Case 26.
Boy, age 16 years.
Heredity: Mother epileptic. Maternal grandmother had convulsions. Father alcoholic and tobacco in excess — weak type.
Developmental conditions: Early disease of the central nervous system.

Delinquencies:
Running away.
Stealing.
Lying.

Mentality:
Abilities irregular, psychic episodes.

CASE 27

Summary: Case of a boy, age 16 years, who told the most extraordinary stories of his vagrant life and the character of his family to officers of several organizations who tried to help him. He understood well that evidences of his unreliability would count against him. His stories, although often repeated, were not credited, and later, after a home had been found for him, he began a new series of lies that seemed almost delusional and somewhat paranoidal. After months during which much had been done for him it was suddenly discovered that he was an epileptic.

John F. appealed to an agency for assistance. He told a story of having wandered with his brother since he was a young boy. "My father was insane from what my uncle did to my mother. He drowned her. The house caught on fire and he blamed her for it. She said she didn't. She was too sick to get up and he took her out of the house and his big son pumped water on her. She was pretty near dead anyhow. We was too little to do anything. I seen it. I remember that all right. I can see that yet. Brother and sister died about 3 years ago. Brother took sick from sleeping out. We slept around in barns for 2 years. Father was in an insane hospital in Kansas. I think my uncle was hanged at N. Junction. We did not stay there. I remember yet when they went to put my mother in the grave. I jumped in with her. We put right out and after awhile folks wrote that father was dead."

So much attention would not have been paid to this gruesome tale had it not been repeated to various people during the course of several months. The boy wrote letters reiterating these incidents. His stories always went on to include the most surprising amount of abuse. It seemed that everywhere he had been illtreated. Farmers had whipped him, or clothed him badly, or defrauded him of his wages.

Physically, we found John to be in good general condition. A strong active country boy. No serious defect of any kind was discovered.

On mental tests he did better than we expected. To be sure he was very backward in arithmetic, but then his story was that he had hardly ever been to school at all. He certainly did well in many of our tests with concrete material, but the results as a whole were curiously irregular, even if we allowed for his deficient schooling. At that time we were disinclined to pass ultimate judgment on his mentality without knowing more about his antecedents.

On the "Aussage" Test he gave only 11 bare items on free recital. On questioning 19 more details were added. Of the entire number only 3 were incorrect, and these were not serious mistakes. Of 6 suggestions offered he accepted 3.

The history of this boy and his family has never been forthcoming. The authorities in his alleged home State have not been able to trace his family, which they could have done had his stories been true   Their report made it clear that the boy's reiterated family history was a fabrication — the *raison d'être* of which is still in doubt. In spite of his lying the boy was found a desirable home in the country at the work for which he was suited. After staying for a few weeks he returned to the city and got lodgings for himself. We next heard of him because he was induced by a "hold-up" man to secrete a revolver on his person while the police were in the neighborhood. Upon looking up his landlady, it was found that while with her he had suffered from epileptic attacks. These had not been observed during the several months we had previously known him, and he had strongly denied them to us. In our court work we constantly inquire for evidences of epilepsy; in this cas we received nothing but negation. After he served his sentence this young man was lost sight of. Even in the institution to which he had been sent he continued his fanciful and often hideous stories, still largely centered about the idea that he had suffered unjustly wherever he had been.

No complete summary of causative factors is possible in this case. The major cause for his lying as well as other delinquencies, particularly his vagrancy, is, of course, the mental traits peculiar to epilepsy.

CHAPTER VI

CONCLUSIONS

CHARACTERISTICS OF THE INDIVIDUAL. DIAGNOSIS

PHYSICAL FINDINGS

OUR 19 mentally normal cases (18 females, 1 male) showed:

Good general condition	14
Fair general condition	2
Poor general condition	1
Poor development	2
Poor development, undersized for age	2
Defective vision	6
Headaches	4
Mild nervous symptoms	2
Tonsils and adenoids	3
Fainting attacks	1
Gynecological ailments	6
Abdominal tumor, etc.	1
Hutchinsonian teeth	2
"Stigmata of degeneracy"	3
Premature sex development	2

Comparing the above with the findings by previous writers we see little chance to draw safe deductions. So many of the foreign cases have been insane; they can be more nearly compared with our 7 border-line types where all sorts of physical conditions may be found. It is notable that a large percentage of our mentally normal cases are in good general condition. Defective vision in 6 cases may be only a coincidence, but perhaps resulting nervous irritation was sometimes a factor in producing misconduct. Headaches, which Stemmermann makes so much of, appear as an incident in only a small number of our cases; her emphasis on periodicity also we cannot corroborate, there are hints of it in only one or two instances, but then her cases for the most part are not comparable to ours. That 6 out of 18 females should have had severe gynecological ailments is not to be wondered at, considering the trend of their lives, but, in turn, there can be little doubt that, as in Cases 16, 18, and 21, the local irritation tended to bring about moral disabilities.

MENTAL FINDINGS

Considering first the question of mental capabilities we can classify our 19 normal cases as follows:

Supernormal in ability 2
Precocious; later, still considered bright 1
Good ability. 6
Fair ability, perhaps not quite up to the former classes . 6
Poor ability 1
Poor ability, hysterical type 1
Poor in general, but with artistic and literary ability . . 1
Dull from physical causes, but later normal 1

Over and beyond the above enumeration there were some intensely interesting facts which came out during the intimate study of these cases. We are at once forced to agree with previous writers that an unusual number of the pathological liar group show great aptitude for language. This is shown by their general

conversational ability and by the fact that many of
them have found out themselves that they had capacity,
for instance, for writing compositions. Taking our
group of pathological liars in the strict sense, as given
in Chapter III, we find that no less than 7 of these 12
have been given to writing compositions and stories.
Three of them had definitely commenced long stories
or novels. It is most unusual among other offenders
to find evidence of any such tendencies. A considerable number of our group were characterized as great
talkers, and several as romantic, dramatic, fantastic,
etc., even by ordinary observers. All this goes to show
clearly that the native traits making for verbal fluency
are strongly correlated with pathological lying. When
it comes to consideration of such an instance as Case 11
we have the point more strongly brought out. Here
the individual is fairly swung down his life's course as
the irregularity of his capacities direct. His language
ability carries him along as nothing else will. In corroboration of this interesting point the conclusions of
other authors should be noted.

The aberrational types which show pathological lying are, several of them, depicted in our Chapter VI.
But little in summary of them needs to be said. The
general mental and moral weakness of the constitutional
inferior very naturally leads him to become a pathological liar; he follows, by virtue of his make-up,
the path of immediate least resistance — lying. The
episodic lying or aimless false accusations of the choreic
psychosis needs no comment — the confusional mental
state sometimes accompanying that disease readily
predisposes toward fantastic treatment of realities.
The relationship of constitutional excitement to pathological lying is less well recognized, but fully explicable

when we recollect the rate at which ideas present themselves in the mental content of such individuals, who have little time, as it were, to discriminate the true from the false. The mental conditions leading to purposeless prevarication which supervene in the real hysterical mental states, or during the course of traumatic psychoneurosis are well known. The individual is to be surely regarded, at least temporarily, as suffering from a psychosis in many of these instances, and falsification, while it may be difficult to distinguish between delusion and lying, is a well recognized phenomenon. The very deliberate lying of psychopathic individuals, such as Case 25, who, though so strongly aberrational, do not fit under the head of any of the classic insanities, is a matter for earnest consideration by all who have to deal with delinquents. There is altogether too little general knowledge of this type of fact. The correlation of the various epileptic mental states with pathological lying is well recognized. In many of the cases cited by foreign writers it has turned out that the individual was subject to epileptic seizures. It is another illustration of the great variety of epileptic phenomena. Something of a point has been made in the literature heretofore that abnormalities of sexual life are unduly correlated with the inclination to pathological lying, and the conclusion is sometimes drawn, as by Stemmermann (loc. cit. p. 90), that the two prove a degenerative tendency. Our material would not tend to show this nearly as much as it would prove that the psychical peculiarities follow on a profound upset caused by unfortunate sex experiences.

A characteristic of pathological liars is undoubtedly a deep-set egocentrism, as Risch states. If one goes over our cases it may be seen that there is exhibited frequently in the individual an undue amount of self-assertion. There is very little sympathy for the concern of others, and, indeed, remarkably little apperception of the opinions of others. How frequently the imagery of the heroic rôle of the self recurs, and how frequently it occupies a central stronghold is seen by the fact that nearly all of our cases indubitably demonstrate the phenomenon.

Most of our cases have been studied by the application of a wide range of tests. Indeed many of the individuals have been studied over and over. It is beyond our point at present to go over the separate findings because there is no evidence of a strong correlation of any type of peculiarity, except the ones mentioned here, with the pathological lying. Memory processes, for instance, as ordinarily tested seem to be normally acute.

We have naturally been much interested in the result of the "Aussage" or Testimony Test work with this present group, on account of the possibility of demonstrating correlations between laboratory work and the individual's reactions in social intercourse, particularly when there has been falsification upon the witness stand. In general we may say that while we have seen normal individuals who are not falsifiers do just as badly as a number of these individuals, yet for the group the findings are exceedingly bad. Perhaps the better way of stating it would be to say that not one case shows the sturdily honest type of response which is frequently met with during the course of testing other delinquents, even as young as the youngest of the cases cited here. Our findings stand in great contrast, we note, to the results on other test work. When looking at the table given above we see that a large share of our 19 normal cases are up to the average in general ability, and yet as a group they fall far below the average on this Testimony Test. Take Cases 8 and 9, for instance — both of them bright girls with, indeed, considerable ability in many directions, and yet both of them give a large number of extremely incorrect items in reporting what they saw in the "Aussage" picture, and also both accept a very large proportion of the suggestions offered. It seems as if frequently in these cases there is no real attempt to discriminate what was actually seen in the picture from what might have been in a butcher shop. In most cases the fictitious items were given upon questioning, but without the offering of suggestions. When the individual was allowed to give merely free recital the result was better. This, however, follows the general rule.

A general survey of work on other tests has not shown anything immediately significant in correlations, and this makes the result upon the "Aussage" much more notable. Perhaps it may be urged that if these individuals had been told to key themselves up to do this test well, being forewarned that otherwise it would reveal their weaknesses, they could have done better. Some hint of this may be seen in our story of the results of tests in Case 3. But of course the same might be argued about the other test work where no such tendency to poor results was discernible.

The following table, with a word of explanation, will serve to bring out results on this test clearly to even the reader unfamiliar with the specific details of this subject. A general description of the test is found in our introduction.

Case	Items Reported		Items Incorrect		Suggestions
	Free Recital	On Questioning	Number	Per cent	Denominator = number offered Numerator = number accepted
16	16^2	12^1	3	10%	$\frac{2}{7}$
15	10	14^3	3	12%	$\frac{2}{5}$
4	12	28^6	6	15%	$\frac{3}{4}$
19	15^2	8^2	4	17%	$\frac{4}{6}$
3	17^2	20^5	7	19%	$\frac{0}{6}$
7	11^2	17^4	6	21%	$\frac{2}{5}$
6	17^1	12^6	7	24%	$\frac{1}{7}$
13	8	21^7	7	24%	$\frac{4}{4}$
8	16	28^{12}	12	27%	$\frac{5}{7}$
9	12	32^{12}	12	27%	$\frac{6}{7}$
14	7	21^8	8	28%	$\frac{4}{4}$
2	10	12^7	7	32%	$\frac{1}{5}$
20	6	9^8	8	53%	$\frac{2}{5}$

Only 13 of our 19 mentally normal cases were found to have had the "Aussage" Test done so uniformly that results could be fairly compared, as in the above table. The reader will find it easy to refer back to the case for noting other correlations with behavior. In the first double column the items which were given in free recital come first, and in the second part the number of positive responses to questions by the examiner. The coefficients attached to these represent the number of egregious errors or entirely fictitious items given. It should be clearly understood that slight deviations from facts, for instance in color, are not counted as errors for our present purposes. In a later study on this whole topic of the psychology of testimony there will be much more complete itemizing. The errors in which we are particularly interested can perhaps best be called pure inventions. In the next double column is given, first, the total number of incorrect items and, then, the percentage of these to the total number of items reported. In the last column suggestibility is dealt with. We have been accustomed to offer 7 suggestions, asking the individual whether such and such things which might well be in a butcher shop really appeared in the picture. For several reasons not all of the 7 suggestions were asked in every case, therefore the result is best viewed as a statement in fractions — the numerator being the number of suggestions accepted and the denominator the number of suggestions offered.

As a last statement on this question which we put to ourselves, namely, whether pathological liars show the same traits in the laboratory as they do on the witness stand or in general social life, we can answer in the affirmative. We may repeat that others have made as bad records as some of this group, but taking the group as a whole, it is unlike any random 13 cases which might be picked out from our other classes of mentally normal offenders. On the other hand, many a feebleminded testifier has done vastly better than the median of this group. The errors themselves are of the purely inventional type, such as your ordinary report from a mentally normal person does not contain. (There is perhaps one interesting exception to this; Case 3. The report given by this subject included egregious denials of some of the main objects in the picture, and so was fictitious to this extent. She did not say that she did not know whether these to-be-expected objects really were in the picture — she insisted that they were not.) So far as suggestibility is concerned, there are great differences among even normal people in all classes. For comparison with the above group, we may take 63 cases of mentally normal delinquents, all of whom had been offered the full 7 suggestions. The median error of this group was two. Lower than the fraction thus obtained was the result on only 4 of the present cases. We have been interested to see that with some of the pathological liars there is no great suggestibility. The person is willing to deal in his own inventions, but not with false ideas which others attempt to put in his mind.

DIAGNOSIS

The essentials for the diagnosis of pathological lying are contained in the definition at the beginning of our book. The above considerations of the physical and mental make-up of pathological liars should leave little question as to what belongs in this class. Of course here, as in the study of any mental traits, border-line cases difficult to discriminate will always be found. Sometimes one will not be able to determine whether the individual is a true pathological liar or merely a prevaricator for a normal purpose. We have already stated our inability to determine this in some cases, and yet the nucleus of the type stands out sharply and clearly, and there can be no doubt as to what is practically meant by the definition.

The differential diagnosis involves consideration of the characteristics of the insane, defective, and epileptic. We repeat that we agree that the mentally abnormal person may engage in pathological lying quite apart from any expression of delusions, and that during the course of such lying the insanity may not be recognized. This occurred in many of the cases cited in the foreign literature, and if the prior histories of many individuals now in insane hospitals were known undoubtedly such lying would be frequently noted. But once the person is recognized as insane he need not be classified as a pathological liar. This term should be reserved, as we stated previously, for normal individuals who engage in pathological lying. Of course other observers have noted such lying in people who could not be designated as being mentally abnormal, but our material is peculiarly rich in examples of this kind.

CORRELATIONS STUDIED FOR CAUSES

Heredity. We come now to a very interesting group of facts — showing at once complete corroboration of previous observers' statements that pathological liars are extraordinarily *"erbliche belastet."* Taking our 19 mentally normal cases we find the following:

Insanity in the direct family (four of these being a parent) 6
One or both parents severely alcoholic 6
Criminal or very dissolute parent 4
Suicide of parent 1
Extremely neuropathic parent 1
Syphilitic parent 2
Epileptic parent 1
Unsatisfactory data 2
Reliable data showing normal family stock 2

Thus, out of the 19 cases there are only three or four which do not come of stock showing striking defects. Now, as we go on to show later that unfortunate conditions or experiences were often causal factors, the total findings seem to show clearly that these latter influences generally bore their unfortunate fruition upon inherited instability.

The heredity in the border-line cases is, as might be expected, even worse. These facts are easily discerned in their respective case histories.

The question of inheritance of similar mental traits is, of course, important. We have found absolutely no proof of the trait of pathological lying, as such, being inherited. The reader will note with interest particularly the facts in Cases 2 and 4, where we at first thought we had to deal with inheritance, but later found there was no blood relationship between the supposed parent and child. In those instances the lying of the younger individual was much more likely to be the result of psychic contagion, and this also may be largely the explanation of Cases 6 and 8, where an older relative was well known to be a prevaricator. The bad inheritance in these cases then turns out to be, corroborating what we found in studying the general problem of criminality,[1] a matter of coming from stock that shows defects in various ways — all making, however, in the offspring for moral instability.

Developmental Physical Conditions. Inquiry into our 19 mentally normal cases gave the following findings: Antenatal conditions were defective in 2 cases on account of syphilis and in one case from advanced age of the mother. The accident during pregnancy to the mother in one case, the severe mental shock in another, and the effect of illegitimacy in still another we can not evaluate. In 2 cases there were operative births with, however, no bad results known. One was a twin. Early severe disease of the nervous system was experienced by one, and convulsions during infancy by two others. Another suffered from some unknown very severe early illness, and one from prolonged digestive disturbance in infancy. Three had in early childhood several severe illnesses, one had a long attack of

---

[1] " Inheritance as a Factor in Criminality. A Study of a Thousand Cases of Young Repeated Offenders." *Edith R. Spaulding* and *William Healy.* pp. 24. Bulletin of the American Academy of Medicine, Vol. XV. February 1914.

"chorea." Two suffered from general nervousness, incited in one case by the excessive use of tea and in the other by a similar use of coffee. One was an habitual masturbator from childhood. Difficult menstruation was reported in only one case. In 5 cases there was a quite normal early developmental period, according to reliable accounts. In 3 cases the early developmental histories are completely unknown, and in 3 others uncertain. The data of developmental history in the border-line types may be easily noted in the case histories.

Previous Ailments. Ailments suffered from in our 19 cases after the early developmental period amount to very little. The several gynecological troubles have been mentioned above under the head of Physical Conditions. In one other case there had been urethritis previously. Head injuries, which play such a significant part in the study of criminalistics, find no place in our mentally normal series, but should always be kept in mind in considering the border-line types. Epilepsy as a possible factor in criminalistic problem cases is to be remembered.

Habits. We have already mentioned the effect upon nervous conditions of excessive tea and coffee in two of our cases. Masturbation, including its indirect effect, particularly upon the psyche, appears to be a very important feature of these cases. We should be far from considering that we have full data on all of our cases and yet this stands out most strongly. We have had positive reports from relatives or from the individual showing this certainly to be a factor in 7 out of the 19 cases. This is a very large finding, when it is considered that the data are frequently unobtainable. Of course we are not speaking here of masturbation *per se*, but only of the fact of its ascertained relationship to the pathological lying. This is only part of the whole matter of sex experience which, we find upon gathering our material together, plays such an enormous rôle.

Age of Onset. It is very easy to see that the tendency to pathological lying begins in the early formative years. Common-sense observation of general character building would tend to make us readily believe that if an individual got through the formative years of life with a normal hold upon veracity he would never become a pathological liar. We can see definite beginnings at certain critically formative periods, as in Case 6 and perhaps in Case 3, but our material shows that most cases demonstrate more gradually insidious beginnings. (Case 21 is in this respect in a class by itself.) As we stated in our introduction, it is clear from the previous studies of older individuals that the nature of the beginnings were not learned because it was too late. Our material offers unusual opportunities in this direction and shows the fact of genesis in childhood most clearly. For specific and often most interesting details we refer the reader to our various case histories.

Sex. Our findings show only 1 male out of 19 mentally normal cases. A general observation by practical students of conduct, namely, that females tend to deviate from the truth more readily than males, is more than thoroughly borne out here. There are certainly several social and psychological reasons for this, but they need not be gone into here. If our figures seem not to be corroborated by the findings of previous students it is only because the figures are not comparable — the latter have mixed the mentally abnormal with the pathological liars proper. It will be noted

that in our examples of border-line cases 5 out of the 8
are males. Cases of pathological swindling by mentally
abnormal individuals, such as we have avoided, make up
much of the foreign literature. We can easily see that
the social opportunities for swindling are vastly greater
for males than those offered to the opposite sex. Sex
differences, as in many instances, must not be taken here
too seriously because social environment, differing so
greatly for the sexes, is largely responsible for the behavior which we superficially judge to be entirely the
expression of innate characteristics.

Environment. We are far from feeling that a mere
enumeration of material environmental conditions tells
the story of environmental influences important for
our present subject. The psyche is frequently most
profoundly affected by environmental conditions which
even a trained observer would not detect. But conditions in the total number of unselected cases show
something, and, for whatever it is worth, we offer the
following enumeration of environment in our 19 normal
cases, who with much more reason might be expected to
be largely influenced by surroundings than our group
of border-line cases.

Reasonably good home from birth 5
Defective home conditions through poverty 2
Very ignorant parents 2
Immoralities in home life 6
Marked defect in parental control 6
Very erratic home conditions — parent abnormal . . 1

Early Mental Experiences. As will have been observed by the reader in going over the case histories,
the early mental experiences of many of our group of
mentally normal pathological liars have been shock-

ingly bad. Full appreciation of this can only be gained through perusal of the text, but here we may call attention to the fact that no less than 8 of the 19 have had very early untoward sex experiences, that 5 were markedly under the influence of bad companions, including even the influence in one or two cases of vicious grown people. The sex experiences we have just enumerated were received through others — we are not here speaking of masturbation, which is discussed above.

Psychic Contagion. Direct contagion of the tendency to lie seems more than likely to take place, at least during the more plastic periods of life. It may be that this only develops when there is some sort of predisposition to instability; our related findings on defective heredity would seem to indicate the fact. It should be noted that in 5 instances out of our 19 mentally normal (Cases 2, 4, 6, 8, 20) some other member of the household, we learned from reliable sources, was known as a chronic prevaricator.

Mental Conflicts. The fact that several of our cases started lying from the time when there occurred some experience accompanied by a deep emotional context, and that this experience and the emotion was repressed, seems to point clearly to the part which repressed mental life may play in the genesis. That as children they kept to themselves secrets of grave import and dwelled long on them, shows in a large number of our cases. Anything deeply upsetting, such as the discovery of the facts of sex life or questions about family relationships, are the incidents which cause the trouble. For students of modern psychology nothing more need be said on this point — the concrete issues are perceivable in the case histories.

Adolescence. Quite apart from the age of onset, we may consider the physical and psychical instabilities of adolescence as effective causes of pathological lying. Of course it is equally true that many other tendencies to peculiarity are accentuated at this period. It has been suggested that cases which have their origin largely in the unstable reactions of adolescence have much the better prognosis, but it seems that not enough evidence has been accumulated as yet to justify us in this conclusion, which, we acknowledge, may prove to be true.

Irritative Conditions. In the same way the various types of irritative conditions, physical and mental, may be considered as exciting moments. Individuals with a tendency to pathological lying will no doubt show aggravation of the phenomenon at periods of particular stress. We have heard it suggested in several cases by relatives that the menstrual period, for instance, brings about an access of tendency to prevarication. We would grant the point without conceding this exciting factor to be a fundamental cause. (Case 21, we may say again, illustrates a special fact.) The periodicity which Stemmermann makes much of may merely mean succumbing during a period of physiologic stress. Social stress also may be met by pathological lying, in the same way that the individual who finds himself in a tight place may attempt to get out of it by running away. We have already spoken of the likeness of social and physical stress as showing when the weak individual is brought to bay. That pathological lying does not run an even course, but shows remarkable fluctuations with powerful exacerbations, is undoubtedly to be explained by changes of inner and outer stress.

Habit Formation. The influence of habit in causing
chronicity must always be definitely reckoned with.
It is hardly necessary to say more than a word on this
subject. Even the individual, as in Cases 8, 9, and 10,
comes to strongly realize it. Particularly is this point
to be estimated in considering the possibilities of a
rapid cure.

Special Mental Abilities. Once more, for the sake of
completeness in giving a category of causes, we should
call attention to the fact acknowledged by all thorough
students of this subject, namely, that, other things
being equal, it is particularly the individual who has
linguistic abilities, who is especially good at verbal
composition, that seems to have most incentive to
dally with the truth. But beyond this we would insist
that a combination of verbal ability with proportionate
mental defects in other fields gives a make-up which
finds the paths of least resistance directly along the
lines of prevarication.

SOCIAL CORRELATIONS

The rôle played in society by the pathological liar
is very striking. The characteristic behavior in its
unreasonableness is quite beyond the ken of the ordinary observer. The fact that here is a type of conduct regularly indulged in without seeming pleasur-
able results, and frequently militating obviously
against the direct interests of the individual, makes
a situation inexplicable by the usual canons of infer-
ence. To a certain extent the tendencies of each
separate case must be viewed in their environmental
context to be well understood. For example, the
lying and swindling which center about the assumption

of a noble name and a corresponding station or affect-
ing the life of a cloister brother, such as we find in the
cases cited by Longard, show great differences from
any material obtainable in our country. In interpretation of this, one has to consider the glamour thrown
about the socially exalted or the life of the recluse —
a glamour which obtains readily among the simple-
minded people of rural Europe. Then, too, this very
simple-mindedness, with the great differences which
exist between peasant and noble, leads in itself to much
opportunity for cheating.

With us, especially in the newer work of courts, which
are rapidly becoming in their various social endeavors
more and more intimately connected with many phases
of life, the pathological liar becomes of main interest
in the rôle of accuser of others, self-accuser, witness,
and general social disturber.

Here again, we may call attention to the fact, which
is of great social importance, namely, that the person
who is seemingly normal in all other respects may be
a pathological liar. It might be naturally expected
that the feebleminded, who frequently have poor discernment of the relation of cause and effect, including
the phenomena of conduct, would often lie without normal cause. As a matter of fact there is surprisingly
little of this among them, and one can find numerous
mental defectives who are faithful tellers of the truth,
while even, as we have found by other studies, some
are good testifiers. Exaggerated instances of the
type represented by Case 12, where the individual by
the virtue of language ability endeavors to maintain
a place in the world which his abilities do not otherwise
justify, and where the very contradiction between
abilities and disabilities leads to the development of

an excessive habit of lying, are known in considerable number by us. Many of these mentally defective verbalists do not even grade high enough to come in our border-line cases, and yet frequently, by virtue of their gift of language, the world in general considers them fairly normal. They are really on a constant social strain by virtue of this, and while they are not purely pathological liars they often indulge in pathological lying, a distinction we have endeavored to make clear in our introduction.

It stands out very clearly, both in previous studies of this subject and in viewing our own material, that pathological lying is very rarely the single offense of the pathological liar. The characteristics of this lying show that it arises from a tendency which might easily express itself in other forms of misrepresentation. Swindling, sometimes stealing, sometimes running away from home (assuming another character and perhaps another name) may be the results of the same general causes in the individual. The extent to which these other delinquencies are carried on by a pathological liar depends again largely upon environmental conditions — for instance, truancy is very difficult in German cities; a long career of thieving, under the better police surveillance of some European countries, is less possible than with us; while swindling, for the reason given above, seems easier there.

Running away from home and itineracy show in a wonderfully strong correlation with pathological lying, both in previous studies and in our own material. Several authors, particularly Stemmermann in her survey of the subject, comment on this. This phenomenon, not only on account of the numerical findings, but also from a logical standpoint, is easily seen to be the expression, in another form of conduct, of the essential tendencies of the pathological liar. It is part of the general character instability, the unwillingness to meet the realities of life, the inclination to escape consequences. As a matter of fact, frequently the pathological liar gets himself in a tight place by lying, and then the easiest escape is by running away from the scene. The delinquencies of our present group as given below can with profit be compared with our previous statistics [1] on a large group of offenders. We gathered the facts concerning a series of 1000 carefully studied youthful repeated offenders. Of 694 male offenders, 261 were guilty of running away to the extent that it made a more or less serious offense. Of 306 female offenders, 76 committed the same type of offense. For comparison with the present group it is to be remembered that 18 out of the 19 mentally normal pathological liars were females.

	NORMAL	BORDER-LINE
Running away	12	6
Stealing	7	6
Swindling	7	2
Vagrancy	0	4
Attempt at suicide	0	2
Sex offenses	8	1
False accusations	10	4
Self-accusations	3	2
Abortion	1	0

We have given figures on false accusations here, including other cases than were enumerated in our special chap-

[1] P. 140 ff. *William Healy.* "The Individual Delinquent." Pp. 830. Boston: Little, Brown, and Co. 1915.

ter on the subject. In that chapter the center of interest was on the false accusations, but it is true that in certain other cases of pathological lying false accusations were indulged in as a somewhat minor offense. The 9 cases enumerated as swindlers showed this offense in varying degrees, as might naturally be expected by the differences in ages, which, if nothing else, makes for variations in the evolution of social and character tendencies. Perusal of the cases shows the small beginnings as well as the flagrant offenses on this order. As we previously have stated, we have avoided dealing with the older careers of notorious swindlers. The nature of the sex offenses can be learned from the case histories by those who wish to make special inquiry. Masturbation we have regarded more as a causative factor, and have spoken of it in a previous section. Truancy we have not enumerated. It goes without saying that it had been indulged in by practically all of the males and by a considerable number of the females in our cases.

The observer of delinquents cannot help being constantly impressed by the fact that the offense of lying seems to the usual offender small in proportion to the commission of other criminalistic deeds. Particularly does this come out when one observes the chronic liar growing up in a household where grave sex and other delinquencies are habitual occurrences. Should his lying be compared with these major anti-social transactions? Indeed, it might be a field for speculation as to whether, given certain qualities of mind, imaginative powers, etc., pathological lying may not play the part of a vicarious delinquency — being to the delinquent apparently less pernicious than more objective offenses. In our case histories may be seen some indications of this.

PROGNOSIS. TREATMENT

In discussing prognosis and treatment we can eliminate at once consideration of pathological lying by the insane. The outcome there, depends upon what can be done for the underlying psychosis. We have avoided intimate discussion of these cases, but many suggestions of the unalterableness of the full-fledged tendencies among the insane are found in the European literature cited by us. Even discussion of the outcome of the border-line cases, such as we have given examples of, needs but short shrift. Everyone knows the extreme difficulties of dealing with constitutional inferiors; marked cases are socially fit only for proper colonization. The epileptic, in default of cure of his disease, is ever going to be prone to many peculiar mental states which may involve pathological lying. The slight mental confusion of chorea, which may lead to false accusation, as we have seen in Case 23, is one of the most curable of all abnormal mental states. With proper attention to diagnosis and treatment, favorable outcome of cases of hysteria, such as that in Case 24, is frequently seen. Another type which cannot be handled except by permanent segregation is the thoroughly aberrational and socially dangerous class represented by Case 25, however one designates the type. Much more, undoubtedly, can be done for such a border-line individual as Case 12, if there is sufficient coöperation among educational and reformatory institutions and the courts. It has seemed to us that the chief cause of failure in this interesting case has been the fact that this young man could go on ever entering new social situations and finding new worlds for exploitation because no one had the means at hand for securing facts concerning his past or for ascertaining what any good diagnostician could easily perceive to be his limitations and tendencies.

Very much more to the point is consideration of the actual and possible outcome in cases of pathological lying by normal individuals. Here, as in other matters where bodily, mental, and social issues are blended, no prognosis or outlook can be rationally offered without consideration of possible changes in the circumstances peculiar to the given case. First and foremost stands out the fact that cure of the tendency sometimes happens even after long giving way to it. In this statement we are not contradictory to some previous writers.

As Stemmermann says, out of the general literature there is not much from which one can deduce any principles of prognosis. But, again, we would insist that one of the great weaknesses has been that earlier studies have not carefully distinguished between the mentally normal and the abnormal cases of pseudologia phantastica. When, for instance, Forel speaks of pathological liars as being constitutionally abnormal individuals who are not curable, he fails to differentiate where profitable differentiation can be made. If our own work is of any practical value it is in offering safer grounds for prognosis and treatment. Stemmermann summarizes well her follow-up work done upon cases seen years previously by other observers. Some of these are still in institutions. After a period of well-doing several of these have become backsliders and reverted again to lying and swindling. Very few appear to have been cured, but yet some of the facts of betterment are most convincing. This author states that, at the most, one dares to ponder over the point as to whether there are not cases which recover, particularly when the pathological lying is a phenomenon of adolescence.

Our own material is, in part, too recently studied to form anything like a generalization concerning prognosis. Many years have to elapse before one can be sure there is not going to be a recurrence. But one is not altogether certain that prognostic generalizations are of practical worth for this group of mentally normal pathological liars. So many incidental factors of physical, mental, and social life, with all of the complicated background of the same, come in to make the total result, that experiment and trial with the individual case, while hesitating to give an exact prognosis, is perhaps the only sane procedure. What we do know definitely is the immensely favorable outcome in Cases 1, 4, 7, 19, and the promising betterment in several other instances — all in direct contradiction to what we had expected from survey of previous literature. In several of these cases the years have gone by with nothing but steady improvement. The difficulty in getting adequate treatment, either in home life or by the necessary individual attention elsewhere, makes it impossible to say that many of the others also could not have been favorably influenced. Frequently a total alteration of environmental conditions is necessary, and this, of course, is often very difficult to obtain. Also it is extremely rare that one can get the whole matter, and its sure social consequences, fairly and squarely met by anybody with influence over the individual. Until this can be done, little in the way of good results may ever be expected. The splendid attack made by relatives or others upon the situation in Cases 1, 4, 7, possibly 14, and 19 tells the story of the prime necessity for adequate handling of pathological lying.

Specific treatment of physical conditions should always be undertaken when necessary. It should go without saying that any individual who is open to the temptations of inner stress should be strengthened at all points possible and relieved from all sources of irritation. But, lest anyone should become too much persuaded of the efficacy of surgical or other treatment, it should be remembered that the psychical reactions, even where there is physical irritation, involve the definite wearing of neural paths, with habit formations, which bodily treatment can only slightly alter. An enticing problem to the gynecologist is always the relationship of pelvic, particularly sexual irritations, to conduct. We cannot confirm the idea of a prime causal connection in this particular, although we have evidence that betterment of the physical ailment may lead to less inclination towards the unfortunate behavior. In Case 1 the lying came long before pelvic disease was acquired, but very likely the irritation of the latter led to an accentuation of the psychical phenomena. In Case 6 the typical conduct was persisted in after remedy of the pelvic disorder; so also in Case 3 after relief of abdominal conditions, and in Case 21 after cessation of pregnancy. Other points bearing upon this may be read in our case histories. On the general problem of the possibility of physical treatment it will be noted that a considerable share of all our cases were in good general condition.

In discussing treatment great emphasis should be placed upon the primary necessity for directly meeting the pathological liar upon the level of the moral failures and making it plain that these are known and understood. It is very certain that frequently this type of prevaricator has very little conception of the social antagonism which his habit arouses. There is faulty apperception of how others feel towards the lying, and to what depths the practice of this habit leads. Appreciation of these facts may be the first step towards betterment. In several of the improved cases we have mentioned that it was largely the acquirement of social foresight which made the first step in a moral advance which finally won the day. In this whole matter the first ethical instruction may well be based upon the idea of self-preservation — after all the backbone of much of our morals. When it comes to specific details of treatment these must be educational, alterative, and constructive. In Cases 1 and 3 under treatment we know that when the lying was discovered or suspected the individual was at once checked up and made to go over the ground and state the real facts. The pathological liar ordinarily reacts to the accusation of lying by prevaricating again in self-defense, but when with the therapeutist there has been the understanding that the tendency to lying is a habit which it is necessary to break, the barricade of self-defense may not be thrown up. An alterative measure of great value, then, is directly to meet the specific lie on the spot, as it were, when it is told.

Next, accuracy of report may well be practiced as a special discipline. In these normal cases we have seen that there could be little doubt about the individual having self-control enough to stick to the truth, if the will was properly directed. Indeed, many of our cases were exceptionally bright individuals with many good powers of observation and memory. Had one the opportunity, there can be little doubt but that training in the power to do well on such a test as that afforded by the "Aussage" picture would have yielded good results. Indeed, there is some suggestion of this in our table of findings on this test, where we note that pathological liars, when left merely to themselves and their first often comparatively meagre report on the picture, give few incorrect details. The difference in their report as compared with other observers of the picture was found when they answered questions. Since this is the case, there can be little question that training in the power to respond accurately might be gained.

It may be of value in considering therapeutics of pathological lying to enumerate the general run of treatment which was carried out in those instances where we know that betterment took place. Nearly always only a part of what we advised could be carried out, but, even so, a brief statement of the conditions under which betterment was accomplished seems worth much.

Case 1 was treated first in an institution for delinquents where every effort was made to cure her disease and where she was taught to employ herself in constructive work. It was found she had ability to design, and this was used to the utmost. Then her lying tendencies were checked by social disapprobation as much as possible. A special effort was made toward this. The girl was undoubtedly made more serious-minded by the after-effects of her experience and perhaps by her disease. She was later successfully handled at home by her sensible mother. Leaving the years of adolescent instability behind her was also undoubtedly a factor in betterment.

Case 4 was taken in hand by a sterling character who restrained very carefully the tendency to lying, and by firm methods showed her the social advantages of self-control in this respect. At the same time she was given a vastly better environment, particularly in the matter of her friends. However, there is little doubt that nothing would have been accomplished in this case without first a deep understanding of the girl's troubles and of her mental conflicts.

Case 7 was treated for her sex difficulties under the constant care of a vigorous mother, who first, naturally, had to gain an understanding of the case. With her bettered physical and mental conditions, the girl was able steadily to hold a position for which earlier she had no capacity.

Betterment in Case 14 came about mainly as the result of an understanding of the child's mental conflicts and somewhat through partially bettered environmental conditions. We learned lately that the severe visual defect had been neglected.

In Case 15 the false accusations were made upon the basis of mental conflict. Investigation of the case, followed by the personal services of a probation officer and by the legal proceedings, served to clear up conditions, including those of the family in general, so that the girl was given a greater chance for success.

Case 19 seems to have been largely cured through the girl herself being able to work out her mental conflicts. Adolescence was a factor and she was tided over this period in a good environment and with friends who understood her type of case and who were willing to put up with her aberrancies for this time. Although we would not minimize the efforts of stalwart friends, we may say that there were more evidences of cure by self-help in this case than in any other we have seen.

Lest we should seem to be placing too much emphasis upon adolescence, with the idea that the mere passing of that period will lead to change in behavior, we cite Cases 3, 5, and 6, where the addition of years has brought no betterment. In neither of these was the essential nature of the difficulty explored during earlier troublous periods.

An interesting consideration for treatment is embodied in the rational idea of utilizing the special powers, so that there may be ample gratification in self-expression, and in use of the imagination. Through this new satisfaction there may be a mental swerving from the previous paths strewn with pitfalls. The inclination to verbal composition, already spoken of as existing in so many cases, may be utilized, and imagination be given full sway in harmless directions. It seems likely that just this deliberate practice may serve to more clearly demarcate truth from falsehood in the individual's mind. Unfortunately we have had too little actual proof of the value of this method, some cases being worked on now are too recent for report, but there is plenty of indication of the possibilities. Had we been able to control environment better, much more of this type of work would have been carried out.

A favorable outcome through this constructive treatment based upon utilizing the characteristic linguistic powers of the pathological liar, is witnessed to by Stemmermann in her story of Delbrück's G. N. In the history of this case a delightful note of comedy is struck. G. N. was found to be a man of considerable literary ability. He had been observed over the period of 13 years. After he was first studied he twice managed to go 3 years without succumbing to his falsifying tendencies, and then found his chance for leading a blameless life by becoming a newspaper man. In fact, he reached an honored place as an editor. Stemmermann suggests, naïvely, that perhaps this calling is especially calculated to give the talents correlated with pseudologia phantastica space for free play, so that the individual's special abilities may not come in conflict with the law, or with social customs, and, on the other hand, may be utilized in fruitful pursuits.

All together, one would certainly advise every effort being made towards specifically stabilizing the pathological liar in the matter of truth-telling — by checking the springs of misconduct, and by diverting energies and talents into their most suitable channels. The problem must ever be one for individual therapy. Failures of treatment there may be, but from our study we are much inclined to believe that well-calculated, constructive efforts will achieve goodly success among those who are mentally normal.

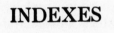

INDEXES

INDEX OF AUTHORS

INDEX OF TOPICS

PATTERSON SMITH REPRINT SERIES IN
CRIMINOLOGY, LAW ENFORCEMENT, AND SOCIAL PROBLEMS

1. Lewis: *The Development of American Prisons and Prison Customs, 1776-1845*
2. Carpenter: *Reformatory Prison Discipline*
3. Brace: *The Dangerous Classes of New York*
4. Dix: *Remarks on Prisons and Prison Discipline in the United States*
5. Bruce *et al: The Workings of the Indeterminate-Sentence Law and the Parole System in Illinois*
6. Wickersham Commission: *Complete Reports, Including the Mooney-Billings Report.* 14 Vols.
7. Livingston: *Complete Works on Criminal Jurisprudence.* 2 Vols.
8. Cleveland Foundation: *Criminal Justice in Cleveland*
9. Illinois Association for Criminal Justice: *The Illinois Crime Survey*
10. Missouri Association for Criminal Justice: *The Missouri Crime Survey*
11. Aschaffenburg: *Crime and Its Repression*
12. Garofalo: *Criminology*
13. Gross: *Criminal Psychology*
14. Lombroso: *Crime, Its Causes and Remedies*
15. Saleilles: *The Individualization of Punishment*
16. Tarde: *Penal Philosophy*
17. McKelvey: *American Prisons*
18. Sanders: *Negro Child Welfare in North Carolina*
19. Pike: *A History of Crime in England.* 2 Vols.
20. Herring: *Welfare Work in Mill Villages*
21. Barnes: *The Evolution of Penology in Pennsylvania*
22. Puckett: *Folk Beliefs of the Southern Negro*
23. Fernald *et al: A Study of Women Delinquents in New York State*
24. Wines: *The State of the Prisons and of Child-Saving Institutions*
25. Raper: *The Tragedy of Lynching*
26. Thomas: *The Unadjusted Girl*
27. Jorns: *The Quakers as Pioneers in Social Work*
28. Owings: *Women Police*
29. Woolston: *Prostitution in the United States*
30. Flexner: *Prostitution in Europe*
31. Kelso: *The History of Public Poor Relief in Massachusetts: 1820-1920*
32. Spivak: *Georgia Nigger*
33. Earle: *Curious Punishments of Bygone Days*
34. Bonger: *Race and Crime*
35. Fishman: *Crucibles of Crime*
36. Brearley: *Homicide in the United States*
37. Graper: *American Police Administration*
38. Hichborn: *"The System"*
39. Steiner & Brown: *The North Carolina Chain Gang*
40. Cherrington: *The Evolution of Prohibition in the United States of America*
41. Colquhoun: *A Treatise on the Commerce and Police of the River Thames*
42. Colquhoun: *A Treatise on the Police of the Metropolis*
43. Abrahamsen: *Crime and the Human Mind*
44. Schneider: *The History of Public Welfare in New York State: 1609-1866*
45. Schneider & Deutsch: *The History of Public Welfare in New York State: 1867-1940*
46. Crapsey: *The Nether Side of New York*
47. Young: *Social Treatment in Probation and Delinquency*
48. Quinn: *Gambling and Gambling Devices*
49. McCord & McCord: *Origins of Crime*
50. Worthington & Topping: *Specialized Courts Dealing with Sex Delinquency*

PATTERSON SMITH REPRINT SERIES IN
CRIMINOLOGY, LAW ENFORCEMENT, AND SOCIAL PROBLEMS

51. Asbury: *Sucker's Progress*
52. Kneeland: *Commercialized Prostitution in New York City*
53. Fosdick: *American Police Systems*
54. Fosdick: *European Police Systems*
55. Shay: *Judge Lynch: His First Hundred Years*
56. Barnes: *The Repression of Crime*
57. Cable: *The Silent South*
58. Kammerer: *The Unmarried Mother*
59. Doshay: *The Boy Sex Offender and His Later Career*
60. Spaulding: *An Experimental Study of Psychopathic Delinquent Women*
61. Brockway: *Fifty Years of Prison Service*
62. Lawes: *Man's Judgment of Death*
63. Healy & Healy: *Pathological Lying, Accusation, and Swindling*
64. Smith: *The State Police*
65. Adams: *Interracial Marriage in Hawaii*
66. Halpern: *A Decade of Probation*
67. Tappan: *Delinquent Girls in Court*
68. Alexander & Healy: *Roots of Crime*
69. Healy & Bronner: *Delinquents and Criminals*
70. Cutler: *Lynch-Law*
71. Gillin: *Taming the Criminal*
72. Osborne: *Within Prison Walls*
73. Ashton: *The History of Gambling in England*
74. Whitlock: *On the Enforcement of Law in Cities*
75. Goldberg: *Child Offenders*
76. Cressey: *The Taxi-Dance Hall*
77. Riis: *The Battle with the Slum*
78. Larson *et al: Lying and Its Detection*
79. Comstock: *Frauds Exposed*
80. Carpenter: *Our Convicts.* 2 Vols. in 1
81. Horn: *Invisible Empire: The Story of the Ku Klux Klan, 1866-1871*
82. Faris *et al: Intelligent Philanthropy*
83. Robinson: *History and Organization of Criminal Statistics in the United States*
84. Reckless: *Vice in Chicago*
85. Healy: *The Individual Delinquent*
86. Bogen: *Jewish Philanthropy*
87. Clinard: *The Black Market: A Study of White Collar Crime*
88. Healy: *Mental Conflicts and Misconduct*
89. Citizens' Police Committee: *Chicago Police Problems*
90. Clay: *The Prison Chaplain*
91. Peirce: *A Half Century with Juvenile Delinquents*
92. Richmond: *Friendly Visiting Among the Poor*
93. Brasol: *Elements of Crime*
94. Strong: *Public Welfare Administration in Canada*
95. Beard: *Juvenile Probation*
96. Steinmetz: *The Gaming Table.* 2 Vols.
97. Crawford: *Report on the Penitentiaries of the United States*
98. Kuhlman: *A Guide to Material on Crime and Criminal Justice*
99. Culver: *Bibliography of Crime and Criminal Justice: 1927-1931*
100. Culver: *Bibliography of Crime and Criminal Justice: 1932-1937*